Library of
Davidson College

THE ENGLISH UNIVERSITY NOVEL

This is a volume in the Arno Press collection

THE ACADEMIC PROFESSION

Advisory Editor
Walter P. Metzger

Editorial Board
Dietrich Goldschmidt
A. H. Halsey
Martin Trow

See last pages of this volume
for a complete list of titles.

THE ENGLISH UNIVERSITY NOVEL

Mortimer R. Proctor

ARNO PRESS

A New York Times Company

New York / 1977

Editorial Supervision: MARIE STARECK

Reprint Edition 1977 by Arno Press Inc.

Reprinted from a copy in
 The University of Illinois Library

THE ACADEMIC PROFESSION
ISBN for complete set: 0-405-10000-0
See last pages of this volume for titles.

Manufactured in the United States of America

Library of Congress Cataloging in Publication Data

Proctor, Mortimer Robinson, 1916-
 The English university novel.

 (The Academic profession)
 Reprint of the 1957 ed. published by University of
California Press, Berkeley, which was issued as English
studies no. 15 of University of California publications.
 Bibliography: p.
 1. English fiction--History and criticism. 2. Universities and colleges in literature. 3. Universities and colleges--England. I. Title. II. Series.
III. Series: California. University. University of
California publications : English studies ; 15.
[PR830.U5P7 1977]   823'.03   76-55197
ISBN 0-405-10030-2

THE ENGLISH UNIVERSITY NOVEL

THE ENGLISH UNIVERSITY NOVEL

By Mortimer R. Proctor

UNIVERSITY OF CALIFORNIA PRESS
BERKELEY AND LOS ANGELES
1957

UNIVERSITY OF CALIFORNIA PUBLICATIONS
ENGLISH STUDIES: 15
EDITORS (LOS ANGELES): LEON HOWARD, J. J. ESPEY,
ADA NISBET, H. T. SWEDENBERG, JR.

Submitted by editors January 27, 1956
Issued March 1, 1957

UNIVERSITY OF CALIFORNIA PRESS
BERKELEY AND LOS ANGELES
CALIFORNIA

◇

CAMBRIDGE UNIVERSITY PRESS
LONDON, ENGLAND

PRINTED IN THE UNITED STATES OF AMERICA

TO ANNE

PREFACE

BEFORE THE publication in 1823 of John Gibson Lockhart's *Reginald Dalton: A Story of English University Life* there was no such thing, strictly speaking, as a university novel. By the end of the nineteenth century, however, the novels about Oxford and Cambridge were so numerous that they clearly represent a striking literary phenomenon. And they are still being written in surprising numbers. Not all have been good novels; some have been very bad; a few have been downright scandalous. The theme of university life has not always been a tractable one for fiction, tending frequently to seduce well-meaning authors into stories of mere juvenile rough and tumble. But it has produced some extraordinary comedy, and some distinguished novels. George Saintsbury, writing on "Novels of University Life" in *Macmillan's Magazine,* in 1898, saw the possibilities of the subject, though he could not yet have seen its most notable products: "... there can be, or should be," he observed, "few passages in life with greater capabilities than that when a man is for the first time almost his own master, for the first time wholly arbiter of whatsoever sports and whatsoever studies he shall pursue, and when he is subjected to local, historical and other influences, sensual and supra-sensual, such as might not only 'draw three souls out of a weaver,' but infuse something like a soul even into the stupidest and most graceless of boys." The purpose of what follows is to show how the capabilities were explored in the novel, how the fictional representation of English university life was developed from an initial stage of crudeness and vulgarity, through a middle period in which humor and the doctrines of university reform were strangely mingled, to the final achievement of a serious and mature statement of the very nature of university education. The statement admittedly came late, and was preceded by much that raised Victorian parental eyebrows; but the form it ultimately took deserves attention still, I think, because the question to which it was directed, What is a university, is as much in need of an answer as it ever was. Few will deny that the concept evolved by the novelists was a noble one.

I cannot state, much less repay, my indebtedness to all who have assisted me with information, advice, and encouragement in preparing this book. Still, to Professors Earl Leslie Griggs and Franklin P. Rolfe, of the University of California, Los Angeles, I owe special thanks for their patient help and criticism at a time when help and criticism were most needed. The members of the Board of Editors in English of the same university, Professors Leon Howard, J. J. Espey, Ada Nisbet, and H. T. Swedenberg, Jr., who advised me in the final preparation of the manuscript, are entirely responsible for extensive revisions a more knowing author would have seen for himself to be necessary; their good judgment and warm encouragement have been invaluable. I am particularly grateful to the American Council of Learned Societies, which, through the grant of a fellowship award, made possible the later stages of my research. The staffs of two libraries, those of the University of California, Los Angeles, and Yale, have done much to make my work easier; I would like to thank especially Mr. Everett Moore and Mrs. Esther Euler of the former, and Mr. Henry M. Fuller of the latter. Also, I must mention the advantage I have enjoyed in having access to two outstanding collections of Oxford books: the Falconer Madan Collection at Yale, and the William W. Clary Collection at the Honnold Library, Claremont, California. Given such help and guidance, I reserve to myself credit for any errors and infelicities that may remain.

Finally, I wish to thank the following publishers who have permitted me to quote from copyrighted materials: Oxford

Preface

University Press, for *Oxford,* by Christopher Hobhouse; Basil Blackwood and Mott, Ltd., for *The Overburian Characters,* edited by W. J. Paylor, and *Picturae Loquentes,* by Wye Saltonstall, edited by C. H. Wilkinson; The Golden Cockerel Press, for *Microcosmographie,* by John Earl, edited by Gwendolyn Murphy; William Heinemann, Ltd., for *The Progress of Hugh Rendal,* by Lionel Portman, *Godfrey Marten, Undergraduate,* by Charles Turley, and *Zuleika Dobson,* by Sir Max Beerbohm; Macdonald and Co., Ltd., for *Sinister Street,* by Sir Compton Mackenzie; Henry Holt and Co., Inc., for *Patchwork,* by Beverly Nichols; Constable and Co., Ltd., for *Hyssop,* by Michael Sadleir, and *A City in the Foreground,* by Gerard Hopkins; and John Lane The Bodley Head, Ltd., for *The Oxford Circus,* by Hamish Miles and Raymond Mortimer.

M. R. P.

UNIVERSITY OF CALIFORNIA, RIVERSIDE
August, 1956

CONTENTS

CHAPTER	PAGE
I. Introduction	1
II. Early Literary Portraits	11
III. Decline of the Universities	33
IV. Reform and the University Novel	51
V. Persistence of the Rowdy Tradition	66
VI. Growth of Realism	88
VII. The Romantic Crichtons	118
VIII. The "Damned Tribe of Scribbling Women"	135
IX. The Cult of Oxford	150
X. Conclusion	182
Notes	203
Bibliography	217
Index	225

Chapter I

INTRODUCTION

The reader who has made his way through the long list of English university novels cannot fail to note the remarkable sameness their plots, and even individual fragments of action, exhibit. Doubtless there are events that can scarcely be omitted from any account of a man's college career. But those that are most useful for fiction have been recorded so frequently by novelists that it is possible to construct a composite plot which would, either in part or in its entirety, provide a synopsis for the majority of university novels. It would proceed somewhat as follows. The freshman, armed with parental advice from either a father who is a country vicar or a widowed mother who plans to live in penury to educate her son, arrives at the university aboard a coach driven by a cigar-smoking, horn-tootling undergraduate (though later, of course, he comes by train from London). The formalities of matriculation performed, he meets his uncongenial tutor to determine a course of study; this, however, is at once neglected in favor of more diverting pastimes when he learns that college life is a highly social affair. Vigorous wine parties, a bonfire in the quad, tricks played upon unpopular students, midnight excursions to screw shut the doors of offending tutors, days in the field with hounds and horses and on the river in punt and shell, all take up too much time to permit him much study. Even if he is a quiet creature, he is drawn by the more sprightly into some form of undergraduate foolishness; if he is a wild one, he lives a very full life indeed. A town-and-gown row, and often a duel, mark the early novels, just as a boat race almost always appears in the later ones. From time to time the scholar takes a much-needed vacation, usually in the company of a friend who is conveniently furnished with a beautiful sister; this girl, blushing and paling interminably and utterly unable to imagine what the young man can be thinking of, soon is obliged to listen to the tender words that will make them the most blessed of mortals. Back at the university the gay life continues, broken perhaps by a serious political effort at the Union, until the awareness of approaching examinations becomes so strong that the scholar locks his door, ignores his friends, and supported by quantities of tea and cold towels attempts to expiate his sins of omission. The days of examination come at last, when pale and trembling he faces his inquisitors; but seldom has the struggle been in vain, for he is quite likely to emerge with a first class. Then, with glory resting heavily upon him, he is ready to enjoy the climax of the college year, when the university is invaded by flocks of fair faces during a week of boat races, college balls, and the ceremonies of awarding degrees; during this eventful time the scholar, plying his guests with lobster and champagne, wrings from willing lips the promise of future bliss. Not infrequently two friends have a sister each, in which event the end of university days takes on an overwhelmingly matrimonial tone.

This general formula, stretched out over college careers of varying lengths, served many authors well; it played tricks on others, who could derive from it only unconvincing banalities; and it was the undoing of some hapless women who, without firsthand knowledge of the universities, drew confidently upon it for their monstrous pictures of undergraduate life. One might suspect, however, that whatever effect such a formula might have on the quality of university novels, it would at least serve to make them readily identifiable. This is only partly true; it is not always easy to say what is and what is not a university novel. The reason lies in the tendency of the subject matter to slip entirely out of sight. In novel after novel there comes a point when the author's exhaustion is evident, when he discovers he has done

Introduction 3

all he can with the university theme and is driven to move on into the more varied world beyond. A clear case of such exhaustion is found in William Winwood Reade's *Liberty Hall, Oxon* (1860). This virulent attack on Oxford's academic integrity presses its case for a volume and a half; the subject amounts almost to an obsession with Reade as he shows how his hero was unfairly forced to leave the university. But having made his point, Reade was left to fill out the cumbersome requirements of the three-decker novel by removing the unfortunate young man to the Shetland Islands, where in spite of some heavy doses of romance and melodrama the reader's interest cannot possibly follow. *Liberty Hall* divides its university and nonuniversity material almost equally, but there are extremes in both directions; some novels deviate from the academic scene even more freely, some not at all. The problem, therefore, of defining a university novel is in part quantitative, in that it must be concerned with the extent to which the author's ingenuity and tenacity have succeeded in making the university theme predominate. And the fact that not all authors could do so without interruption not so much obscures the genre as gives to it one of its dominant characteristics. In what follows, therefore, some works—Thomas Hughes's *Tom Brown at Oxford* (1861) and Max Beerbohm's *Zuleika Dobson* (1911), for example—will stand out as easily discernible "university" novels in that their whole concern is with undergraduate life, but others will be included whose qualifications might seem questionable in terms purely of the amount of university subject matter they contain. Yet these could hardly be omitted. They are a part of university fiction in that they either pronounce significantly upon university education, or serve to fill out the pattern of development of the university theme in fiction, or actually influence (as did Thackeray's *Pendennis*) the growth of the genre itself.

A second generalization regarding subject matter may also

be made here. Historically speaking, the university novel has been the Oxford novel. Just why there should be an overwhelming preponderance of Oxford novels of all kinds is not at once clear, but the unbalance is so great that it cannot be ignored: approximately 85 per cent of the novels which form the subject of this study are about Oxford, most of the rest being about Cambridge.[1] To account for these figures one is inclined to wonder if Oxford's traditional emphasis on classical learning and literature might not have been more conducive to producing novelists than Cambridge's devotion to mathematics. Of the nineteenth-century novelists listed in the *Cambridge Bibliography of English Literature* nearly half (44 per cent) of those who were university-educated went to Oxford (see accompanying table). The relationship of these figures to the authors of university novels (most of whom have not won their way into the

	Oxford	Cambridge	Others	None
Early nineteenth-century novelists	8	4	4	91 (47 women)
Mid-nineteenth-century novelists	12	10	8	71 (28 women)
Later nineteenth-century novelists	15	8	11	63 (28 women)
	35	22	23	225

Cambridge Bibliography) is not very close: of the Oxford graduates listed by Bateson, for example, only eight (Lockhart, Ward, Hughes, Newman, Hewlett, Froude, Merivale, and Tyrwhitt) wrote at length about their university; of the Cambridge graduates, only two (Rice and Farrar—though Thackeray must be considered as well). Yet there does seem to be a curious connection between Oxford and the nineteenth-century novel. As for the host of "unknowns" of university fiction, when one real-

---

[1] For notes to chap. i, see pp. 203–204.

izes that with few exceptions ("Cuthbert Bede" of Durham is a notable one) these authors wrote of their own universities, the conclusion seems inescapable that Oxford men were inclined to write of their undergraduate days as Cambridge men were not. This inclination has, in fact, been noted before: in Gerard Hopkins' *A City in the Foreground* (1921) one of the characters remarks of a recent Oxford graduate, " 'He has fallen prey to the first infirmity of Oxford minds—he is writing an Oxford novel.' "[2]

From another and less statistical point of view, it seems that Oxford's historical associations must contribute—both directly and indirectly—to the multitude of Oxford novels. The home of lost causes and particularly of royalist sympathies has had, for the novelist and reader alike, a romantic appeal scarcely to be found in Cambridge's Whiggish and Puritanical past. Evidence of this is found in the fact that although several novels are devoted to incidents in Oxford's history, I have been unable to find one such novel about Cambridge. A favorite theme, of course, is the Oxford of Civil War days: the Rev. W. E. Heygate's *The Scholar and the Trooper* (1858), a well-documented work of high adventure, concludes with the reflection that it is well the hot and hasty days of rebellion are over, and Oxford is left to retirement and meditation; *John Inglesant* (1881), by J. H. Shorthouse, although not really an Oxford novel, contains a long section (in chaps. 8–13) on the fortunes of the king during his stay in the university town; the Rev. Alfred Church, in *With the King at Oxford* (1886), gives a detailed account of undergraduate life in the seventeenth century and the way in which it disintegrated during the rebellion, and pictures the political division within the university and the Parliamentary visitation which followed the king's surrender; and *A Young Oxford Maid in the Days of the King and the Parliament* (1890) by "Sarah Tytler" (i.e., Henrietta Keddie) describes the incongruity of court intrigue within the halls and quadrangles that had lost their scholars. All of these novels, it need hardly be said, reflect royalist sympathies. The royalist cause of the 1640's did not, however, represent the only source of historical material from which to construct novels based on Oxford's romantic past. *A Clerk of Oxford and His Adventures in the Barons' War* (1898), by Evelyn Everett-Green, is a convincing picture of Oxford in the Middle Ages, with its haphazard organization and its riotous student life. *The Black Rose* (1945), by Thomas B. Costain, is set in part in thirteenth-century Oxford, and narrates the story of a poor scholar who makes his way to Cathay and back, achieving knighthood and royal favor for his efforts. James Baker's *The Gleaming Dawn* (1896) tells of the days of Wycliffe and the brawls between his followers and those who wished to drive him out of Oxford. *Towers in the Mist* (1938), by Elizabeth Goudge, is an eminently cheerful book about Elizabethan Oxford, with a cast of characters that includes Sidney, Campion, Raleigh, Bodley, and the queen herself on her visit to Oxford in 1566. It would be difficult to prove that Cambridge's history has been so drab that comparable narratives could not be drawn from it, but the evidence that they ever were seems strangely lacking. Whether the reason is to be found in Oxford's past or Oxford's present, the majority and by all means the best of university novels are also Oxford novels.

And finally, a question that must occur to the reader who encounters the long roster of university novelists is surely this: who on earth were these people? Certainly the authors of university novels form a fairly large and well-defined fraternity, but also a very undistinguished one unfamiliar to even the best-informed students of nineteenth-century literature. To most scholars only a few of the names that will appear—among them Lockhart, Thackeray, Hughes, Benson, Beerbohm, Mackenzie—will carry any suggestion of a "literary" reputation. Similarly, the novels themselves are with only a few exceptions distinctly second-rate as "literature," and today as unknown as their authors, the Battys and Cokes, the Gulls and the Goldies, who walked so freely in a domain where most competent novelists in the great age of the novel apparently hesitated to tread.

One explanation may lie in the fact that most authors of university novels were qualified for their task in a way that their betters were not: most of them had had a university education. For better or for worse, very few of the major Victorian novelists were university men, and very few, consequently, possessed the intimate knowledge of university life which must lie behind a university novel.[3] Scott studied at Edinburgh, as did Stevenson; Thackeray was a Cambridge man, and Charles Reade and Charles Dodgson went to Oxford. Of these, only Thackeray and Reade introduced the university theme in their novels. And these five represent the total among those of the *Cambridge Bibliography*'s leading novelists who were university-educated. The number and literary stature of the rest are impressive, for the list contains the names of Peacock, Marryat, Borrow, Disraeli, Dickens, Trollope, Meredith, Gissing, Moore, Hardy, and Kipling (as well as Maria Edgeworth, Jane Austen, Mrs. Gaskell, the Brontës, and George Eliot, who, being women, could not have been admitted to either Oxford or Cambridge). The evidence would seem to indicate, then, that one reason at least why most of the major novelists did not write at length about university life is that they did not know much about it. And they were probably wise in not probing too deeply into the subject. Attempts by the uninitiated, like the more preposterous of the women university novelists, to imagine successfully the complexities of life at Oxford and Cambridge, demonstrate how precarious such an undertaking might be; it simply was not true, as "Belinda Blinders" thought it was, that "knowledge like this one acquires one knows not how; but still one has it."[4]

This is not to say that the better-known novelists as a group ignored the subject altogether. Incidental comments—even whole chapters—in well-known works are plentiful. Admittedly, treatments of the university theme which were created however seriously and thoughtfully, yet more or less freely from the imagination, are at best likely to be disappointing, and with few exceptions fail to convey anything like a picture of college life. Frequently they are limited to the delineation of a curious academic character—an obstreperous undergraduate, or a peevish don—or to a generalization about the state of university education. Yet even these have their special interest, for coming from authors of indisputable literary stature they contribute to the climate of opinion surrounding the nineteenth-century universities. Disraeli, for example, began early and continued long to write spiritedly about the disadvantages of a university education. Perhaps as a young and ambitious political figure he felt that his competitors from the universities enjoyed an advantage he lacked; a degree could open up a political career more easily than could hard work. Whatever the cause, *The Young Duke* (1831), *Contarini Fleming* (1832), *Coningsby* (1844), and *Sybil* (1845)[5] all suggested that the puerility of university education could overwhelm a man's natural talents and goodness, and on the whole such an education was an impractical waste of time, a "deplorable and disgusting study of a small collection of imperfect books, written by Greeks, and preserved by Goths."[6] Eventually, however, his natural conservatism seems to have tempered this view (and he received an honorary degree from Oxford in 1853); both *Lothair* (1870) and *Endymion* (1880) speak highly of what could be expected from a double-first.[7] Most of Disraeli's earlier opinions were shared by his contemporary, Bulwer-Lytton, who in *Pelham* (1828) expressed two particularly clear, though not very original, ideas of what was wrong with the universities: the inequalities of university social life which permitted the unearned privileges enjoyed by wealthy students, and the tradition of classical education.[8] Here appears the notable portrait of Christopher Clutterbuck, the debilitated scholar, the machine of a memory laboring endlessly and uselessly, the unknowing victim of "the curse of an English education."[9] Unlike Disraeli, Lytton did not temper his criticism; forty-five years later, in *Kenelm Chillingly* (1873),[10] he was still saying very much the same thing. This is all, of course, quite fragmentary, the expression of ideas about university education rather than anything like a substantial representation of university life. The same must be said of what one finds in Trollope—a fast undergraduate in *Doctor Thorne* (1858), the character of Mr. Arabin—the "double-distilled quintessence of university perfection"—in *Barchester Towers* (1857), and throughout a feeling for Oxford's conservatism and orthodoxy; little more.[11] Or in Charles Reade, whose *Hard Cash* (1863), *Foul Play* (1869), and *A Simpleton* (1873) contain enthusiastic praise for the mental and muscular attainments of university men, together with the conviction, rare for the time, that the universities provided a practical education after all.[12] Or in Samuel Butler's *The Way of All Flesh* (written between 1873 and 1885), in which Ernest Pontifex demonstrates the triumph of mediocrity at Cambridge.[13] Or in Hardy's *Jude the Obscure* (1896), with its bitter and scolding remarks about the bigotry, gloom, and decay of Oxford.[14]

There is material in Charles Kingsley's *Alton Locke* (1850) and in the works of Thackeray which deserves fuller comment; this will be found below. But aside from a few other instances, some of which will probably occur to most readers, this is the extent of what the more prominent Victorian novelists had to say about university education. It is little enough. So little, in fact, that one must ask if there is not another reason, beyond simple ignorance of the subject, that kept serious novelists away from the university theme. In what follows it will be a cause for reflection that the subject matter of university fiction for long suffered from inherent limitations, due sometimes to its scandalous, sometimes to its merely juvenile, qualities. These were in fact grave limitations. Insofar as they affected the tone of university fiction they could only have discouraged serious men of letters from attempting to subdue the fractious material that constituted tales of college life. But this fact in turn will serve to throw useful light upon a remarkable transformation. For changes did occur which freed the university novelist from his earlier handicaps and permitted the development of the university novel toward its final achievement, a profound exploration of the function and purpose of the university itself.

CHAPTER II

EARLY LITERARY PORTRAITS

THE ENGLISH university novels which appeared in such numbers in the nineteenth century offer a problem not common to better known Victorian fiction. Inasmuch as they deal with Oxford and Cambridge they are concerned with the peculiarities of life within two exclusive and inbred communities, and they constitute a narrowly specialized body of literature built around codes of behavior and thought which at times appear artificial to the outside world. The societies of Oxford and Cambridge are, in fact, unique to the extent that they can be compared only with each other. One difficulty in comprehending the life of their undergraduates as novels have portrayed it lies, at least for the outsider, in official academic terminology unlike that of any other university. To this is added the complication of a highly developed vocabulary of slang. That the Progger of Quagger should also be the Provost of Queen's College, Oxford, or that tufts lionizing their toasts during Commem. should be the simple way of describing young noblemen playing the gallant during the festivities at the end of term before the Long Vacation requires, except for the initiated, a watchful eye and a patient mind. But vocabulary itself is not a serious obstacle. More important is the fact that by 1800 the traditions that governed England's older universities had had some six hundred years in which to grow; in this time they had produced some strange customs and even stranger personalities. University lecturers who did not lecture, and undergraduates who freely enjoyed all the pleasures of depravity, seem very odd creatures indeed if viewed in any light except the background that produced them. But their existence, which is luridly confirmed by a host of shocked witnesses, may be accounted for in the pages of any history of the universities. There may be found, similarly, historical explanation for most of what seems exaggerated or incomprehensible in university novels. Not only does the past explain their peculiarities of characterization and incident, but it also explains the varying critical attacks upon the universities by which they are so consistently marked—and too often marred. A neutral attitude toward the universities is seldom found in nineteenth-century fiction, and it was the changing bias of personal and popular opinion which in large measure determined the several courses taken by the novels. The critic must, therefore, be also part historian if he is to make much sense of what he finds before him in this curiously twisted avenue of literature.

He must, as well, try for a time to ignore the fact that the university novel is so distinctly a nineteenth-century phenomenon. An overwhelming proportion of all such novels was written during the reign of Victoria, almost none before; and by the end of the century so many had been produced that they clearly represent one of the major literary fads of the period. In this time they underwent nearly all the transformations that led to their final accomplishment, and since the first quarter of the new century they have appeared less frequently. It would therefore be justifiable in many ways to confine the study of them to relatively modern times. Yet literary influences are always at work, and when the subject matter of literature is so strictly limited as is this, they seem to work with special potency. The university man did, in fact, flourish in fiction long before anyone saw fit to devote a full novel to his academic exploits. He not only flourished; he became tainted with such an odious reputation that the first novels about him could only allow him to continue his long existence as either villain or fool. The earlier literary tradition which established him in these discreditable roles also provided the first university novelists with the stereotyped pattern of incident, and the bitter denunciations, which accompanied the university rake in his progress through so many Victorian novels. The literary backgrounds of the university novel are therefore quite as important as the historical, and indeed the two are quite inseparable.

It is a hazardous literary temptation to trace all things to Chaucer, but at least one attempt has been made to show that his Clerk of Oxford established the character of university fiction from the fourteenth century to the nineteenth.[1] This does not seem to be the case. Chaucer's Clerk, learned but no pedant, poor but no beggar, and reticent from becoming modesty rather than from bumbling ignorance, was the first of his kind in English fiction, and the last until more than four centuries of caricature had poked fun at these admirable qualities. If there is any persistent line of descent from Chaucer, it begins rather with his other clerks, whose ways suggest those of many an undergraduate since their time. That even they, however, seem unlike their immediate descendants is owing to the fact that Chaucer shows consistent sympathy and admiration for his scholars. For example, although Jankyn's peculiarly one-sided study of troublesome women brought him to no good end, he was merely an intelligent man whose misfortune it was to demonstrate that marriage to the Wife of Bath was an undertaking for which no university could have prepared its best scholar. In *The Reeve's Tale,* Aleyn and John of Soler Hall, Cambridge, proved by their outrageous nocturnal vengeance that the Miller who thought he could get the better of smart young college boys disastrously underestimated the advantages of a college education. So too with Nicholas of *The Miller's Tale,* who outwitted the credulous carpenter by an absurd prediction of a second flood. Chaucer came close to discrediting the university man in his portrayal of the foolish dandy Absolon (again, in *The Miller's Tale*), whom Oxford had taught to be "jolif and amorous," but not to curb his vanity. Yet the poet seems to have avoided any disparagement

---
[1] For notes to chap. ii, see pp. 204–205.

either of honest learning or of the high spirits and ingenious devices of fourteenth-century scholars. In this respect his portraits differ sharply from those which followed soon after.

But then, Chaucer wrote while both Oxford and Cambridge held unquestioned leadership in the intellectual life of England. So long as the scholastic philosophy to which they were dedicated remained unchallenged, there was no serious attempt to ridicule either them or their members. To Oxford, especially, came England's most learned men: there taught Adam Marsh, Scotus, Ockham, Roger Bacon, and Wycliffe; at both universities gathered scholars intent upon an honored pursuit, scholars whose devotion to learning overshadowed the poverty and discomfort which were conspicuously a part of university life in the Middle Ages. It should not be implied, of course, that the scholarly life was all sweetness and all light. A tendency toward mayhem is one of the most persistent traits of the university man in fiction, and it had its origin in these early times. Almost constant fighting among students, as well as between gownsmen and townsmen, frequently ended in astonishing scenes of bloodshed and death. Early accounts lament an almost frontierlike atmosphere of violence in the university towns, and reveal that numbers of students who were obliged to support themselves while they studied did so quite efficiently by becoming armed brigands. Yet even rioting and lawlessness did not detract seriously from the good name that honest scholars enjoyed. It was for them that the earliest of the college foundations were established, whose charters pointed the way toward the support of learning and the encouragement of more suitable government of the university communities. And it was from them that Chaucer drew his almost saintly Clerk of Oxford.

In the fifteenth and sixteenth centuries, however, the reputation of the universities began to disintegrate. For one thing, though scholastic learning gradually became outmoded, and

Early Literary Portraits

vexed by sophistications that could only exhaust the patience, the forms of the schoolmen continued to dominate the intellectual atmosphere of both Oxford and Cambridge. Not even the new humanism of Grocyn, Linacre, Colet, and More could effect the necessary break with the past, and as a result, the scholar's learning became suspect. In addition, there arose a serious administrative difficulty: new colleges increased rapidly in number at both universities, and by 1600 these corporate bodies had acquired wealth and power not dreamt of by their founders. Whereas the universities nominally continued as governing bodies, which alone had the powers of examining and conferring degrees, they found themselves eclipsed by their federations of autonomous and independent colleges, whose tutorial teaching came more and more to replace university professorial lectures. Moreover, the increasing wealth of college foundations, coupled with the fact that college heads found themselves the *de facto* heads of university government, led to an unfortunate misuse of patronage in the awarding of college preferments. Poor scholars who should have received assistance were neglected in favor of the wealthy, who could contribute in their own more spectacular way to the colleges' prestige. Favoritism in this direction led to similar abuses in the awarding of clerical livings to university graduates, and it seems to have been this latter evidence of decay that most moved the early critics. Hoccleve, in his *De Regimine Principum* (*ca.* 1412), exclaimed in shocked tones that the deserving men of both universities were being neglected in the distribution of church offices:

> Allas! so many a worthy clerk famous
> In Oxenforde, and in Cambrigge also,
> Stonde unavauncede, where as the vicious
> Favelle hathe chirches and prebendes mo
> Than God is plesede withe; allas! of tho
> That wernen vertu so to be promotede;
> And they helples in whom vertu is rootede.[2]

Caxton, appending an epilogue to his edition of *Aesop's Fables* (1484), showed precisely what was happening by his little tale of the poor but conscientious priest. There were once, he said, two Masters of Arts at Oxford, one a man who knew his way about in the world, the other a simple scholar. In time the first rose high in the clerical hierarchy, and drew to himself a large number of wealthy benefices. As he one day was traveling in state about the country he came into a small but pleasant parish whose priest he discovered to be his Oxford fellow. He was visibly jolted to discover that so plain a man had actually found such an agreeable niche, but recovering himself he addressed the honest priest almost as an equal and inquired of him, man to man, how much the parish was worth to him annually. The priest had no idea—had never, it seems, bothered to notice. To the great man such a thing was incomprehensible, but even his shocked exclamation was silenced as the priest added that he was sure the parish was worth a great deal to him, inasmuch as it would be, if he worked hard, the means of his reaching heaven.

This sense that all was not well in the world of learning, that wealth often spoke louder than good works, continued to flourish while the world of learning itself continued to deteriorate. The Reformation, with its confiscations, burnings, and hasty alterations in prescribed teaching, brought compounded difficulties to the universities. Anthony à Wood, writing of these troubled years, observed (and the university *Register* confirms it) that Oxford was hurt by a dropping off of students, its halls were falling into decay, the schoolmen were scorned while their successors had not yet been accepted, and there was little encouragement to take degrees.[3] And he noted, concerning the disturbances of Edward's reign, that poor students were suffering from the misuse of patronage, theological contention was driving out serious study, and the university was letting its own standards drop while its properties and possessions disappeared. The situation was no better at Cambridge. The universities, said Wood, were despised as "Stables of Asses and Stews of the Devil."⁴ Perhaps they were not quite so bad as that. But it is true that the follies indulged in by the universities, and the troubles imposed upon them, produced in the sixteenth century a new and devastating concept of the scholar. Clearly the qualities in Chaucer's Clerk which made him modest, industrious, and withdrawn from the world, could be interpreted in a new light when viewed against the changes that had taken place in university life. They provided, in fact, materials for the portrait of the scholar-fool— one given over to worthless knowledge, and so naïve and ignorant of the ways of the world that he could be put upon by the slenderest ruses. Together with this unhappy man there appeared another kind of fool and a more dangerous one, the hopelessly ignorant scholar who was just bright enough to win by bribery and deceit the awards that should have gone to the learned. And finally, a third type was portrayed in the scholar who, far from being stupid, had so mastered the tricks of fraud that he could outwit the world. This latter type would appear superficially to resemble Chaucer's Nicholas were it not for the fact that in his maliciousness and knavery he made startlingly clear the curse of worldliness which afflicted the universities.

These new types are to be found abundantly in two collections of tales that were assembled in early Elizabethan days; the stories themselves are much older. *The Merie Tales of Skelton*[5] was licensed by the Stationers' Company in 1567 and purported to be the jests of the poet laureate himself, though the fact that nearly forty years had passed since his death in 1529 adds to the probability that they are apocryphal. In them, Skelton, who had actually been educated at both Oxford and Cambridge, is represented as a Master of Arts addicted to all kinds of sharp practice. He once, we are told, was summoned from his parish to explain charges that he kept a mistress. Armed with two capons for bribes, Skelton abused his bishop with insolence and then returned to warn his parishioners that if they objected further to his mistress (she had borne him a healthy son, whom he displayed from the pulpit) they would suffer for it by being made cuckolds.⁶ This is by no means the coarsest of the tales, most of which show Skelton as a rogue. Yet rogue or no, there exists throughout the tales the implication that the old scoundrel was making good use of his talents.

The Jests of Scogin (Scogan, Scoggin, etc.) was recorded by the Stationers' Company in 1565,⁷ and goes even further in debasing the world of learning. A John Scogan (fl. 1480) is said to have been a fool at the court of Edward IV and perhaps a Master of Arts at Oriel College, Oxford; but it is unlikely that the tales about him have any more validity than do those about Skelton and he may have been an entirely fictitious character. He is shown as a resident Master of Oxford who, after selling sawdust as flea powder, advised his disappointed customers to hold open the mouth of each flea and pour in sawdust until it choked.⁸ Like the fictional Skelton, he was a swindler and a knave, and represented the scholar who could live by his wits; but he moved among lesser men. Bribed by the gift of a horse, he once undertook to prepare for orders a slovenly fool who only after hard work was able to master the alphabet. When the time came for him to be examined, Scogin assisted him before the examiners and won for him the order of subdeacon. The scholar's father would next have him a deacon, to which end he gave Scogin a sum of money; but the boy's stupidity defied even Scogin's coaching in the next examination, so that only by bribing the examiner himself was Scogin able to get him through. Still not content, the scholar now decided to advance further and become a priest:

> After this, the said Scholler did come to the next Orders, & brought a present to the Ordinary from Scogin, but the Schollers father paid for

all. Then said the Ordinary to the Scholler: I must needes oppose [i.e. examine] you, & for Master Scogins sake, I will oppose you in a light matter. Isaac had two sons: Esau and Jacob; who was Jacob's father? The Scholler stood still, & could not tell. Well, said the Ordinary, I cannot admit you to be Priest untill the next orders, & then bring me an answer. The Scholler went home with a heavy heart, bearing a letter to master Scogin, how his Scholler could not answer to this question: Isaac had two sons, Esau and Jacob: who was Jacob's father? Scogin said to his scholler: thou fool and asse-head! dost thou not know Tom Miller of Os[e]ney? Yes, said the Scholler. Then Scogin: thou knowest he had two sonnes, Tom and Jacke. Who is Jacke's father? The scholler said: Tom Miller. Why, said Scogin, thou mightest have said, that Isaac was Jacob's father. Then said Scogin, thou shalt arise betime in the morning, & carry a letter to the Ordinary, & I trust he will admit thee, before the Orders shall be given. The scholler rose up betime in the morning, & carried the letter to the Ordinary. The Ordinary said: for Master Scogin's sake, I will oppose you no farther than I did yesterday. Isaac had two sons: Esau and Jacob—Who was Jacob's father? Marry, said the Schollar, I can tell you now that was Tom Miller of Os[e]ney. Goe, foole, goe, said the Ordinary, & let thy master send thee no more to me for orders; for it is impossible to make a foole a wise man.[9]

It was, however, possible to make a fool a priest, and Scogin's scholar, by bribery, finally became one. The scholar-fool was the butt of the joke in this instance, as was the freshman in another tale who, poaching rabbits with his fellows, cried *"Ecce cuniculi multi!"* when he saw their prey, and as the frightened rabbits ran off was astonished to reflect that they should have understood Latin. But the humor of such incidents is secondary to the ridicule heaped on the want of even common sense in the university clerk. And more biting than the ridicule is the cynicism of the compiler of *The Jests of Scogin,* who observed of the imbecile scholar's success, "Heere a man may see that money is better than learning."[10]

Ephemeral literature of this sort contributed to a bluntly derogatory form of criticism which lasted throughout the Elizabethan years. Crude, and often vulgar, the tales seem to have been something more than scandalous exaggerations; they were, in fact, popularizations of a prevailing attitude which from time to time received more dignified literary expression. That the universities were acquiring an increasingly bad name from intrigue and bribery among college heads and officials is suggested, for example, in the second part of Philip Stubbes's *Anatomie of Abuses* (1583). Here it is maintained that

> except one be able to give the regent or provost of the house, a peece of mony, ten pound, twentie pound, fortie pound, yea, a hundred pound, a yoke of fatte oxen, or a couple of fine geldings, or the like, though he be never so toward a youth, nor have never so much need of maintenance, yet he comes not there, I warrant him. If he cannot prevaile this way, Let him get letters commendatory from some of reputation, and perhaps he may speed, in hope of benefite to insue. So that the places in the universities and free schooles, seeme rather to be solde for mony and frienship [*sic*], than given *gratis* to them that have neede, as they ought to be.[11]

The decay of learning was lamented in the complaint of *Tom Tel-Troths Message* (1600), when the poet observed:

> Englands two eyes, Englands two Nurceries,
> Englands two nests, Englands two holy mounts,
> I meane, Englands two Universities,
> Englands two Lamps, Englands two sacred founts,
>   Are so puld at, puld out, and eke puld downe,
>   That they can scarce maintaine a wide sleev'd gowne.
>
>   Lately as one CAME ore a BRIDGE, he saw
>   An OXE stand ore a FORDE to quench his drouth:
>   But lo, the Oxe his dry lips did withdraw,
>   And from the water lifted up his mouth.
>   Like Tantalus, this drie Oxe there did stand:
>   God grant this darke Ænigma may be scand!

Early Literary Portraits

> The Liberall Sciences, in number seaven,
> Which, in seaven ages, like seaven Monarchs raigned,
> And shin'd on earth as Planets seaven in heaven,
> Are now like Almesfolkes beggerly maintained,
>   Whilst in their roome, seaven deadly sins beare sway,
>   Which makes these seaven Arts, like seaven slaves obey.[12]

And in the *Parnassus* plays (*ca.* 1600) appears almost a summary of the ills which had, by the end of the sixteenth century, tarnished the universities' reputation. The *Pilgrimage to Parnassus* shows by allegory how the well-intentioned Philomusus and Studioso traveled to Parnassus through the trivium of medieval study, fully as intent on reaching their goal as was a later and more famous pilgrim on his progress to heaven; neither the wine-bibbing of Madido, nor the "melting venerie" of Amoretto, nor the worldly ambition of Ingenioso, could deflect them from their purpose. But once arrived (i.e., after long years at the university), the scholars became bitterly disillusioned. In the *Return from Parnassus* they found that though they had sacrificed their youth to learning, the price had been paid in vain; the most ignorant boor was better off than they, and cynically they concluded that since fortune and virtue did not go together, they would henceforth strive for fortune.

By the time the *Parnassus* plays were enacted at St. John's College, Cambridge, at the end of the century, adverse criticism of the universities had created a foreshadowing of many of the unsavory characters who later pervaded the university novel—the conniving Master, the corrupt student, and the scholar-fool. There was not yet, however, any appreciable body of literature that might be called university fiction. This was owing in part to the fact that only during the reigns of the Tudors did the universities begin to emerge from the relative seclusion of their medieval existence. They had from the first belonged to churchmen and scholars, and little went on within their walls that directly concerned anyone not a churchman or a scholar. But with the sudden decision of Henry VIII to thrust the settlement of his first troublesome divorce into the unwilling hands of his universities, they began to play a more immediate part in England's affairs. Under Elizabeth, they became important agents in the establishment of the new church. They also were developing new scientific thought despite their Aristotelian heritage, and it was from Oxford and Cambridge that Sir Thomas Gresham in 1596 drew the teachers for his new Gresham College in London. The drama early became a popular student amusement; it was Cambridge that sent Nashe, Greene, and Marlowe on to London. At Cambridge, too, appeared the poor scholar Edmund Spenser, who with pedantic Harvey threshed out the future of English poetry. Perhaps nothing could demonstrate more clearly the new place the universities held in the public consciousness than Elizabeth's visits to Oxford and Cambridge. She went twice to each, and was feted on all four occasions with a ponderous succession of sermons, masks, and disputations for which she showed an enthusiasm that wonderfully survived the heavy outpourings of Latin. Her evident pleasure in what she found there and the mutual esteem which was apparent between the queen and her universities made of these visits events of national importance and gave clear evidence of the extent to which the universities had emerged from their earlier obscurity.

Change of this sort obviously did much to prepare the ground for popular fiction about university life. Yet an even more important development was taking place which was to have a profound effect in stimulating writers to use university material. So long as characters drawn from the academic world were represented as being merely despicable, or stupid, or abused, they were at best suited to outraged complaint, and at worst, to the bawdy tales of *Skelton* and *Scogin*. But by the end of the sixteenth century the university scene was being drastically altered by increasing numbers of young men of wealth and birth. It was then that it became fashionable for young men to go to the universities for a few markedly pleasant years of undergraduate life, and, as a result, distinct social classes within the student ranks became clear. This need not necessarily, perhaps, have been a change for the worse. But wealthy and titled students, pampered outrageously by solicitous college authorities, quickly evolved their own ideas of higher education. By 1600 many of them were in residence without the slightest intention of taking a degree, but with large followings who demonstrated that there was more to university life than attendance at lectures. Charges of idleness and dissipation began to flow freely against undergraduates who affected rich clothes, long, curled hair, and the manners of court society, while they spent their time bullbaiting, cockfighting, and brawling in taverns. The increasing comfort of university life encouraged this new race of students. Rooms in colleges now showed signs of luxury—paneling, fireplaces, pictures, books, and soft beds. Never again were the universities to be, as they once had been, the home of poor scholars; henceforth these were on the fringe of university life. They were scorned both for their poverty and for their industry, and quickly took on, in the eyes of their betters, the musty attributes of pedants.

This change in the composition of both Oxford and Cambridge enriched significantly the range of characters from which fictional representations might be drawn. The earlier scholar-scoundrel was perhaps comparable to the new scholar-libertine, just as the earlier scholar-fool was comparable to the new dullards of university life. But the new race of scholars was far more colorful than its predecessors, and it included conflicting groups of personalities which were admirably suited to the purposes of fiction. For a time, the development that had taken place was reflected chiefly in indignant explosions berating the new state of the universities. John Lyly complained in *Euphues* (1579) that "it has become a byeword among the common people that they had rather send their children to the cart than to the university," and he explained that the cause was to be found in the rioting, drinking, dancing, and corruption of university life.[13] In the *Pilgrimage to Parnassus,* it was the tippling of Madido and the amorousness of Amoretto that aroused the author's scorn. And while the *Parnassus* plays decried the high life and low ways of the frivolous, they also demonstrated that the poor and hard-working student was something of a martyr; so did the character of George Pyeboard in *The Puritan* (1607), who told how while others wasted their time at Oxford, he worked conscientiously for the period it took to wear out six gowns, only to be expelled for having been driven by hunger to the desperate expedient of stealing a cheese from Jesus College.[14] These academic characters early established the line, observed in novels later on, between spectacular villains and rather dull heroes. Meanwhile, the humor inherent in descendants of the scholar-fool was being exploited. The pedantic Holofernes of *Love's Labour's Lost,* and Fungoso, the awkward student of *Every Man Out of His Humor,* may have been drawn from the tradition of Italian comedy and *novelle,* but they are completely in agreement with other academic portraits, shortly to be examined, and as character types they helped to establish a pattern as important to the university novel as that which set the wild young men against the studious bores.

But these were only beginnings. It seems to have been left to character writers of the seventeenth century to exploit for the first time the startling and humorous incongruities that were now to be found in the academic scene. There would be some difficulty, no doubt, in proving that the Overburian characters (which began to appear in 1614) and John Earle's *Microcosmographie* (1628) directly influenced nineteenth-century university novelists, but it is very easy to show that between the seventeenth

Early Literary Portraits

and nineteenth centuries there was no significant alteration, in popular literature, of the character-types they established. They succeeded in joining the themes of poverty, pedantry, and wasted youth to create pictures of university life which later became stereotypes in university fiction. And in their divergent attitudes they set forth the opposing points of view that motivated the plots of almost all the novels: the group known as "Overburian," though certainly not all written by Sir Thomas, agree in speaking for the world of fashion, scoffing at the uncouth ways of the scholar; Earle, on the other hand, countered by uttering the world of learning's scorn for the "meere Gallant."

The Overburian "A Meere Scholler" makes its point abruptly when it identifies its subject as "an intelligible Asse" who can speak longer than any man can listen to him.[15] This creature knows Latin better than he knows English, just as he knows the rest of the world better than he knows England. Yet his interests are narrow: his only conversation is of the university, and his only ambition is to be a Fellow of one of its colleges. He is at pains to argue on all matters, so that "his whole life is spent in *Pro & Contra*," yet his ignorance is profound and his pedantry complete:

'Tis a wrong to his reputation to be ignorant of any thing; and yet he knoes not that he knowes nothing. He gives directions for Husbandry from *Virgils Georgicks;* for Cattell, from his *Bucolics;* for Warlicke Stratagems, from his *Aeneides,* or *Caesars Commentaries.* Hee orders all things by the Booke, is skilfull in all Trades, and thrives in none. He is led more by his eares then his understanding, taking the sound of words for their true sense: and do's therfore confidently beleeve, that *Erra Pater* was the Father of Hereticks, *Rodolphus Agricola,* a substantiall Farmer; and will not sticke to averre, that *Systema's Logicke* doeth excell *Keckermans.* His ill lucke is not so much in being a foole, as in being put to such paines to expresse it to the world: for what in others is naturall, in him (with much adoe) is artificiall. His poverty is his happinesse, for it makes some men beleeve, that he is none of fortunes favorites. That learning which he hath, was in his Non-age put in backward like a Clister, and 'tis now like Ware mislaid in a Pedlers packe; a ha's it, but knowes not where it is. In a word, he is the Index of a man, and the Title-page of a Scholler, or a Puritane in moralitie, much in profession, nothing in practise."[16]

The intensive "meere" only sharpens the edge of these remarks, which were reinforced by the portraits in "A Pedant" and "The True Character of a Dunce."[17] Equally cutting is the character of "A Meere Fellow of an House" (i.e., of a college), a pedant who "respects no man in the *Universitie,* and is respected by no man out of it." He is inevitably a pauper whose poverty is exceeded only by his pretentions. He laughs to think what a fool he could have made of Solomon. It is his chief delight to lead a faction, and to compete for offices he seldom wins. But the Fellow appears at his worst when he tries to mix with society, in which he is painfully awkward, unfashionably dressed, and given to conversation "wherein hee commits more absurdities, then a Clown in eating of an egge."[18]

These unkind thrusts were parried by John Earle. "A Downe-Right Scholler," he wrote, does indeed have many faults: he talks too much of the university, his table manners are atrocious. "He cannot kisse his hand and cry *Madame,* nor talke idly enough to beare her company. His smacking of a Gentle-woman is somewhat too savory, & hee mistakes her nose for her lippe.... He ascends a horse somewhat sinisterly, though not on the left side, and they both goe jogging in griefe together."[19] But these failings are unimportant; the scholar doesn't bother himself with trivialities because he has better things to think of. Though he is rough without, he is actually made of good metal inside, and he has "much learning in the Ore"; it is only his rough exterior that draws upon his head the rebukes of the courtier, who is his exact opposite—finely finished on the outside, but empty within.

Early Literary Portraits

The time ha's got a veine of making him ridiculous, and men laugh at him by tradition, and no unlucky absurdity; but is put upon his profession, and done like a Scholler. But his fault is onely this, that his mind is somewhat too much taken up with his minde, and his thoughts not loaden with any carriage besides.... The Hermitage of his Study, ha's made him somewhat uncouth in the world, and men make him worse by staring on him. Thus is he silly and ridiculous, and it continues with him for some quarter of a yeere, out of the Universitie. But practise him a little in men, and brush him o're with good company, and hee shall out-ballance those glisterers as farre as a solid substance do's a feather, or Gold Gold-lace."[20]

Not all scholars, to be sure, earned this kind of praise, for not all scholars were quite so "downe-right." In "A Plodding Student," Earle poked fun at one who he noted "...ha's a strange forc't appetite to Learning, and to atchive it brings nothing but patience and a body. His Study is not great but continuall, and consists much in the sitting up till after midnight in a rug gowne, and a Night-cap, to the vanquishing perhaps of some sixte lines...."[21] And in "A Pretender to Learning" Earle describes the man who "never talks of any thing but learning, and learnes all from talking.... He ha's taken paines to be an Asse, though not to be a Scholler, and is at length discovered and laught at."[22] But whereas Earle too laughed at foibles such as these he saved his most damaging caricature for another student who deserved it more: the idle young blood. "A Young Gentleman of the University" describes one who enters the university only because he wants to call himself a university man, and because his father thinks he should learn fencing and dancing. He is distinguished by velvet on his gown and by a certain skill at tennis. Although his rooms are handsomely decorated with fine bindings, he does not study for fear of misplacing and losing his books; the only reading he indulges in takes place in the library, on rainy days, when he pores over books of heraldry and the peerage. In fair weather he is busy with sports and the pleasures of the tavern. This young man dreads above all things being mistaken for a scholar—a possibility surely more fancied than real."[23] Here, almost fully formed, is the new kind of undergraduate who was to appear spectacularly in the pages of so many novels of a later day.

At this time there appeared as well, and apparently for the first time, a secondary group of characters who were soon to be established as accessories to the university scene. Earle described "An Old Colledge Butler" who was as shrewd, unscrupulous, and domineering as the scouts and gyps of Victorian times,[24] and "An Universitie Dunne," waiting doggedly outside doors that were forever closed to him and upbraiding scholars who, if caught at all, paid him only with abuse.[25] And in the work of still a third character writer, Wye Saltonstall, is to be found a lively portrait of "A Townesman in Oxford," "one that hath liv'd long by the well of knowledge, but never sipt at it."[26] He is amiable, but only until he has emptied the purses of undergraduate victims, whom he then pursues with fanatic zeal as "a seducer of hopefull wits, & one that strives to wrythe the pliantnesse of youth to all ill actions."

The character writers dealt with university life for the most part in a spirit of good humor. In fact, despite occasional expressions of genuine anguish and contempt, early critics did not utterly condemn the world of learning represented by Oxford and Cambridge. They recognized some obvious failings, but these were neither so dangerous nor so pervasive as others which were soon to attract attention. A more perceptive observer might have seen that by the time of the Restoration the foundations had been laid for the disastrous days of the eighteenth century, when both Oxford and Cambridge were obliged to endure the consequences of a number of serious wrongs wrought by them and upon them during the reigns of the Tudors and Stuarts. At least three important reasons for their deterioration may be

Early Literary Portraits

found in the history of the years between the Reformation and the Restoration. The first of these was the nagging problem of religion. Beginning with the visitations (i.e., inspections) despatched by Henry VIII in 1535, the universities were under the constant scrutiny of outsiders determined that they should reflect the orthodoxy of the moment. The agents of Thomas Cromwell were ruthless in wiping out the vestiges of a discredited clergy; the visitors under Edward VI confirmed the triumph of the reformers; those sent out by Mary were ordered to uproot, demolish, and add whatever was held necessary for the reëstablishment of the Roman Catholic faith, and their demands for conformity added many university men to the tide of Marian exiles which flowed to the Continent. Interference of this kind brought only distress to the universities: Henry's heavy hand wrought a too-violent break with their cultural past; Mary's lighted the flaming stakes in Oxford which consumed Cranmer, Ridley, and Latimer; and throughout the troubled days of the Reformation the stability necessary to academic life was impossible so long as theological contention raged so violently. When Elizabeth ascended the throne a period of relative peace did, to be sure, come to the universities, but it was induced by a measure whose effects were unfortunate and lasting. Elizabeth's Act of Supremacy meant, among other things, that matriculating students were required to subscribe by oath to the Thirty-nine Articles and to the doctrine of royal supremacy in the church; it was not until the reforms of 1854–1856 and 1871 that the universities were released from this restriction which made them denominational, rather than national, in character, and which forbad them to offer degrees to those outside the Church of England.

Political interference accompanied the disturbances brought on by religious controversy. From the time of Henry VIII to that of Elizabeth, political alignments fluctuated as wildly as did the concepts of orthodoxy. Elizabeth, however, made sure that law should determine the political allegiance of Oxford and Cambridge; in 1571 she established, by an act of Parliament, the subjection of both to parliamentary control. Elizabeth merely followed well-established precedent when she took a direct hand in university government through the proclamation of statutes covering all aspects of university life. But though by the end of the sixteenth century the practice of governmental interference with the universities was to be expected, even in the hands of enlightened reformers it was too often a harmful imposition. Its dangers can be seen nowhere more clearly than in the period of parliamentary rule in the next century, when the right of university government was assumed by Parliament itself. The outbreak of the civil war found Oxford loyal to church and crown; it became Charles's headquarters while he waged his unequal struggle, and it defended so stoutly its greatest lost cause that it shares still in the tradition of cavalier tragedy and the fall of an ill-fated and imprudent king. By contrast, Cambridge, which had become increasingly Puritan in its sympathies, was promptly seized by Parliamentarians who ruled it so harshly that the Restoration brought relief even to those who had earlier opposed the crown. During Puritan rule, university life at both Oxford and Cambridge was little more than a succession of expulsions and dispossessions which destroyed the remnants of a vanquished cause and drove out all who would not subscribe to Parliament's authority.

    The third source of serious trouble within the universities was in part the outgrowth of these confusing demands for religious and political conformity. It is obvious that under such troubled conditions academic achievements could not be great. Intellectual life was of course never wholly destroyed, but the atmosphere of oppression was nearly fatal to university curricula that still lacked the vigor to escape the domination of Aristotle. The humanist revival had all but expired, at Cambridge as well as Oxford, in the chaotic years of unrest; until well into the seventeenth century it survived chiefly in the faltering study of Greek. It was in fact the inadequacy of the standard curriculum which drew forth a substantial body of criticism in the years after 1600. This was the first great period of educational theorists in England, and a number of them had a great deal to say over and above horrified comments about the downward path of the undergraduate. These are in many ways typified by Thomas Hobbes, who had been at Magdalen Hall, Oxford, and knew what he was talking about when he savagely charged the universities with their neglect of practical knowledge in general and the sciences and mathematics in particular.[27] Then came Milton, with even more violence. The studies he had met with at Cambridge had been, to say the least, uncongenial—an "asinine feast of sow-thistles and brambles" he called them in *Of Education* (1644)—and his own plan was for something more practical. So was Cowley's, when he complained in his *Proposition for the Advancement of Experimental Philosophy* (1661) that the universities were only too likely to breed "impossible mermaids."

Not all of this criticism was quite fair. Although it was scarcely possible that the universities should, in such difficult times, have been able to effect the necessary revolution in their studies, there were signs that the devil had not taken all. In 1658 John Locke received his degree of Master of Arts at Oxford; in 1661 Isaac Newton entered Trinity at Cambridge, where he wrote most of his *Principia;* in the middle of the century the little group known as the "Invisible College" was working so effectively in Oxford and Cambridge that with the Restoration it emerged as the Royal Society. The Restoration saw, also, the flourishing of antiquarians at Oxford, and the start of the great university press; and it was the Cambridge Platonists who won praise from Bishop Burnet for having preserved the Church of England's "esteem over the nation." Nevertheless, it would be an understatement to say that the universities were conservative in their attachment to the older forms of learning. This failing, coupled with their subservience to the Church of England and their unfortunate concern with politics, contributed largely to the increasingly painful abuse that was heaped upon them.

CHAPTER III

DECLINE OF THE UNIVERSITIES

DETRACTORS of eighteenth-century Oxford and Cambridge have not been able to say enough against them, and most of what they have said is justified.[1] Following 1688 the political involvements became even more complex. William was welcomed at Cambridge, which emerged from the Revolution firmly Whig and low-church in its sympathies, but he was pronounced a boor and an intruder in Tory Oxford. Anne won Oxford completely, but was cool toward Cambridge. And the first two Georges showed almost no interest at all in either university save in their resentment toward an Oxford that still defiantly toasted the Jacobite cause. During this time the party struggles which were so prominent in the English political scene were mirrored in the universities, determining appointments and preferments on all levels. It is not surprising, though many felt it was deplorable, that professors who for long had had little to do while the real work of teaching was carried on by the colleges, now were inspired to engage in a discreditable scramble for positions and to quarrel energetically among themselves for power and wealth. A good example is Richard Watson of Cambridge. The vigor with which he accumulated offices and worked to make them more profitable to himself was completely uninhibited. Beginning as a scholar of Trinity, he was in 1764 appointed Regius Professor of Chemistry, a subject of which he openly claimed to know nothing; the office was unendowed when he took it over, but he arranged for an annual payment of £100. In 1771 he realized one of his fondest ambitions when, as he put it, "through hard travelling and some adroitness," he was made Regius Professor of Divinity; though he conceded

---
[1] For notes to chap. iii, see pp. 205–206.

that he "knew as much of divinity as could reasonably be expected of a man whose course of studies had been directed to, and whose time had been fully occupied in, other pursuits" (he certainly had no degree in divinity), he raised the awards of this post from £300 to at least £1,000. And in 1782 he became Bishop of Llandaff. Yet through these profitable years he spent much of his time on his pleasant estate in Windermere, where he improved his land and lived the life of a country gentleman. Predatory ambition like this left little peace in Common and Combination Rooms, and helped to make the reputation of the eighteenth-century dons, as they were by then called, almost completely unenviable. The situation was not improved by the fact that thoroughly unfitted men who happened to be the descendants of college founders could receive automatic college appointments. It was not improved, either, by the immunity which incumbents of most senior offices enjoyed against removal for nearly any offense short of actual crime. And it was decidedly worsened by the universal requirement of celibacy among dons, which made for evils of a peculiarly unacademic nature. One can hardly wonder that the commonest picture of an eighteenth-century don is that of an idle old sinner, fat and coarse, too vain and lazy to attend to his students beyond toadying to the wealthy ones, content to feast and slumber, drink vast quantities of brandy and port, engage in amours with the college bedmakers, and aspire to the profitable consequences of being college head, professor, and bishop all at the same time.

As for the undergraduates, those who paid their own way had become by 1700 far more numerous and prominent in college life than the scholars who won their places on the college foundations. They were headed by the noblemen, young chips off the old title who were distinguished by gold tassels, or "tufts," on their caps, and gowns of brilliant colors (though purple came more and more to be in vogue). They enjoyed, together with a great deal of prejudice in their favor among the dons, a number of privileges such as the right to a degree in two years rather than the three or four required of humbler men. Beside them, there was a large class of aspirants to the dignity that accompanied a title: the gentlemen commoners of Oxford, and the fellow commoners of Cambridge. These were ambitious young men who, by paying twice the normal college fees, earned the privilege of eating with the Fellows, snubbing everyone (including the dons) except their titled superiors, and wearing gowns only slightly less conspicuous than those of noblemen. The universities of the eighteenth century drew a very sharp line between the rich and the poor, and these two groups stood very clearly on one side of it. Middle ground was occupied by the commoners at Oxford and the pensioners at Cambridge, in both cases students who paid regular fees but who often were comfortably well off, lacking only the pretentions of gentlemen and fellow commoners. Last in the scale, and very much on the other side of the line, were the Oxford servitors and Cambridge sizars, students who were really poor, and could not qualify as foundation scholars, but worked their way through the university by performing duties for the colleges or menial work for the noblemen and gentlemen commoners. These were, of course, greatly scorned by the upper ranks; the stringent rules of university etiquette which forbad a junior to speak first to his senior, or indeed anyone to speak at all until proper introductions had been performed, also forbad any intercourse between sizars or servitors and their social superiors. It need hardly be added that the decay which beset the dons struck also at this body of undergraduates, and in the obvious places. The line between rich and poor corresponded exactly with the line between dissipation and ignorance on the one side, and hard work and learning on the other. Unfortunately, dissipation and ignorance appeared to hold the field so long as the majority was preoccupied with dress, gaming, drinking, and wenching, in a frenzied and moderately successful effort to practice the arts of the beau monde.

There is, to be sure, a kinder word to be said about eighteenth-century scholars. The tendency to caricature what was undoubtedly a remarkable accumulation of abuses has in some measure obscured the less spectacular accomplishments of quieter men—"reading men," as their somewhat rare occupation distinguished them. From the Restoration to 1800, Cambridge could boast the names of Newton, Bentley, and Porson, Gray, Prior, Horace Walpole, Sterne, and later Wordsworth and Coleridge, as well as Chesterfield, the younger Pitt, Castlereagh, and Wilberforce. To Oxford went the senior Wesley, his three sons, and Whitefield; there also went Christopher Wren, Bishop Butler, Fox, the elder Pitt, Adam Smith, Gibbon, and for four unhappy terms, Samuel Johnson. In the light of such names, one can scarcely say that the universities were wholly unproductive of good. And though most of what was wrong with Oxford and Cambridge was not to be corrected until the reforms of the following century, reform was beginning, even in this time: curricular and examination systems were being overhauled, and appointments were gradually subjected to more impartial control. But to most eighteenth-century critics, the picture was on the whole pretty black, and the state of the universities discouragingly corrupt. Serious scholars found it difficult to work with tutors who could not be bothered to instruct and who in fact resented academic intrusions into their more compelling affairs. It was perfectly possible to pass through the universities with distinction but without the slightest pretense of study beyond picking up a sufficient number of tricks and ruses to satisfy examiners who had no intention of placing any hurdles in the path of those claiming their degrees. The Acts and Disputations, which terminated the university course, were meaningless forms carried on before dons whom the thoughtful candidate had feasted into apathy and into whose ears he poured memorized answers to stock questions that had become traditional. At Oxford the six lectures that were the final test of the aspiring Master of Arts' ability to teach came to be called "wall lectures" for the sufficient reason that no one bothered to attend them.

The preface of a 1732 edition of Earle's *Microcosmographie*, commenting on its collection of characters, observed that the portrait group, being drawn from unchanging nature, stood out as true then as when it had been originally composed. If the adherence to type in live academicians was noticeable, as this suggests, certainly fictional characters showed an even more marked continuity. With monotonous regularity pictures of university life included wily townsmen and college servants; tutors who were pedantical pedagogues after the pattern of the Overburian "meere Fellow"; and fast young men like Earle's "young gentlemen," who threatened violence to their creditors and led—as "Smarts," "Slicers," "Loungers," "Dashing Men," and "Men of Fire"—lives of pleasure unspoiled by the sobering presence of stolid reading men who were the descendants of both "meere Schollers" and "downe-right Schollers." Moreover, the sharp distinctions between classes of undergraduates, and between undergraduates and dons, made the problem of literary characterization both increasingly easy and increasingly stereotyped. The terms "fast men," "slow men," "reading men," "bloods," and "tufts" carried familiar connotations to eighteenth-century readers. The activities in which the widely differing "sets" normally engaged became fully prescribed. One group was expected to hunt, drive forbidden tandems, steal unseen into their colleges after the midnight curfew, journey surreptitiously to London, and feign illness to avoid bothersome lectures and chapel services. These men drank hugely, fought (duels were fashionable for a time), kept mistresses in nearby towns, and affected an elegance of dress matched only by that of their living quarters, where they entertained hordes of their friends with the costliest fare their unlimited wealth could provide (it was a point of honor, though, to pay no bills), held riotous wine parties, and relaxed in the comforting fumes of a narghile. In the meantime their humbler fellows, the "slow" and "reading" men, kept to their bare rooms, studying until dawn with their heads wrapped in cold towels, their walls covered with charts of easy reference detailing the progress of the Punic Wars.

A sampling of eighteenth-century periodical literature will serve to illustrate the perpetuation of the earlier characters in popular literature. One familiar theme which drew upon the older tradition was that of the difference between the scholar and the gentleman.[2] *The Babler* (No. 77, July 17, 1764) tells of young Tom Welbank, who for six months after his return from the university was so encumbered by the manners of the scholar that society considered him a madman. At a welcoming party intended to give him the opportunity to show off his erudition, he made a fool of himself with academical declamations and harangues, sprinkled with Latin and Greek quotations, defending impossible arguments until the comment circulated about the table that " 'Mr. Welbank is a very pretty scholar, but he seems a little unacquainted with the world.' "[3] In *The Tatler* (No. 39, July 9, 1709), Steele struck a little-heard note by eulogizing Oxford as a great democracy of learning; and in *The Guardian* (No. 62, May 22, 1713) he praised both universities as nurseries for the service of the church, and the homes of culture. Elsewhere, however, *The Guardian* was on more familiar ground: No. 94 (July 29, 1713) raised an objection against the universities for their concern with deep learning to the exclusion of "all the little qualifications and accomplishments which make up the character of a well-bred man."[4] Jack Lizard, in No. 24 (April 8, 1713), undertook after his university career to be "the mouth of the company" with such deplorable results that he had to be given strict rules of conversation, which eventually turned him into an acceptable companion.[5] Yet Jack conceived of himself as a gentleman, and affected a giant sword at his side to add gallantry to his person (No. 143, August 25, 1713). Dr. Johnson in *The Rambler* (No. 157, September 17, 1751) pictured the heavy scholar who sneered at the way the "ambition of pretty accomplishments found its way into the receptacles of learning," but was embarrassed into stupid silence by fashionable ladies who had heard he was a wit and pressed him for bright conversation;[6] it is in *The Rambler,* too (No. 179, December 3, 1751), that Gelasimus is described, a learned scholar "who [first] fully explained all the properties of the catenarian curve," but was a social misfit when he tried to conform to the demand for wit and an easy manner.[7]

Another theme was equally prominent. *The Connoisseur* (No. 82, August 21, 1755) offered to a young gentleman going to the university a letter of advice which warned him not to become a pedant, but at the same time cautioned him to avoid the atheists, drunkards, rakes, and liars whom he was bound to encounter there. This reflected the general assumption that an introduction to sin would necessarily accompany a university career. In the same periodical (No. 11, April 11, 1754) appeared a comment on Oxford coxcombs, idle and debauched, who were to be found most commonly in the taverns, theaters, and bagnios of London, and (No. 41, November 7, 1754) a letter from a young Cantab describing the exploits of the sporting set at Newmarket. Throughout the periodical literature of the time, in fact, are found the fast men and the scholar-nimrods who possessed all the graces that scholars lacked, together with vicious tendencies that made university life a colorful, if not uplifting, experience. And just as some dons were dismally pedantic, others were represented as living in delightfully sybaritic idleness, as content to waste away their time as were the most casual students. The academic atmosphere of the eighteenth-century universities is devastatingly revealed in a portrait that appeared in *The Idler* (No. 33, December 2, 1758, written by Thomas Warton).[8] Here is the "Journal" from a week in the life of "a Senior Fellow, or Genuine Idler," whose sole preoccupations were his wine cellar, the state of his weather glass, which told him whether it would be agreeable to ride out into the country, and the relative merits of his friends' tables. The only annoyances in this leisurely week arose when his meals were ill-prepared, when his bedmaker woke him at eight (for which she was dismissed), and when his seamstress ("the baggage has got a trick of smiling") lost the measurement of his wrist. There follows, after the extract from the "Journal," a mild recantation and apology beginning with the hope that the reader would not see in this an attempt to decry the universities which, "however degenerated," preserved in the memories of Hooker, Hammond, Bacon, and Newton a "Genius" that inspired learning, and did, after all, teach pure religion even in the midst of "general depravity of manners and laxity of principles." This righteous thought is really no more convincing than the author's conclusion that the English universities of the eighteenth century "render their students virtuous, at least by excluding all opportunities of vice." Opportunities for vice would seem to have knocked more than once on academic doors of the period.

Novels of the eighteenth century, insofar as they contain university subject matter, are generically the most immediate ancestors of the university novels. But although literary portrayals of university life such as those just reviewed were lively, they were hardly substantial enough for expansion to novel length, and for a time they were best put to use to add flavor rather than substance to the novels in which they appeared: a few somewhat

Decline of the Universities

raw incidents of high life among undergraduates, a sketch of a don or two—these were used most effectively as components of episodic and often picaresque tales. Later, changes within the nineteenth-century universities made available more varied and significant subject matter, though even then the novelist found it difficult at times to sustain variety or even interest in his work. The eighteenth-century novelists did not even attempt to do so, but they did make an important contribution to what was to follow. It is obvious that writers of fiction were bound, sooner or later, to find "the young gentleman of the university" a more colorful figure than his slower fellows. His escapades, his extravagance and dissipation, as well as his attractive ornaments of wealth and perhaps a title—these were perhaps not heroic qualities, but they could and did make the first university hero in the novel. It was in the novel that the rake became the leading figure in the scene, and he kept his place in the center of the stage for generations to follow. It was in the novel, too—and for somewhat the same reason—that the dons completed their evolution from bad to worst possible. Villainous tutors related to the harsh "meere Fellow" became even more pompous and incapable. Senior members were caricatured as "heavy, stupid recluses," such as those for whom the *Devil's Almanac* for 1745 predicted that "they would be so insensibly translated from the animal to the vegetable world, that men would hardly perceive any material alteration in the individual."[9]

The episodic nature of the early attempts to employ this material is exemplified in what seems to be the first appearance of university life in a novel—the story of the Man of the Hill in Fielding's *Tom Jones* (1749). The narrator relates how he spent four thoroughly debauched years at Oxford in the company of one Sir George Gresham, who was for a time his mentor in wickedness. Sir George, enjoying an annual allowance of £500, "kept his horses and his whore, and lived as wicked and as prostitute a life as he could have done, had he been never so entirely the master of his fortune."[10] He, by the way, was the first of the undergraduate villains who appreciated the full humor not only of running into debt but also of plotting the ruin of more sober youths. It was not long, however, before Sir George's pupil became even more profligate than he:

> I had not long contracted an intimacy with Sir George, before I became a partaker of all his pleasures; and when I was once entered on that scene, neither my inclination, nor my spirit, would suffer me to play an under-part. I was second to none of the company in any acts of debauchery; nay, I soon distinguished myself so notably in all riots and disorders, that my name generally stood first in the roll of delinquents, and instead of being lamented as the unfortunate pupil of Sir George, I was now accused as the person who had misled and debauched that hopeful young gentleman; for though he was the ring-leader and promoter of all the mischief, he was never so considered.[11]

Like many another young man, he discovered that this conduct did not sit well at home; he was cut off without a penny. It was now that the "great art" of Sir George was brought into play, to put Oxford's worst delinquent hopelessly in debt. When he realized the trap that had been set for him, his first thought, quite reasonably, was of suicide. But "a more shameful, though perhaps less sinful" alternative was at hand: he managed to complete his degradation by stealing a large sum of money from a fellow student, and was forced to flee Oxford. That he had managed to stay there for four years must remain either a cause for wonder or a confirmation of the gossip that condemned the universities for the vice they encouraged.

This pretty story is almost obscured, in the novel, by the more important events in the life of Tom himself; so are the admirable caricatures of the learned gentlemen Thwackum and Square. But in its defiant affirmation of the worst that could be said of an undergraduate its tone was soon enlarged and amplified. Francis Coventry's *The History of Pompey the Little* (1751) contains four chapters in which the degeneracy of life at Cambridge is gleefully exposed.[12] Coventry, writing while still at Cambridge (M.A., 1752), tells how the little dog Pompey was adopted by a young Cantab, Qualmsick by name, who was on his way to Cambridge for his first term. That Qualmsick became immediately one of the university's uncontrollables is not surprising, for his earlier education at Westminster had included a thorough grounding in the life of London's bagnios, where he had learned to conduct himself as one of the gentlemen of the town in the company of the best-known ladies of the town. He was entered in Cambridge only for the sake of fashion and, appropriately, as a fellow commoner determined not to profit from anything he found there. Coventry devoted a long paragraph to the iniquities wrought by this breed of undergraduate upon both the peace and the good name of Cambridge. Then, dropping his stern mood, he happened to think of one especially droll exploit of Qualmsick's, a prank played upon a master of arts of his college, Mr. Williams. Williams had won his post because he could bow lower than anyone else, and once it was his, he had decided that he would never have to work again; instead, he fussed continually at tidying up his rooms, rode abroad in fine weather, ate and drank frequently and well, and above all, made himself agreeable to the less scrupulous young ladies of Cambridge. It was, in fact, Williams' amorousness that nearly got him into trouble. Qualmsick, spotting his man's weakest point at once, deposited one morning on his doorstep an ominous blanket-covered basket with a note pinned to it, the whole purporting to be from an outraged college bedmaker who had finally been brought to bed and wanted nothing more to do with, as she put it, Williams' bastard. For some reason Williams felt this was unfair, and arranged for a meeting of the college officials to clear his name. These dignitaries, many of whom felt it was only good luck that had kept the basket from *their* doorsteps, agreed with the college head that though there was little doubt the child was Williams', the offending girl who made such a disturbance should be punished. At this point Qualmsick's wit had its triumph as Pompey sprang from the basket, where he had been bundled up throughout these sorry proceedings.

Coventry wrote at length (chap. 13) on the character of Williams, and came to the conclusion that the man was "an egregious trifler." Williams' cousin was a milliner, who forwarded on to him bits of gossip dropped from and about the great ones in society; these he took to heart, and unaware that his conversational coinage was almost always counterfeit, passed it freely among those as ignorant as he. Williams did, however, affect a certain politeness, a clumsy imitation of the polite world. Nothing pleased him so much as the chance to exercise his charm in the role of guide, showing strangers (preferably female) about the university, and Coventry, remarking that Williams could, if he wished, act rather like a human being, showed him at his happy task. Other dons, however, lacked even this frail grace: Qualmsick's tutor, for example, who "knew no more of the world than if he had been brought up in a forest";[13] and the ancient recluse (chap. 14) who, frustrated in all his ambitions for advancement, finally withdrew to his rooms to live in solitude for the remainder of his life. This hermit, interrupted one day by the horrifying presence of ladies at his door, shuddered with alarm when he was asked to conduct them through the colleges; frantically he advised them to find a younger man, since he would probably no longer remember the sights they wanted to see.[14]

If the university was no longer familiar ground to the old man, he and others like him were among its best-known figures—at least in fiction, where the list of the incompetent is a long one. There are, to be sure, exceptions to this depressing rule. Sir Thomas Amory in *The Life of John Buncle* (1756–1766) described John's studies at Trinity College, Dublin, and showed by pages of ponderous discourse that they must have been rewarding. Richard Graves, an Oxford graduate, gave to one chapter of *The Spiritual Quixote* (1773) the title "Universities defended, &c."; here Mr. Geoffrey Wildgoose, who had been a diligent scholar at Oxford, upheld the universities as repositories for the sciences, quite necessary to keep the nation from "Gothic ignorance and barbarism."[15] At the very end of the century (though her novels did not appear until 1811 and after) Jane Austen created a small group of virtuous, intelligent, and cultivated young men in the persons of Henry Tilney (*Northanger Abbey*), Edmund Bertram (*Mansfield Park*), and Edward Ferrars (*Sense and Sensibility*), all of Oxford and—as a group—unique at the time for being both university men and gentlemen. Others of her university characters fall short of this standard: James Morland and John Thorpe of *Northanger Abbey,* and Mr. Collins of *Pride and Prejudice,* are, respectively, a nonentity, an empty-headed swell, and a smug fool. But even these men are only weak, not vicious. Far more typical of the eighteenth century is the heroic figure of Smollett's Peregrine Pickle, a contemporary (1751) of the unattractive Qualmsick. Armed with avuncular advice to avoid immodest women and mind his learning, and with £500 a year to maintain himself in the rank of gentleman commoner, Pickle became the leading young buck of his university (presumably Oxford), where he smoked more pipes, drank more ale, and supported more mistresses than any of his envious fellows—and spent the better part of many terms incognito in London. It is somewhat curious to discover in Pickle the first university hero who made friends among the leaders of the "sedate" set as easily as among the fastest men. During periods of regeneration, in fact, he studied hard, and he had always the good sense to go into retirement rather than into debt when his allowance was consumed. The reader is tempted to regard such discretion as almost a weakness in an otherwise splendidly unregenerate character. Certainly Pickle the terrible was a more familiar figure to eighteenth-century readers than was Pickle the wise and good.

Yet of all the terrible fellows, one stands out as the rascal who brought the eighteenth-century legend of academic depravity to its climax. Nowhere have the English universities been more vulgarly portrayed than in an otherwise insignificant book with the appealing title of *The Adventures of Oxymel Classic, Esq.: Once an Oxford Scholar* (1768), an anonymous slander which is probably the earliest approach to a university novel. Whether its author bore a grudge, or simply had a taste for the obscene, he reveled far more delightedly in the sour than in the sweet of the ancient compound suggested by his title. Oxymel, in spite of his name, "was not... blindly devoted to antiquity" and in fact scorned Latin and Greek (along with work of any kind) save as they could provide flavor to his conversation like "those pretty smirking gentlemen, who make a figure in the world, and are esteemed the very pretty scholars of the age."[16] Nevertheless, Oxymel had no less than two university careers, for he managed to be expelled from not only Oxford but Cambridge as well, which gave him a rather broader view of university life than most fictional heroes are able to attain to. His first attempt to matriculate at Oxford proved to him that his distaste for learning would have nothing to do with his progress at the university, for "a single line from any nobleman would have been of more service to him than if he had been the author of the Iliad itself";[17] and he was refused admission until he procured just such a recommendation, together with some practical advice:

Decline of the Universities 47

My good sir, replied his friend to him, when he had heard his story, you are come to the worst place in the world to succeed in without a good name or a recommendation. A vote for any paltry borough in the kingdom would be of more service to you here, than all the Greek and Latin you have picked up in school. The great men of Oxford are as good politicians as the great men at London; and I am afraid, you'll not find them very ready to oblige you, unless in your turn you can oblige them.[18]

This word of warning, however, became irrelevant when Oxymel began his education. He learned first to smoke, then to drink, and to kiss his bedmaker without blushing, and finally proceeded to the arts of staying out late at night, avoiding chapel, and running into debt. Some of his time was devoted to routine practical jokes such as the substituting of tobacco juice for tea in the cups of a friend's guests, but Oxymel was also capable of decidedly unusual attainments. At one period he shared his rooms with a prostitute who had been cast off by a Doctor of Divinity. Disguised as a student, she lived quite happily there until a peevish scholar gave the hoax away to the tutor Carfax, a beast whose immediate reaction was one of jealousy (he himself, it is noted, "had never ventured himself beyond the embraces of a musty bedmaker").[19] Carfax's raid on Oxymel's quarters did turn up the girl, but the unhappy tutor was locked in the cellar until he promised to forget the whole matter; Oxymel, in his turn, promised to get rid of her. But the upshot was that he brought her right back in again, and the reader is granted a startlingly suggestive picture of their subsequent congenial employments.

Tutors are pictured here as being not only bestial, but incredibly stupid. Yet the senior dons are even more contemptible. The Dean of Oxymel's College (which must, then, have been Christ Church, the only college headed by a Dean) was, like "almost all the heads of colleges in either of our universities," a monster who with unmerited advancement grew so insolent that he was dreaded by all the members of his college; strutting gigantically, he cowed them with a countenance so fierce that it successfully hid the waste of ignorance that lay behind it. "In one word, he was a composition of pride and ignorance, insolence and stupidity. A wit amongst bedmakers and undergraduates, and a fool amongst men of learning and his equals. A most imperious tyrant in his own college, and a most abject sycophant everywhere else."[20] In the same college was one of those who were, says the author, "to be found in all the colleges of our two renouwned universities, a set of invalids, whose distemper is of the mind, rather than of the body." This invalid was a Doctor of Divinity whose eccentricity bordered on lunacy when he became convinced that he was pregnant. When his bedmaker one day used his chamber pot, and thereby provided the Doctor's physician with some astounding evidence of genuine pregnancy, his desperation mounted to the point where Oxymel was obliged to find him a midwife. By common conspiracy the Doctor was then delivered of a large Hebrew concordance—to his happy astonishment, for, as he told Oxymel, he had never studied much Hebrew, and that not since he was a young man.[21]

Oxymel's Oxford career was full, but it was brief; he was expelled by the monstrous Dean for drunken fighting. At this point the hero reflected that college life was, indeed,

> never suited to his disposition; and the meannesses he observed practiced there every day, served only to fill him with indignation and disgust. On examining the discipline of our colleges, he condemned them all as most absurd institutions; nor was there so much injustice in his decision, as may be apprehended by those who live at a distance from the universities, and in consequence of that, entertain the most profound veneration for them. Those scandalous badges of subserviency and dependence, which every undergraduate is compelled to wear, might be suitable enough to a despotic government, but in a place of freedom, are most intolerable grievances.[22]

However hard it is to reconcile such a statement with Oxymel's own egregious conduct, it is almost harder to accept his next move. Off he went to Cambridge, hoping that things would be better there. But, displaying a wholly unforeseen love for scholarship, he promptly ran into trouble for defending the classics in what was by then considered the home of mathematics, where "it would be much safer to speak against the holy trinity, than against the use of triangles, curves, telescopes and fossils."[23] For a time he was made happy by the discovery that Cambridge was not quite lost, that where Dryden, Prior, and Milton once had dwelt there was still wit and genius "in the midst of systems, problems, lemmas and philosophy, as gold and diamonds are often found in the midst of dirt and rubbish."[24] The damage had been done, however, his blasphemy had been uttered, and Cambridge too expelled him. There being no other university in England to which he could apply, Oxymel turned to the life of a rake in London, and for another volume engaged in a succession of seductions and escapades for which his training at Oxford had abundantly prepared him.

This repulsive book is in its way a remarkable commentary on university life. But it really adds nothing except colorful details to the scholar's reputation that had long been current. So widely was this reputation accepted that the titles of at least two novels capitalized upon it to adorn their heroes with raffish qualities that were assumed rather than portrayed. One, entitled *Memoirs of an Oxford Scholar* (1756),[25] is perfunctory in its treatment of Oxford. Its main character, Mr. ———, there learned to drink and run into debt, but once armed with these accomplishments he departed prematurely to take up the life of a roué in search of a beauty known only as Chloe. At the conclusion of his somewhat immoral adventures he unexpectedly reflected: "Everything at Oxford contributes to strike a young Student with venerable Awe for that sacred Seat of Learning.

... I retain the most dutiful Regard for my Alma Mater."[28] This unlikely palinode is scarcely justified by any evidence of venerable awe in the scholar himself. A second work of this kind is *The Oxonian: or, The Adventures of Mr. G. Edmunds, Student of Brazen-Nose College, Oxford* (1771).[27] Mr. Edmunds' college career is even more nebulous than Mr. ———'s. We are told that he studied for the degree of Doctor of Divinity, but on the eve of receiving it he suddenly discovered that the idea of taking orders was unbearable, and left Oxford, remarking that its control over its students was too rigorous. Since the plot motivation of this novel is not its greatest merit, Mr. Edmunds next unaccountably embarked on a career of debauchery on the Continent, and finally, just as unaccountably, ended his life in perfect virtue, carried off by a malignant fever. Neither of these books is of even modest importance beyond the attempt each makes to endow a young man with an aura of wickedness by the simple expedient of identifying him with Oxford. Both, however, suggest the near-exhaustion of university fiction which was unable to refrain from snickers of delight at what it professed to condemn.

CHAPTER IV

REFORM AND THE UNIVERSITY NOVEL

THAT THE UNIVERSITY THEME in literature should ever have revived from the debasement to which *Oxymel Classic* had subjected it is almost entirely the result of the great changes that took place within the universities during the nineteenth century. The movement for university reform arose with such force, accomplished so much, and worked so effectively both to create and to dignify the large body of university fiction produced during the Victorian years, that it will probably be of some advantage to review briefly the events that took place. Enough has been said, no doubt, to indicate that change was badly needed. It should of course not be concluded that even during the eighteenth century, when English university education was at its lowest level, the need for change was not recognized. As early as 1747 Cambridge instituted the terminal examination called the Mathematical Tripos, but covering natural religion, moral philosophy, and the works of Locke as well, which in time came to determine the university's honor students. If this did not cure the ills of an outmoded examination system, it was at least a step toward such a cure. Not until 1800 did the Oxford Public Examination Statute initiate the same badly needed tightening of standards. But perhaps it was even more important that by the 1780's reform was also being undertaken in both universities to ensure the impartial appointment of fellowships. Complaints from within Oxford and Cambridge themselves had begun to discredit the practice of awarding unmerited appointments, which had served to perpetuate the sins of omission and commission on the part of so many college Heads and Fellows. But how clearly the reform movement was the product of the first half of the nineteenth century is perhaps suggested in the following observation by Oxford's Mark Pattison. For long the Rector of Lincoln College, and always a vigorously attentive critic of his university, Pattison in 1883 recalled what to a liberal educator must have seemed a miracle:

> If an Oxford man had gone to sleep in 1846 and had woke up again in 1850 he would have found himself in a totally new world. In 1846 we were in old Tory Oxford; not somnolent, because it was as fiercely debating, as in the days of Henry IV., its eternal church question. There were Tory majorities in all the colleges; there was the unquestioning satisfaction in the tutorial system, *i.e.* one man teaching everybody everything; the same belief that all knowledge was shut up between the covers of four Greek and four Latin books; the same humdrum questions asked in the examination; and the same evasive arts of reply. In 1850 all this was suddenly changed as if by the wand of a magician. The dead majorities of heads and seniors, which had sat like lead upon the energies of young tutors, had melted away. Theology was totally banished from Common Room, and even from private conversation. Very free opinions on all subjects were rife; there was a prevailing dissatisfaction with our boasted tutorial system. A restless fever of change had spread through the colleges—that wonder-working phrase, University reform, had been uttered, and that in the House of Commons.[1]

As it did to Pattison at Oxford, the change which took place in mid-century gave hope to men of both universities that reform could be effected; and by the end of the century it proved to be so. No single cause can be credited as the start of the reform movement, but several contributed to it. For one thing, the large and powerful merchant class which had been created by the Industrial Revolution contained within its numbers many Nonconformists who felt strongly about the religious restrictions that barred them and their sons from Oxford and Cambridge. For another, many felt just as strongly, and as justifiably, that

---
[1] For notes to chap. iv, see pp. 206–207.

Reform and the University Novel 53

they were excluded by the expense of an education which had come to belong to those who could afford to support their sons in the country-house atmosphere of the colleges. But ultimately it was the problem of the curriculum which did most to point up the obvious inadequacies of the universities. The phenomenal growth of science in the nineteenth century, with its accompanying marvels of invention and industry, created the inevitable and violent agitation for instruction in useful and practical knowledge.[2] And of course Oxford, where the authority of Aristotle was still unquestioned, and Cambridge, where Newton had scarcely been fully accepted, were glaringly ill-equipped to provide any such thing. From directions such as these, then, the universities had reform thrust upon them. It is probable that the depravity and decay with which they were burdened, and which no one really exaggerated, would sooner or later have impelled correction from within, but the abuses which their members took advantage of were so pleasant and profitable, and indulged in so universally, that few critics were optimistic enough to conceive that the unwholesome fabric would fall of its own weight. And so, impulsion came from such unofficial sources as the *Edinburgh Review*, which from the time of its inception (in 1802) produced scores of bitter and brilliant articles about the inadequacies of English university education.[3] By the time of the Reform Bill of 1832 Oxford and Cambridge had been well illuminated as targets in the fight against the strongholds of privilege. The exposure was painful to them. It must be said to their credit that they both made some progress; they improved their examination statutes,[4] and at Cambridge Trinity (in 1844) and St. John's (in 1849) obtained new college statutes. But the instruments of official correction—the Royal Commissions that visited both universities in 1850—encountered an uncertain welcome from their Chancellors: the aged Wellington at Oxford, and the Prince Consort at Cambridge.[5] Oxford, in fact, refused to give the Commissioners any information they could not find out for themselves.

The Commissioners were able to find out a great deal, however, and their reports, issued in 1852, resulted in the University Acts of 1854 (Oxford) and 1856 (Cambridge), which together did much to set things right. The reports were exhaustive in what they had to say about university government, but they were important especially for their recommendations in three specific fields. First, regarding curricula, they declared that undue importance was being given to classical languages and literature at Oxford, and modern studies were similarly being neglected at Cambridge; this, though, was a matter the universities had taken upon themselves to correct.[6] Second, they were concerned with a number of related problems arising from the ascendency which the colleges had enjoyed over the universities since the statutes of Elizabeth and Laud and which had become absolute by 1800. Heads of colleges held in their hands the government of the universities through domination of the Hebdomadal Board at Oxford, and the Caput at Cambridge. These men lived their lives as a group apart, unapproachable by tutor and undergraduate alike. The story is told of William Whewell that while he was Master of Trinity at Cambridge (1841–1866) he was once obliged to take shelter under the umbrella of an undergraduate; he tersely and in official voice cautioned the young man to make any communications to himself through a tutor, and then lapsed into becoming silence as the rain poured down. Apocryphal, no doubt. But these great men earned their reputations. Personally, of course, they were not always offensive, but their government was arbitrary and dictatorial, and should have been in the hands of the universities. A parallel difficulty lay in the continuing decline of the professoriate. By 1800, the lectures of university professors were considered, by reading men, to be only interruptions, and were consequently unattended; for so long as classics and mathematics were the major requirements for degrees, it was not to be expected that undergraduates would spend their time in attending lectures on other subjects which could not assist them in passing examinations—for which college tutors could better prepare them. As a result, university professors very often did not lecture at all. The narrowness of this arrangement was aggravated by the manner in which college tutors were obtained. Scholarships and fellowships had come increasingly to be awarded on the basis of the locality, school, or family from which applicants came; they were, that is, "closed" by the terms of the endowment which provided them. Tutors were selected from the fellows, and as a result of their backgrounds were usually capable only of perpetuating the classical and mathematical formulas they themselves had been taught. The resulting in-breeding could not have been more complete, and the situation was worsened by the fact that the pay of tutors was too low, and their advancement too slow, to permit colleges to get and keep first-rate men, particularly young men. Yet these tutors constituted the most important body of teachers in the universities, and, with the development of the examination system, exercised increased control over the instruction of students dependent upon their methods of "cram."

The third area of major concern to the Royal Commissions was the vexed problem of religion. Since the time of Elizabeth, religious tests had barred from degrees all except members of the Church of England. In addition many college offices required that their incumbents be ordained in the church. The universities were, in effect, controlled by a clerical oligarchy. Attendance at chapel was compulsory in all colleges, though services were often slovenly and perfunctory, and were generally resented by undergraduates, who had to rise early to attend them. Yet the tendency of nineteenth-century education was away from denominational teaching, as attested by the foundation of the nondenominational University of London (1836) and of the secular universities which followed its example during the century. Oxford and Cambridge resisted firmly any suggestion of removing their religious barriers, though this was the subject of some agitation by reformers in 1832; in 1834 a bill actually passed through the House of Commons which would have removed the disabilities of Nonconformists at the universities, only to be rejected by a two-thirds majority in the Lords— to the vast relief of university conservatives, who were enjoying their last untroubled days.

The University Acts, which followed upon the Commissions' findings, meant, for one thing, additional weight behind the already strong pressures working for new curricula. A subsequent Royal Commission appointed in 1872 to report on Oxford and Cambridge resulted (in the Oxford and Cambridge Act of 1877) in specific stipulations regarding such details as the funds that colleges were to contribute to the universities for scientific teaching and equipment. The statutes written between 1877 and 1882, at the instigation of the 1872 Commission, governed the academic organization of both universities for the rest of the century, and left any further advancement in the teaching of modern subjects to the momentum that by then had been effectively built up. In the Acts of 1854 and 1856, also, the universities were partly restored to their proper functions and importance by the revival of the Hebdomadal Board and Council of the Senate as elected bodies, and restoration of the deliberative powers of Congregation and Senate. The majority of scholarships and fellowships were opened for competition, the professoriate was enlarged and provided with funds from the colleges, and the college tutor's career was made more attractive. The Act of 1877 provided statutes removing the ban on marriage for college fellows and improving the conditions of their residence. And finally, in 1854 and 1856 the abolition of religious tests was ac-

Reform and the University Novel

complished, with certain reservations: Nonconformists were still barred from fellowships and from degrees qualifying their holders for office in the Church of England. In the following years requests from residents of Oxford and Cambridge to remove these restrictions were plentiful; and in 1871 Gladstone pushed through the Universities Test Act, which nearly completed the reform. Religious restrictions were now limited to the divinity degrees and chairs and to the offices that required ordination; college chapel services and religious instruction were no longer compulsory.

The reform by legislation, which began in 1850 and continued during the remainder of the century, was concerned as well with one of the most conspicuous products of university mismanagement, the undergraduate. There were, to be sure, diligent and serious young men enough. They were to be found at Cambridge, for example, in the group that called itself The Apostles and included in its membership Maurice and Sterling, Tennyson and Hallam; the Cambridge Union Society was founded in 1821, and the Oxford Union, somewhat abortively, in 1823; the Tractarians were at Oxford even at a time when it was a popular complaint that compulsory chapel services were desecrations frequented by scholars who were often drunk and always inattentive. But it is also true that both fact and fiction made it luridly clear that the universities were still the domain of fresh spirits who did little more than waste their fathers' money and their own time. Fellow commoners and gentlemen commoners, free of responsibilities (they were exempt from examinations), were triumphantly capable of a great deal of reckless nonsense. The presence of these men did nothing to lower the cost of a university education, encouraging as it did the widespread temptation to play the man and to enjoy the full advantage of the unlimited credit offered to students in the university towns. Vicesimus Knox, taking a very stern view indeed, wrote:

In no places of education are young men more extravagant; in none do they catch the contagion of admiring hounds and horses to such a violent degree; in none do they learn to drink sooner; in none do they more effectually shake off the fine sensibilities of shame, and learn to glory in debauchery; in none do they learn more extravagantly to dissipate their fortunes.[8]

If this was overstatement, there was still much truth to it. The Cambridge Commission deplored expensive habits, which it said were formed at home and contributed to the bad name of the university; the Oxford Commission found that the whole expenses of even "prudent and well-conducted students" greatly exceeded £300 annually—and shuddered at the thought of what imprudence might cost. Fortunately, the Acts of 1854–1856 were salutary in this respect as they were in others. The class distinctions enjoyed by gentlemen and fellow commoners were abolished. In addition, the unhappy servitors and sizars, at the bottom of the social scale, were relieved of the onerous label of poverty which these names carried; they no longer had to perform the menial tasks that had accompanied their old status and together with scholars on the foundations now received support in the form of scholarships—Oxford and Cambridge called them exhibitions. And perhaps of even more importance, the Commissions, feeling that many students were barred from the universities and more were distracted from academic pursuits by the expense and social life of the colleges, recommended that residential halls be a part of the university organization (as indeed they had been in the Middle Ages); their charges were to be moderate and they would permit students to share the advantages of university instruction. The new halls never challenged the prestige of the colleges, but the way was open for a new class of students and the process of democratization was begun.

Quite obviously, legislative reform affected almost every aspect of university life. And, as has been already pointed out, it was the reform movement that perhaps more than anything else was responsible for the rapid growth of university fiction in the nineteenth century. This came about for several reasons. First, the noisy agitation created by the reformers—notably in the *Edinburgh Review*—did much to increase public interest in the universities. Second, reform brought with it an extended range of subject matter. It has been suggested that, in earlier days, antics performed by the more restless members of the university, and scandalous portrayals of bibulous dons, left much to be desired as materials for a novel. Reform, however, brought new causes to urge, and a new cast of characters to add to the traditional rakes. With reform, it became more plausible to take an interest in the success of scholars; examination halls became the scenes of triumphs and disasters in which good very nearly always triumphed over evil. And the years of reform brought forth new subject matter as well, as extracurricular activities were gradually removed from the taverns and billiard rooms. Now were founded and expanded the debating clubs, amateur theatrical societies, undergraduate publications, and competitive athletics, which came to play such a large part in the lives of undergraduates both real and fictional. Boating races in particular were of universal interest—the first intercollege race took place at Oxford in 1815, and the first race between Oxford and Cambridge in 1829; after 1856, when this became an annual event, few university novels neglected to include the college boating hero, or the excitement of a hotly contested race. And finally, the most fundamental alteration produced by the spirit of reform was reflected in the tone and point of view adopted by novelists concerned with the university scene. Whereas early experimenters took, on the whole, obvious pleasure in making their revelations of evil at Oxford and Cambridge, and appreciated fully the humor of what they found there, novelists who were in any way concerned with the progress of reform treated the university theme as a matter of great seriousness. This was at least a step away from the earlier superficial observations.

The new point of view was expressed early in Thomas Holcroft's *Hugh Trevor* (1794), an undeservedly neglected novel that narrates with sympathy and perception the revulsion of feeling suffered by a youth who came to hold, with William Godwin, that evil is the result of ignorance, and "man becomes what the mistaken institutions of society inevitably make him."[9] The novel is a study of the making of a philosophical radical through his progressive disillusionment with human institutions, of which the university was the first. Hugh Trevor, a poor boy, was suddenly enabled to enter Oxford, which he approached with the excited anticipation that he would find there a society of scholars devoted to learning. His dream was destroyed when he found that undergraduates delighted more in vicious words and deeds than in study, and poor scholars were scorned while tutors spent their time toadying to the wealthy. In an effort to find what he still hoped might be the real Oxford he associated himself with a band of "severe" students, some of whom were Methodists (the butts, incidentally, of good men and bad at this time; Oxymel Classic enjoyed making them drunk, and was especially proud of having seduced the wife of a Methodist preacher). The university authorities who shut their eyes to debauchery in others were quick to condemn Trevor for this unhealthy association and rusticated (i.e., suspended) him for two terms. At the end of his forced absence he returned to take up his studies, only to have a Master of Arts deprive him unfairly of his degree by speaking against him in Convocation. Nothing that he discovered later about corruption among churchmen and politicians hurt him more than this injustice.

Holcroft's treatment of Oxford in *Hugh Trevor* is notable not only because of his evident sincerity in condemning its evils,

Reform and the University Novel

but also because of the realism with which he drew the Oxford scene, its dons, and its undergraduates. Others were to do this better, of course, but none before him had done it so well. And yet Holcroft was not a university man. In the nineteenth century the employment of established conventions of plot and characterization was to become common enough in university novels, some of which are from the pens of authors who knew the universities only at second hand. That these conventions should have provided Holcroft, in 1794, with examples of a degenerate society, and that he should have used them so tellingly, is perhaps evidence of the strength of the tradition which had its start early in the seventeenth century.

Godwin himself uttered what was becoming a familiar complaint when in *Fleetwood* (1805) he courageously devoted more than fifty pages to the telling of how Oxford could make "an accomplished pickle" of an honest man, and the castigating of rituals of undergraduate drinking bouts and licentiousness[10]—courageously, because he too had not attended Oxford; and he concluded that Oxonians, and Cantabs too, were dull, dissipated, and ill-tempered, an opinion that was of course hardly unique at the time.

Another novel, of lesser—or perhaps no—stature, which deals with the theme is the anonymous *Frederick: or, The Memoirs of My Youth* (1811). This is a surprising book for the emphasis it places on the good qualities of Oxford. Its narrator, to be sure, knew well the bad, for he was thrown out of the university for writing "A Satirical Poem on the Fellows of the College" attacking what he called "an inexcusable instance of gross partiality in the election of some members to vacant scholarships."[11] But he arrived at Oxford with the great hopes Trevor had felt: "I was now on classic ground. Amid these aisles the spirits of the illustrious dead might be supposed to flit. In *this* grove a sage had meditated; in *those* schools an orator declaimed."[12] In this exalted mood, Frederick was fortunate enough to find some of the things he sought; the dons, he said, who had been so maligned, were actually a harmless lot and full of much sound learning; and among the undergraduates, though there were "a few professed and exclusive votaries of pleasure...I have never found profligacy, or ignorance, or infidelity, triumphant."[13] This doesn't sound much like a plea for reform, and it isn't; the book is anomalous in its good cheer about the state of Oxford. But beneath the cheer is a critical attitude which permits the author no joy at the evil he does find.

A far more important novel is John Gibson Lockhart's *Reginald Dalton: A Story of English University Life* (1823).[14] It is the tale of the son of a poor country vicar who had by legal manipulation been deprived of his rightful inheritance of a large estate. Expecting nothing from life, therefore, save what his own talents could win for him, Reginald entered Oxford with serious intentions of improving himself. He quickly, however, fell under the influence of a fast group led by his old friend Frederick Chisney, embarking on a life of drinking, gambling, and rioting which not only put an end to hard work but placed him seriously in debt. Despite the steadying influence of a kindly Catholic priest, with whose ward Ellen Heskith he fell in love, Reginald finally reached the point where he had to admit to his father the serious state of his affairs. The subsequent sale of the vicar's beloved library to settle his debts shocked him into better ways, and he applied for and won a servitorship which would have permitted him to support himself. But his good intentions came too late; an affront to his fiancée by Chisney involved Dalton in a duel which resulted in his expulsion from the university. The concluding part of the novel, therefore, departs from Oxford, and describes the ultimate restoration of the family estate to the Daltons, and the happy outcome of Reginald's affairs.

In the course of his novel, Lockhart established a number of precedents for university fiction. The journey to Oxford by coach, the first exciting view of its towers, the violent town-and-gown fight, undergraduate exploits in the town and field, the problem of debt, the effects of snobbery, and the duel—all are elements that became conventional in later novels. More important, however, is Lockhart's point of view. Obviously much of the novel is similar in tone to works of the preceding century which took it for granted that university life had more than its share of undesirable aspects. Chisney is in every way a villain of the earlier type: a heavy drinker, a rowdy fighter against the townsmen, and a bad example for students generally. The dons of other days are here too, in the guzzling, red-faced Fellows who were the ornaments of the high table in the college hall. But unlike his predecessors, Lockhart was a reformer with some positive suggestions: if the young bloods of Christ Church are corrupting influences, tame them; put an end to the spirit of snobbishness which rejected Dalton the moment he became a servitor; put an end to the credit system by which men can accumulate disastrous debts; and, naturally, put an end to dueling in the universities. These are his recommendations. For the rest, Lockhart was perfectly content to savor the affection he felt for Oxford. In 1808 he himself had entered Balliol, where he was a witty and industrious scholar, though not always a tractable one, for the next five years. Much of his novel is the direct reflection of his life at Oxford, which he never ceased to regard with affection and delight.[15] His personal feeling, coupled with an antipathy toward all that emanated from the *Edinburgh Review,* is responsible for his original and heartfelt homage to his university. Dalton (and Lockhart) admired the medieval buildings, the ancient traditions, and the true scholars like Dalton's tutor, Mr. Barton. Mr. Barton had some of the deplorable qualities that critics had been complaining about: he was ancient and emaciated; he set foot outside his study only to eat and attend chapel, and was reluctant to undertake the intrusive duties of a tutor; he scorned any work more recent than Johnson's *Lives;* he was not, Lockhart makes clear, the right man to attend to the needs of undergraduates, to whom he was almost inaccessible. And yet, in his devotion to learning, this kind and scholarly man was almost saintly. The love of Oxford and its people was to emerge, after the middle of the century, as one of the most prominent characteristics of the university novel, but Lockhart gave it its first effective expression in fiction, just as he did the cause of university reform.

One realizes Lockhart's skill in making both innovations convincing if one reads an early imitator who followed him. Robert Plumer Ward in *De Clifford: or, The Constant Man* (1841) produced a plot and a protagonist rather like those of *Reginald Dalton*. Its hero might better have been called the constantly dissatisfied man, for he spent four tedious volumes wrestling with the problem of how to marry above his station. Among the social rebuffs he suffered, none was more painful than those which stemmed from Oxford's social caste system, and it is obviously the prerogatives of wealth and birth among undergraduates that Ward, even more than Lockhart, meant to condemn. But though he made his point forcefully enough, he also made it clumsily; and though he tempered his criticism with praise, it is difficult to catch the fervor of his love for Oxford even in de Clifford's most impassioned declaration, in which he saluted "the abode of science, of genius, of an inexhaustible mine of learning, the haunt of cultivated spirits, holding their arms open to myself to become one of them."[16] Lockhart did the thing much more skillfully.

The novels just noted are not the only ones, and certainly are not the most significant ones, which had a word to say about university reform in the nineteenth century. As a group, however, they represent the initial approach to the subject in fiction, and were, especially in the case of *Reginald Dalton,* instrumental in demonstrating that more could be done with the university theme than had been accomplished in the preceding century before reform had become a significant issue. If they are not at all times convincing in their portrayal of the universities, they only share in a failing common to the time before realism became a deliberate aim, and even an end in itself, in the representation of university life. When this happened, the university novel moved still closer to offering a valid interpretation of that tormented abstraction, university education.

CHAPTER V

PERSISTENCE OF THE ROWDY TRADITION

THE DAYS OF THE Oxymels, however, were not quite over. University life continued to be described in terms that at worst were disreputable and at best were frivolous. *Confessions of an Oxonian* (1826) was published anonymously by one Thomas Little. It is a very curious mixture of two opposing points of view which so contradict each other that neither can be taken very seriously. The plot is chaotic. The hero (who is also the narrator) undertook one colorless term at Oxford, at the end of which he departed for a life of merriment in Paris. Returning to Oxford, it was his intent to do some real work, but his intentions fell so far behind his taste for excitement that he was rusticated almost immediately. The following year he spent with his Jewish mistress Jessica in picaresque adventures in India. When she met an untimely death he returned to Oxford and an orderly life in which his interests were suddenly turned to speculation about the state of the university—the ugliness of its new buildings, the good and lively conversation of the members of New College, the envied fellowships of Christ Church, the gentlemanly retirement offered by Merton and All Souls, and the intellectual leadership of Oriel, Brazenose, and Exeter. Tours about the Oxford countryside inspired him to discourses upon the historical associations which it called to his mind. All of this came to a sudden end when his other nature asserted itself in the seduction of his cousin Laura, whose subsequent death brought on the suicide of her uncle and a somewhat dismal conclusion to a tale that is in many ways incomprehensible.

Its most conspicuous characteristic, however, is the relish with which its narrator relates the least creditable phases of his Ox-

Persistence of the Rowdy Tradition

ford career. The demise of his intent to work is epitomized by his decision to give an elaborate supper "a l'Athenienne," an orgy which is probably not equaled in all university fiction: after serving a meal whose dishes are itemized in four pages of small type, the host introduced a group of "nymphs" from the town, and what followed was brought to a tardy conclusion only by the arrival of the Proctor and his assistants. During the well-deserved rustication which ensued, this outspoken hero encountered an old Oxford friend with news of the university: a mutual friend had run off with a milliner and brought her back pregnant; a tutor had been found drunk in a ditch with a gypsy; and the Provost of ———— College had been seen making love to his cook while he read to her from the Bible. The picture of dons throughout is derogatory; even when they are not vicious they are incompetent, as was the examiner who, uncouth, ugly, affected in speech and manner, was so worn out with study that he failed a student whose papers his weak eyes could not see to correct.

The appearance of anything approaching a sober appraisal of Oxford in the midst of these affairs is incongruous, but it is there. Apparently unconscious of hypocrisy, this vagabond reflected upon his dismissal with the words, "Oxford! dear Oxford! how delighted did I, always, feel, to approach the sphere of thy venerable halls and spires. How delighted, even now, when there are few things which can please me, to think upon thee, and in my recollections, again to visit thee!" This surprising reflection led him to others, which can hardly be explained in the light of what had passed. After paying homage to the society and mirth of Oxford which presumably he was qualified to discuss, the author put up a vigorous defense of a classical education and delivered a short sermon on the sins of poor men who spent more than they should while their families were

---

[1] For notes to chap. v, see pp. 207–208.

struggling to see them through the university. Clearly the spirit of reform could turn up in odd places and in the mouths of highly improbable spokesmen.

A weak and conventional romance entitled *The Oxonians: A Glance at Society* (1830), by Samuel Beazley, who went to no university, is of little significance save for the use it made of the university name to give color—as had been done before—to characterizations which otherwise have little of the undergraduate about them. Like the *Confessions of an Oxonian*, it proceeded on the assumption that the undergraduate was either a gay sporting blade or a dissipated wreck. It did, however, offer some serious criticism in the form of objections to the useless education which ill equipped young men to make a living. Truer to type in the eighteenth-century tradition was Charles Lever's *Charles O'Malley* (1841). Lever was a graduate of Trinity College, Dublin, and it was there, quite naturally, that he pictured his recollections of college life. *Charles O'Malley* is not properly a university novel, devoting as it does only three chapters (13-15) to O'Malley's academic life. But it could hardly be omitted from this study if only for the fact that it is one of the earliest novels to portray the undergraduate who entertained a cheerful disregard for learning and yet stopped short of the almost criminal activities of his predecessors. For this reason the novel represents an important turning point in university fiction. Here the character of Frank Webber, living in happy disorder in rooms given over to whist, boxing, and loud music, sets the example for his fellows:

...we rose about eleven, and breakfasted; after which succeeded fencing, sparring, billiards, or tennis in the park; about three, got on horseback and either cantered in the Phoenix or about the squares till visiting time; after which made our calls, and then dressed for dinner, which we never thought of taking at commons, but had it from Morrison's, we...being reported sick in the Dean's list, and thereby exempt from the meagre fare of the fellows' table. In the evening our occupations became still more pressing; there were balls, suppers, whist parties, rows at the theatre, shindies in the street, devilled drumsticks at Hayes's, select oyster parties at the Carlingford; in fact, every known method of remaining up all night, and appearing both pale and penitent the following morning.[2]

There is a note of delighted exaggeration in Lever's portrait of life in Trinity College, and of unreality when one realizes that Webber's college career extended over a period of fifteen years (from 1800 to the Battle of Waterloo). But an oversight such as this does not mar an enthusiastic description of fast but agreeable young men who were to have many literary descendants. Lever showed unusual perception when he described Dr. John Barrett, Vice-Provost of Trinity from 1807, who was called by a reviewer in *The Athenaeum* "one of the strangest pieces of pedantic simplicity and eccentricity that a college ever saw."[3] Adapting Dr. Barrett to the tradition of donhood would not have been difficult, but instead Lever affectionately portrayed this "singular" and "eccentric" man, than whom "a greater or more profound scholar never graced the walls of the college; a distinguished Grecian . . . a deep Orientalist . . . [but] in affairs of the world he was a child"; he was required by the rules of the college to take holy orders in order to hold his fellowship, but this infliction sat lightly on one who was known for his exploding oaths in moments of excitement.[4]

Later university novels were indebted to one more work which cannot be included in their numbers yet cannot be omitted from a study of them. Thackeray's *Pendennis* (1848) drew together in four chapters the boisterous tradition of the eighteenth century, the *bon vivant* atmosphere of *Charles O'Malley,* and the voice of reform which had been heard in *Reginald Dalton*. In addition, Thackeray gave to his picture of life at "Oxbridge" (clearly his own Cambridge, but true to Oxford as well)[5] a gaiety and sense of whole-hearted fun which not even

Pen's sudden remove could spoil and which spread to a group of novels that contributed much to the development of the genre. The story of Pendennis' career at St. Boniface, of how the idol of his widowed mother so exceeded his wordly uncle's advice to cultivate good society that he was sent down from the university in disgrace, does not need retelling here. Pen is one of the greatest dandies of university fiction:

> We have mentioned that he exhibited a certain partiality for rings, jewellery, and fine raiment of all sorts; and it must be owned that Mr. Pen, during his time at the university, was a rather dressy man, and loved to array himself in splendour. He and his polite friends would dress themselves out with as much care in order to go and dine in each other's rooms, as other folks would who were going to enslave a mistress. They said he used to wear rings over his kid gloves, which he always denies; but what follies will not youth perpetrate with its own admirable gravity and simplicity? That he took perfumed baths is a truth; and he used to say that he took them after meeting certain men of a very low set in the hall.[6]

This young fop was one of the first to return home on vacation to alarm and then to dazzle the quiet loved ones with cigar smoking, drinking, and a taste for French novels. Pen was a great man at Oxbridge, a paragon in undergraduate eyes not yet trained to detect a coxcomb and unable as yet to tell which was the greater, Pendennis of St. Boniface or the Proctor. His brilliance astonished all:

> His name is still remembered at the Union Debating Club, as one of the brilliant orators of his day. By the way, from having been an ardent Tory in his freshman's year, his principles took a sudden turn afterwards, and he became a Liberal of the most violent order. He avowed himself a Dantonist, and asserted that Louis the Sixteenth was served right. And as for Charles the First, he vowed that he would chop off that monarch's head with his own right hand were he then in the room at the Union Debating Club, and had Cromwell no other executioner for the traitor. He and Lord Magnus Charters, the Marquis of Runnymede's son, before mentioned, were the most truculent republicans of their day.[7]

Persistence of the Rowdy Tradition

The irony in the picture of "Pen the superb, Pen the wit and dandy, Pen the poet and orator"[8] is applied in large quantities, but it cannot conceal Thackeray's own good-natured amusement at the foolishness and foppery of undergraduate swells. Pen was "no better nor worse than most educated men,"[9] but how much better than the Oxymels and even the Webbers! He was not the first of the heroes who committed sins enough to justify the alarms of vociferous witnesses of depravity in the universities, but he was himself untouched by depravity. The pretentious optimism of his plans for a prize poem, the elaborate outfitting of his rooms, his defeats at the dice table, the downward progress of his studies, and the astonishing ascent of his debts—all these were the workings of one whose only faults were the vanity and selfishness of youth. Insofar as Pen was not conspicuously virtuous he belongs in the ranks of his predecessors; at the same time, he was the progenitor of a long line of university characters of whom it would be difficult to deny the goodness of their hearts in the midst of their most errant follies. Pendennis suggests, in fact, what Tom Jones would have been like had he been a university man. Thackeray made doubly sure the establishment of a new breed of university men when he created Harry Foker with the same sure conviction that a good heart can beat beneath the most absurd fur waistcoats and cheese-plate buttons. This indomitable little man, a dunce at school but at Oxbridge "the humorous, the sarcastic, the brilliant Foker" who ordered turtle and champagne for dinner, the familiar of coachmen and noblemen alike, the ornament of St. Boniface, whose quadrangles he made hideous with the tootlings of his horn, was a completely affable worldling whose good humor made it impossible for him to give or feel the slightest offense.

It is surprising in a way that Pen and Harry Foker escaped as easily as they did from the harsh pen of their creator, who was not always so tolerant of their foibles. *The Book of Snobs,* which appeared almost simultaneously with the first serial issues of *Pendennis,* shows what could have been the fate of both. What Thackeray treated so tolerantly in the individual was devastatingly ridiculed in the abstract. In *The Book of Snobs* the characters of the seventeenth century come to life again as Thackeray points out the abuses which had been the chief substance of university fiction since the Man of the Hill first told his story. The chapters "On Clerical Snobs" are a condemnation of the social distinctions which favored the titled and wealthy while disgracing the poverty of sizars and servitors.[10] Thackeray proceeded to demolish Mr. Crump, the vain and domineering President of St. Boniface, and the tutor Mr. Hugby, a cringing worshipper of the nobility and their sons.[11] How narrowly Pen and Harry Foker escaped damnation is seen in still another chapter, on student snobs.[12] Here, in fact, are the very portraits of these young gentlemen, in the "Dressy Snobs," who flattered themselves that they set the fashion, and the "Sporting Snobs," who drove the London coach, arrayed themselves in pink in the early morning, indulged in dice in the evenings, and attended in the company of their bull terriers many more races and boxing matches than they did lectures. The "Philosophical Snobs" of the Union were "audacious free-thinkers, who adored nobody or nothing, except perhaps Robespierre and the Koran, and panted for the day when the pale name of priest should shrink and dwindle away before the indignation of an enlightened world."[13] And the worst snobs of all were those who, like Pendennis, ruined themselves "from their desire to ape their betters."[14] That the picture of Pen was softened is due in part to the fact that it was Thackeray's fancy to create a hero who had enough good qualities to preclude a thoroughly blackened character, and in part to the spirit of affectionate reminiscence with which Thackeray looked back on his own days at Trinity, evident in the musing paragraphs in which he calls attention to the sentiment with which university men regard their college days.[15] Thackeray was a reformer at heart, but his university characters are not the blackguards of less tolerant authors.

After *Pendennis,* novels in the rowdy tradition took two differing directions. For one, the classic pursuit of scandal in the universities drew to its inevitable end in diluted and somewhat romanticized treatments of undergraduate wickedness. *The Cambridge Grisette* (1862), for example, by Vaughan Morgan, writing pseudonymously as Herbert Vaughan, tells the story of how the sophisticated freshman Carnby fulfilled the terms of a wager by carrying off the belle of Cambridge milliners, Polly Darlington, to London. When she discovered his knavery the deceived girl fled, and placed herself under the protection of the once-fast undergraduate Dick Roughly, who had reformed to the extent of concluding that Carnby was a cad, and now challenged him to a duel. Carnby refused to satisfy him until a public horsewhipping changed his mind; in the resulting duel, fought in France, both were seriously but not fatally wounded, and Polly, flying to the side of Roughly, nursed him into health and marriage. A more anemic tale is that of *Une Culotte, or, a New Woman: An Impossible Story of Modern Oxford* (1894), by Horace Bleackley. Just how impossible a story it is becomes evident in the opening chapter, in which two girl graduates of Girton College, Cambridge, concluded during a visit to Oxford that the majority of undergraduate males were so weak and effeminate that it would be a lark to enroll among them and pose as men. The result is what one might fear, though not quite so amusing as one might hope. The girls were invited to a breakfast at which the conversation about women, full of *doubleentendres,* brought pretty blushes to their cheeks; they were forced to ride horseback astride the saddle, like men, and to engage in drinking bouts which were very nearly their undoing;

and worst of all, they were obliged to try out for the eights, a disastrous effort which wrecked the college boat. The conclusion, in the best-old-fashioned style, showed just how bad college men could be when they put their minds to it. A few glasses of claret unleashed the beast in the "effeminate" men of "St. Chad's," who were determined to punish the pair that had caused their defeat on the river, and the two girls, still disguised, were saved only by a harried scramble over the tiles of the college roof and the resolute assistance of the one don who had the courage to stand up to the maddened and bloodthirsty mob.

Fortunately, anachronisms such as these are relatively scarce, and the inheritance of the eighteenth century, although it was long a-dying, was adapted to better ends in a second development of university fiction, the comic novel. This was largely uncritical in tone, and its purpose was simply to amuse by transforming, after the manner of *Charles O'Malley* and *Pendennis,* the discreditable escapades of academic libertines into materials for a comedy of undergraduate errors. In 1841, the year in which *Charles O'Malley* was published, there appeared a collection of tales which had much in common with Lever's work. *Peter Priggins, the College Scout,* by Joseph Hewlett, is a very imperfect book, but it influenced later university fiction, not least by its point of view that however rough-and-tumble life in the universities might be, it was no more than an expression of healthy spirits that required no apology. Hewlett adopted the device of narrating the observations of an Oxford scout, a device which permitted him to write, from a vantage point below stairs, with a sympathetic boys-will-be-boys attitude that was admirably suited to his taste for broad, slapstick humor. He set forth at the beginning of the book his intention "to remove as much as possible of that ignorance which is observable every where *out* of Oxford [by providing] an insight into what goes on *in* Oxford,"[16] but the violence of his narrative brought forth so many

Persistence of the Rowdy Tradition

protesting letters to the editors of the *New Monthly Magazine,* in which it appeared serially, that Hewlett was obliged in his fifth chapter to concede that he had colored the picture somewhat: "... many such scenes as I have described have really been witnessed in Oxford—(and in Cambridge too, I've no doubt *similes similibus gaudent*) unsanctioned, of course, by the authorities. To please the taste of the public, which, in these days, requires highly-seasoned dishes, it is absolutely necessary to embellish... to overdraw and overcolour,"[17] from which one may conclude that Hewlett was admitting a distortion of emphasis only.

Certainly it would be difficult to find in all university fiction a more consistently rowdy picture of undergraduates at play, and nowhere else are such floods of alcohol consumed. In the chapter on "The Henley Boat Race, between Oxford and Cambridge,"[18] for example, a brief but effective description of Oxford's victory is barely able to find a place between the accounts of wild doings on the road to and from Henley; practical jokes and acts of alcoholic bravado follow one upon the other with no respite. For Hewlett, it is all good fun. "Great allowances are to be made for young men in the heyday of their youth, and just freed from the restraint of school, with the command of a little ready money and unlimited credit. While boys, they fancy themselves men (for many enter at fifteen), and rush into indulgences and extravagances, which they would not do if they were a little older."[19]

His indignation was reserved not for the violent but for the weak. The chapter describing "Mr. Singleton Slipslop's Great-Go Party"[20] tells how an effeminate only-child was induced to celebrate his success in examinations. Singleton, receiving no mercy at Hewlett's hands, is revealed as having literary ambitions which had so far brought him a ten-pound note from his grandfather for a work beginning with the lines,

Brave General Wolfe! uncommon brave!! particular!!!
Who for our sakes climbed rocks quite perpendicular!

But the reading set at Oxford did not suit Singleton, nor he them. In absurdly over-decorated rooms, surrounded by all the implements of the sporting man, which were as useless to him as they were expensive, Slipslop lived a perfumed existence with others of his kind,

... beings who never read, because it was a bore; never hunted, because they wanted pluck for it; never rowed, because it spoiled their hands; and never fished, because it spoiled their complexions. Their mornings were passed in dressing, lounging in each other's rooms, and indulging in talk—it could not be called conversation—about music, of which they did not know a note.—Green-rooms, the interiors of which they had never seen—and women whom they only knew by name, though they let fall sundry hints of the expensiveness of their favors. They strolled down the High Street once or twice, to show their coats, took a quiet drive or ride, and then dressed for dinner, vying with each other in stocks, waistcoats, and silk stockings; dined quietly, and talked of the merits of their respective tailors and bootmakers, sipped a few glasses of light wine with their dinner, a little claret afterwards, and after an early cup of coffee, with its accompanying *chasse,* lounged again, and talked again of the virtues of their tailors and their women, and fancied they had passed a "gentlemanly quiet day."[21]

There was an emasculated quality in these youths which was lacking in the equally idle Frank Webber and Pendennis, and seems to have annoyed Hewlett; one feels that he resented the "few glasses of light wine" as much as anything else. He was, at any rate, enthusiastic in narrating how Singleton's party, supported by fantastic quantities of brandied claret and beer, resulted in the complete destruction of his bower. And the disreputable undergraduate Mr. Sponge, who engineered the catastrophe, received a pat on the back for his night's work.

This somewhat negative point of view did not encourage

Hewlett to go beyond the noisy violence of undergraduate revelry. Writing at the height of the Tractarian movement he nevertheless referred to it only as a potentially dangerous plot of "tea-and-tract men" to bring about the abolition of boating as an amusement.[22] At times a serious thought did strike him, particularly in regard to the debts men incurred while celebrating their attainment to the years of indiscretion. But his interests were predominantly those of the man who is a perpetual undergraduate at heart (he was himself of Worcester College, Oxford). He was one of the first to utilize the excitement of a boat race just as he was one of the first to fill his pages with the slang and colloquialisms of Oxford. If he modified the exploits of eighteenth-century scholars he did so chiefly by giving them the quality of robust good nature.

Two more books followed in which Hewlett tried unsuccessfully to continue the vigorous style of *Peter Priggins*. *College Life: or, The Proctor's Notebook* (1843) is a collection of tales too heavily burdened with both sentimentality and improbable incident to permit a favorable comparison with the earlier work. They show how difficult Hewlett found the task of continuing an unbroken series of stories about Oxford, for some of them have only the associations of the Oxford countryside to support their claim of having anything to do with college life. Typical of those which pertain most nearly to Oxford is the sentimental story of Matthew Scrawler, a poor boy befriended by a wealthy family and sent by them to Oxford. There he was an ideal student: he won a scholarship at "St. Peter's," studied hard, behaved at all times like a gentleman, cheerfully accepted his poverty and refused to indulge in what he could not afford, won the prizes for the English and Latin essays, the Latin poem, and the Newdigate, and finally emerged as a double-first in classics and mathematics. The type was in time to become popular and familiar, but Hewlett seems to have been the first to portray such dazzling undergraduate virtue, which in this case equipped young Scrawler with more than enough ability to carve a career for himself and to rescue at last the fallen fortunes of the family that had given him his start.[23] Hewlett's third collection of purportedly college stories is *Great Tom of Oxford* (1846), in which his fancifulness in finding narrators led him to settle on the great bell hung over the gate of Christ Church. Great Tom, however, had even more difficulty than did the Proctor in confining himself to the Oxford scene, and after the first of three volumes gave up the effort entirely. Of Hewlett's works, only *Peter Priggins* contributed significantly to the development of the university novel. It is related on the one hand to the broad and often disreputable humor of earlier university fiction, and on the other to the later taste for the harmless merrymaking of undergraduates whose worst offenses were practical jokes. From the cheerful nonsense of *Peter Priggins* it is but a short step to the more subtle portrayals of Pendennis and Foker, and from them it is a still shorter step to the work of "Cuthbert Bede," which fixed the style of the comedy of university life.

The Reverend Edward Bradley chose the pseudonym of Cuthbert Bede from the names of the two patron saints of Durham, from whose University College he had received his degree in 1848. The work for which he is most famous, *The Adventures of Mr. Verdant Green* (1854–1857),[24] is an account of the trials of a freshman so ignorant of the ways of the university that he was at once made the gull of more knowing undergraduates. The sheltered child of doting parents, he began his university education with the signing of matriculation oaths so formidable that he was at a loss to understand them. He was promptly taken in hand by the scheming scout Filcher, who established him in cramped and shabby rooms and gave him copious advice calculated to result in more profit to himself than to the bewildered Verdant. But it was at the hands of his new undergraduate acquaintances, the fast Charles Larkyns and the irrepressible Mr. Bouncer, that his education was carried forward along the lines which, they assured him, would make him a man of the world. These lively tutors saw to it that he was thoroughly taken by tradesmen, made hideously drunk, thrown from a horse, overturned on the Isis, and filled full of outrageously erroneous information about the life and traditions of Oxford. Verdant was an apt, if not very knowing, pupil. He learned to smoke, to drink, and to gamble; he invested ruinously in a bulldog, dressed himself ornately, took lessons in boxing, and made a fool of himself before the Union. At the end of his first term he rightly concluded that he had learned a great deal, and in his second he was able to enjoy duping others as he had been duped. But he never lost the naïveté which made him the butt of practical jokes, and when later he appeared on the broader stage of country-house life and in the company of less scheming companions, he was still the shy and unworldly being of his first colorful Oxford term.

Verdant was, for all his blundering, a highly appealing character. His author's own drawings show a gangling, awkward youth, dressed in absurd imitation of high fashion and peering nearsightedly through eyeglasses that won him the nickname of "Gig-lamps." Yet the figure who gives the book its touch of greatness is not, after all, Verdant, but Mr. Bouncer. This festive little gentleman, whose only mood was one of gaiety, is clearly the reincarnation of Harry Foker and is in every way as triumphant a creation. His allegiance to the fast set of his day was formed not through any vicious tendencies but through unfailing spirits and good humor which made it impossible for him to take anything seriously. His preposterous wardrobe, his terriers Huz and Buz, his unlimited vocabulary of slang, and his affectation of worldly ways which sat incongruously on his undignified figure, were all fitting accompaniments to a nature that could not be dampened either by reverses in the Schools or by the arrival of two Shetland ponies from "the Mum" to whom he had announced that he was "short of the ready" and in need of "two ponies" of a far different sort.

Verdant Green, with its lively narrative and farcical comedy, is written in the Hewlett manner, but with far greater coherence and skill in adapting frivolous materials to a convincing picture of university life. Bradley did not, of course, try to achieve realism any more than did Hewlett; both *Verdant Green* and *Peter Priggins* frequently sacrifice credibility to the demands of humor. But whereas Hewlett secured his effect through violent and often grotesque incident, Bradley contrived a better balance between the comic and the simply violent. As Hewlett never did, he idealized undergraduate exploits which in time became part of the conventional notion of what a collegian's life is like. The rise of Verdant and Mr. Bouncer added color to university literature for the next fifty years. Bradley's skill in catching the irresponsible spirit of college life at Oxford, and in making *Verdant Green* the very *locus classicus* of that spirit, appears the more remarkable for the fact that he was himself of University College, Durham, and had never more than visited Oxford.

The book had, incidentally, an interesting publication history. It began as a series of illustrations intended first for *Punch* and then for the *Illustrated London News;* neither periodical, however, published them. Finally Bradley wrote his book around his pictures, and succeeded in persuading the very reluctant Nathaniel Cooke to publish it. The work came out in three parts (and ultimately from the hands of three separate publishers) as a railway library paper-back at one shilling an issue; by 1854 the first part had reached a fourth edition, in twenty years the whole work had sold 107,000 copies, and today the total sale is estimated at more than 250,000. From all this, largely because of his own ineptness regarding the terms of publication,

Persistence of the Rowdy Tradition

Bradley made only £350, and to the end of his life he never ceased referring to this financial tragedy. The book cost him further pain, too, by the very qualities which made it popular. As a churchman, Bradley discovered that it damaged his professional standing. This was so evident to him that he declined to write further books in this vein (including a Cambridge Verdant Green series) until he obtained a permanent clerical living. In 1871 he finally became rector of Stretton, and two years later published *Little Mr. Bouncer,* a book which has the same fresh quality and gaiety of *Verdant Green* but adds little to the style of university comedy established by the earlier work. His *Tales of College Life* had appeared in 1856, but its three short stories have little to do with college life at all. *Verdant Green* remains Bradley's remarkable, though troublesome, triumph.

One of the most conspicuous of Bradley's imitators was James Rice, who under the pseudonym of "Martin Legrand" published in 1871 *The Cambridge Freshman: or, Memoirs of Mr. Golightly*.[25] The similarity between this work and *Verdant Green* is striking, but the novels are not of equal merit; like most imitations, Rice's comes off second best, handicapped as it is by feeble characterization and by incidents and hoaxes which are too forced and improbable even for so playful a work. Mr. Golightly is a shy, unsophisticated, and unsuspecting freshman like Verdant, and even more of a fool than his predecessor. As Verdant had been the pupil of Mr. Bouncer, Samuel Golightly found himself in the hands of Mr. Pokyr, a young gentleman cut from the same pattern that produced Foker (one suspects a play on the name) and the great Bouncer. But again, the characterization of this untrustworthy guide fell short of its originals; he lacked their gaiety and worldly swagger—or rather, he could not wear them quite so well. The tricks he played on Golightly often were born of a malicious spirit sadly inferior to the spontaneous eruptions of Bouncer's good nature.

The incidents of the story follow very closely those of *Verdant:* the journey by coach to Cambridge, the knavery of the gyp John Sneek, practical jokes of the broadest humor, a ride on a horse that was too wild, disastrous adventures with tradesmen, the surreptitious purchase of dogs—these are common to both novels. Like Verdant's, Mr. Golightly's eyes were finally opened, so the later terms of his college career he spent in amusing himself with any more gullible than he. There are good touches such as the description of Mr. Eustace Jones, a serious mathematical recluse whose rooms above Pokyr's reverberated from time to time with the vigorous racket he set up playing croquet while working off the emotion of having solved a "prob.," and the account of the tutor Mr. Bloke, distinguished for having sent 10,003 corrections to Liddell and Scott. But the novel is for the most part a reworking of materials that had already been assembled by an abler hand.

Also, it was getting late in the day for a treatment of university life which was as juvenile as Rice's. The slapstick tradition did not, to be sure, die out for some time: W. F. Traill's *Tales of Modern Oxford* (1882) tells a story of life in "St. Boniface's" which is full of anecdotes such as those in which a drunken college porter is blackfaced with burnt cork and robed in academicals for the amusement of the undergraduates, and a latter-day Slipslop is persuaded to give a party at which he is made dreadfully drunk. The pseudonymous "John Bickerdyke," actually Charles Henry Cook, wrote his *With the Best Intentions: A Tale of Undergraduate Life* (1884) merely to exploit a ludicrous rag in which three undergraduates hoaxed the entire university with an elaborately staged lecture exposing spiritualism. *Red Paint at Oxford* (1904), by the pseudonymous "Pish" and "Tush," narrates a series of frolics which include the joyful calamities of an automobile trip to London. But works such as these became an outmoded minority. *Verdant Green* is at best a literary trifle, but its humor is mature and its admirable fooling was propitiously in tune with the popular conception of the universities, which had not yet come to feel the effects of subsequent reforms. In most of the later university literature, even in the purely comic, there was evident an effort to penetrate more deeply into undergraduate life than is shown in the horseplay of *Mr. Golightly*. The sources of comedy were transplanted from the broadly humorous exploits of juvenile delinquency to the somewhat nostalgic re-creation of ordinary undergraduate weaknesses.

A comic novel of this later sort is *The Babe, B.A.: Being the Uneventful History of a Young Gentleman at Cambridge University* (1896), by Edward F. Benson. In his Dedication, the author points out that in company with old college friends he once set out to list the "remarkable and stirring events" he could recall from his own experience as an undergraduate. The upshot was that he found no such events at all.

Then it was that the uncomfortable conviction dawned upon us, gradually illuminating our minds...that in the majority of cases, remarkable and stirring events do not befall the undergraduate, and that if [this] book were to be made at all, it must be made of homely, and I hope wholesome, ingredients, a cricket ball, a canoe, a football, a tripos, a don, a croquet mallet, a few undergraduates, a Greek play, some work, and so forth.[20]

The Babe is a thoroughly amiable book, a leisurely narrative of unconnected and insignificant events that make no show of extravagance but are for that reason more convincing than the antics described in earlier works. The delineation of indolence and misdirected ingenuity in the undergraduate, which achieved its full expression in *Verdant Green*, is here brought down to a level that puts these qualities within reach of the most uninspired loafer. The book is full of warm and convincing scenes such as the first meeting of the "work club" of a pair of students who, after wasting a full day sharpening their pencils and their wits for study that never was accomplished, departed exhausted from their labors, convinced that they had put in an honest six hours of work.[27] The chapter entitled "A College Sunday" catches the ennui of normal young men who could not bring themselves to study, found it too cold to walk out, and complained because the meals on Sunday came all on top of one another. The Babe himself, congenial, flippant, and lazy, was no better or worse (though somewhat more gifted) than the men about him, but he took part in what is probably one of the few interesting croquet games in all literature, and performed brilliantly in a ludicrous presentation of *Agamemnon*. He conducted himself throughout as a comedian whose language was that of understatement rather than the cheerful guffaws and horn tootings of Mr. Bouncer *et al.*

A novel which has much in common with *The Babe* is Archibald Marshall's *Peter Binney* (1899)—and it is in fact dedicated to Edward Benson. It tells the amusing story of how the elder Binney, of "Binney's Food for Poultry," entered Cambridge as an undergraduate with his son Lucius, determined to win at last the education he had missed in his youth. Unfortunately, he was ill-prepared for the grinding normalcy he found there. Not only was he shocked to discover that the authorities "fail to grasp ... that Latin and Greek *are not spoken nowadays,*"[28] and he must work hard at them to stay in the university, but he had a disastrously conventional view of the high jinks undergraduates indulged in. As a result, he made a fool of himself and embarrassed his son by acting like "the second rate undergraduate who wishes to be taken for a sporting character"[29] while the younger men about him lived far more quiet lives. Marshall, like Benson, saw clearly how commonplace the events of college life really were, and Peter Binney gave added emphasis to the quiet charm of the prosaic by showing how ridiculous the old man's determined wildness appeared to the critical eyes of youth.

On the other hand, the dry humor of *The Babe* is transferred to the realm of donhood in Hilaire Belloc's *Lambkin's Remains* (1900), in which the deflation of the academic ego is ensured by the inanities of an Oxford bursar's "unpublished works." The first two paragraphs of his address to the undergraduates of his college, on the day of their departure for vacation, reflect the tone of this delightful book:

"MY DEAR FRIENDS; MY DEAR UNDERGRADUATE MEMBERS OF THIS COLLEGE, the end of Term is approaching—nay, is here. A little more, and we shall meet each other no longer for six weeks. It is a solemn and a sacred thought. It is not the sadness, and even the regret, that takes us at the beginning of the Long Vacation. This is no definitive close. We lose (I hope) no friends; none leave us for ever, unless I may allude to the young man whom few of you knew, but through whose criminal folly the head of this foundation has lost the use of one eye.

"This is not a time of exaltation, so should it not be a time for too absolute a mourning. This is not the end of the Easter Term, nor of the Summer Term. It is the end of Michaelmas Term. That is the fact, and facts must be looked in the face. What are we to do with the approaching vacation? What have we done with the past term?"[30]

Here too is found Lambkin's Newdigate poem (rejected by the judges) on the subject, "The Benefits Conferred by Science, Especially in Connection with the Electric Light." It begins:

> Hail! Happy Muse, and touch the tuneful string!
> The benefits conferred by Science I sing.
> Under the kind Examiners' direction
> I only write about them in connection
> With benefits which the Electric Light
> Confers on us; especially at night.
> These are my theme, of these my song shall rise.
> My lofty head shall swell to strike the skies,
> And tears of hopeless love bedew the maiden's eyes.
> Descend, O Muse, from thy divine abode,

> To Osney, on the Seven Bridges Road;
> For under Osney's solitary shade
> The bulk of the Electric Light is made.
> Here are the works, from hence the current flows
> Which (so the Company's prospectus goes)
> Can furnish to Subscribers hour by hour
> No less than sixteen thousand candle power,
> All at a thousand volts. (It is essential
> To keep the current at this high potential
> In spite of the considerable expense.) ...[31]

How much the reserved humor of such works reflected changing times within the universities and how out of place the ebullition of Verdant Green's day seemed at the end of the century is seen in a novel that deliberately resurrected Verdant's antics for the purpose of consigning them once and for all to the realm of outmoded jokes. *The Adventures of Downy V. Green, Rhodes Scholar at Oxford* (1902),[32] by George Calderon, is the story of Verdant Green's grandson, whose father Tony Green had emigrated to America, made a fortune in soap, and decided, when Downy was ready, to send him back to Oxford to follow in the steps of the distinguished Verdant. For this undertaking Downy prepared himself by carefully reading and rereading *The Adventures of Mr. Verdant Green,* upon which he planned to pattern his actions at Oxford. He had been at the university only a few hours, however, before he discovered that his behavior was regarded as eccentric: the loud clothes his grandfather had affected were incongruous amid tan Norfolk jackets and gray flannels; when he bellowed for his scout in Hall his voice rang out embarrassingly clear over the mumble of subdued dinner conversation; his winking assurances that he for one was not going to be trapped by rags and tricks were met with astonishment by his hosts of the philosophical Swipes Club, which was in fact a philosophical club and not the drinking society that Downy suspected. Downy's education in the ways of modern Oxford revealed to him that so completely had the tribe of Bouncer passed from the university scene that the undergraduates were afflicted with inertia rather than rowdyism; his own enthusiasm was conspicuous in the midst of the dogged reserve typified by this fragment of conversation at a tutor's breakfast party:

"I would give a thousand dollars," said Downy, "to have been up here with Newman!"

None of the undergraduates looked as if he would have given a Greek grammar for it. Only one of them showed signs of life; he cleared his throat and moved uneasily in his chair for a few minutes.

"Which Newman do you mean?" he asked.

"Why, Newman, sir; *the* Newman."

"Do you mean W. G. Newman who fielded point, or T. P. Newman who broke the roof of the pavillion in the M.C.C. match?"

All the freshmen glared at Downy.

"Neither, sir, neither; Cardinal Newman, the eminent divine!"

"Never heard of him!" said the bold freshman, and went on with his egg.

"Never heard of him!" echoed two or three others; and a short silence ensued.

"Wahl," said Downy, "that beats the bugs!"[33]

As a result of his encounters with the real Oxford, Downy set aside the history of his grandfather, adjusted his behavior, and entered with zest into a matter-of-fact life which would have been inconceivable in the days of Verdant Green. Downy's experiences point up the entire development of comic university literature, a development which gradually departed from the crudeness of the early broad and physical humor to emerge in more subtle forms derived not so much from the visible defects of the preform universities as from the vagaries of undergraduate life which were as harmless as they were amusing.

Chapter VI

GROWTH OF REALISM

MANY OBSERVERS, unable to smile at what they saw in Oxford and Cambridge, must have felt that a novel like *Peter Priggins* was offensive for at least two reasons. First, it took the side of the devil by glorifying the lamentable celebrations of a tribe of delinquents. Second, in failing to wag a disciplinary finger at the troublemakers it failed also to show how they might be brought into the paths of virtue. To anyone with a righteous bent of mind, the answer was obvious: the curtain had to be pulled back, the ugliness revealed, and the way prepared for moral improvement. And so the course of the novelist-reformer was clear. Admittedly it was often obscured in practice by reason of a weakness inherent in the crusader's ways—the tendency to paint life-as-it-is in terms of life-at-its-worst. Thus in attempting to reveal the evils that were to be removed, a number of zealous but clumsy novelists produced distortions that were more violent (and far less entertaining save for the unconscious humor in them) than were the excesses of *Peter Priggins*. But as the nineteenth century progressed, university fiction came more and more to be characterized by vigorous—if heavy-handed—portrayals of undergraduate life deliberately labeled as revelations of the truth and adjurations for reform.

A dreadful portent of what was to come is found in a very pious work bearing the title *Truth Without Fiction, and Religion Without Disguise: or, The Two Oxford Students, in College, London, and the Country* (1838), by "a Country Rector." The author's purpose is made explicit on a second title page: "A true tale of characters and occurences in real life; exemplifying the influence of FEMALE WISDOM AND PIETY: intended to be a Mentor to all Young Persons in commencing the journey of life—warning them against snares and animating them to virtue, religion, and duty." The novel employs a very slight plot, which is too weak to be damaged even by the frequent exhortations to virtue which interrupt it. Two friends, Charles Mortimer and Rowland Clinton, shared an almost unhealthy preoccupation with the problems of Life, Religion, and Oxford. In their moments of lighter conversation, however, they indulged in flights that by comparison with their normal intellectual fare seem almost frivolous:

"I seldom," said Rowland, "have enjoyed Thomson more in any place than in these meadows. Reclining on one of these seats, in a little nook, I can look over one of those fields, and view the villagers at their toil, and in a moment turn me around and contemplate the scenes of studious ease and of dignified retirement..."

"Yes," said Charles, "and, to a mind rightly formed, Oxford presents advantages of no common kind for the pursuit of study and for mental recreation."

"A change, however," said Rowland, "is pleasant; I enjoy the thoughts of the long vacation. The sports of the country, the entertainments of London—the panoramas, parks, exhibitions, preachers, and novelties of London delight me in the prospect."[1]

It seems clear from what has already been observed of Oxford and its literature of the 1830's that these two men represented a departure from the norm. They were, however, set among inferiors who made of Oxford the bad school that it was, where scholars were, the Country Rector informs us, more in Christ Church than in Christ's fold.[2] Charles and Rowland discovered that in their college there were only "about a dozen... whose minds were fixed on heavenly things, and these formed an association to meet once in the week for the discussion of religious subjects."[3] These men were of course safe enough from corruption and, like Charles, spent a good deal of their time in wander-

---

[1] For notes to chap. vi, see pp. 208-209.

ing through orchards, reading pocket editions of the Greek Testament. The two friends enjoyed at least one long vacation in traveling from one rectory to another up and down the length of England, absorbing righteousness as they went; at the conclusion of this tour they rejoined their families, to receive congratulations on moral improvements for which the reader can hardly be convinced there was ever room. The appeal which *Truth Without Fiction* made for morality in the universities was not founded on a very profound examination of the universities themselves; written at the height of the Oxford Movement, it reflected religious extremes only in one scene in which Charles and Rowland slipped into a popish chapel and made scathing remarks to each other as the priest performed his ritual. Rather, the work is a tedious piece of moralizing by one who in his preface declared himself a spokesman for "the ardent wish breathed by the fond parent, as she says 'Farewell' to her beloved child."⁴

Godfrey Davenant at College (1849), by the Rev. W. E. Heygate, was another appeal, well larded with sermons, for high moral life in the universities. Godfrey was a fresh, intelligent young man with sound ideals, but idleness led him into the clutches of the fast and fashionable set—and, we are told, he was not wholly to blame. If the universities, said Heygate, had more and better religious services, this sort of thing would never happen. But the author had other causes at heart as well, which he explained in his preface. The present reformers, he said, were worrying about the wrong things in that they were concerned too much with secular improvements; it was "the ecclesiastical idea" that needed refreshing. Specifically, Heygate wanted strict observance of the wills of college founders, the perfection of ecclesiastical acts and ordinances, the assumption of college duties by the Fellows, increased social intercourse between juniors and seniors, provision for religious advice and assistance for undergraduates, and the exercise of plainness and economy in the conduct of college life. He felt, too, that most tutors were either well-meaning but too ignorant, or learned but not sufficiently Christian, to be proper guides for young men.[5]

These two novels have in common a concern for the state of religion within the universities, and it may be well to pause for a moment to consider other university novels given over to the religious theme. The first observation that must be made concerns a puzzling scarcity of such novels. Until Oxford and Cambridge were opened, in 1854 and 1856, respectively, to students outside the Church of England, one of the most warmly debated issues of reform was, as we have seen, the relaxation of matriculation oaths that required subscription to the Thirty-nine Articles; conservative elements within both universities fought to maintain them as adjuncts of the Established Church in the face of arguments that claimed denominational restraints should be removed. In addition, both Oxford and Cambridge produced religious movements of importance; Tractarianism, in particular, was for a time an issue of national interest. Still, while no one can deny the impact of Oxford's Tractarians and Cambridge's Evangelicals on the intellectual life of England, it is very easy to overestimate the effect they had on Oxford and Cambridge. The career of Charles Simeon and the Evangelical movement at Cambridge continued that university's tradition, begun in the sixteenth century, of disaffection toward high-church Anglicanism. Similarly, the Tractarian movement grew in the most likely ground in all England for the flourishing of high-church sympathies; Oxford had never lost its inclination to encourage Tory sentiments in either religion or politics. But Simeon's enthusiasm was not much liked at Cambridge. And Oxford was opposed to the views of Newman—as it had been, for very different reasons, to those of the Wesleys. The Oxford Movement grew up within the walls of a single college—it was an "Oriel" rather than a university movement. Oriel, which had opened its fellowships to outsiders late in the eighteenth century, now drew to itself Keble (from Corpus Christi), Pusey (from Christ Church), and Newman (from Trinity); these men, with Oriel's own Richard Hurrell Froude, made Oriel the heart and center of Tractarianism. No other college was similarly affected. Though the universities' religious leaders did much to rouse them from their eighteenth-century lethargy, Cambridge only tolerated the Evangelicals and Oxford sighed with relief when the Tractarian controversy was over.[6]

One might at first be justified in presuming that matters ostensibly so intimately related to the life of the universities—matters that aroused such deep interest during the very years the university novel was developing as a literary genre—would have produced a sizeable body of fiction, but this seems not to be the case at all. Novels that are the results of religious controversy fill a very small corner in the realm of university fiction.

Those which do exist fall into two classes: novels which uphold the position of the Church of England, and those which are concerned with the Oxford Movement. Of the former, two have already been mentioned: *Truth Without Fiction,* in charting a moral course for young men, offered the Church as the indispensable guide amid the temptations of university life; *Godfrey Davenant at College* defended the original clerical establishment of the Oxford colleges as that best able to provide the religious guidance undergraduates require. A third, *Perversion: or, The Causes and Consequences of Infidelity* (1856), by the Rev. W. J. Conybeare, is the very voice of middle-of-the-road orthodoxy; in painfully explicit scenes the perverseness of Evangelicals, the narrowness of Anglo-Catholics, and the blindness of unbelievers all represent forms of the perversion of true faith referred to in the title. Novels about the Oxford Movement are no more plentiful. Probably the best known is Newman's

Loss and Gain (1848), a work which, as one might expect, reveals a good deal more about Newman than it does about Oxford. Newman's preoccupation here was the problem of conversion to Roman Catholicism as it affected the individual, and he made little effort to draw Oxford into the story of how one of its undergraduates found his way to Rome. The book consists largely of interminable theological discussions during which Charles Redding, a projection of Newman himself, appeared conscious of Oxford only when he reflected on his love for the university and his pain at its hostility to those who were "papistically inclined." As a result, the work qualifies as a university novel chiefly by default; its author, its Oxford setting, and its theme make its exclusion impossible so long as other contemporary treatments of Tractarianism in fiction are so conspicuously lacking. Two other novels which touch upon it are both by James Anthony Froude. *Shadows of the Cloud* (1847) is an unsatisfactory account of one who was for a time a student at Oxford and was influenced by Newman, but who, when he found that all the elements of religion beyond a profound faith in God were "but shifting cloud," turned away (as Froude himself did) from Catholic thought to latitudinarianism. *Nemesis of Faith* (1848) tells of a similar religious struggle, but one which ended in tragedy: Mark Sutherland, another Oxford scholar, after a period of blind devotion to the faith of Newman, passed to Anglican orthodoxy, and thence to skepticism and moral confusion; because, Froude pointed out, he had never adequately distinguished between the outmoded acceptance of the Bible as divine writ and the more reasonable views of the latitudinarians, faith became his nemesis instead of his salvation.

The novels of orthodoxy, it seems clear, are poor things at best, products of the tendency to reduce the real religious problems of the university world to personal issues involving the choice between upright conduct and downright misbehavior.

And if one looks to the novels which touch on the Oxford Movement for any serious consideration of what Tractarianism meant to Oxford, one finds a similar preoccupation with personal, not university, problems. Of the few attempts that were made, Newman's is probably the most effective; his sensitive and introspective mind worked out one answer to the questions that many must have asked. Even in retrospect the theme proved to be a difficult one. *The Vision Splendid* (1913), by D. K. Broster and G. W. Taylor, is a historical novel (time: 1840) about the Tractarian vision of a life of abnegation and self-sacrifice spent in the service of God within a truly Catholic English Church. In spite of a great deal of Oxford scenery and convincing argument from Newman and Keble, the thesis of conversion stumbles and nearly founders in the course of two unhappy love affairs which left the participants with little choice as to the amount of self-sacrifice they would have to endure in the future.

Issues other than the religious, however, continued to find a place in university fiction.[7] The early novels of reform suffered almost without exception from an affliction ironically characterized by the title of *Truth Without Fiction:* their authors, though choosing the medium of fiction, were not at all inclined to let fiction prevail at the expense of truth, and plots that were perilously frail to begin with usually expired altogether under the weight of long didactic passages. For example, *The Life and Adventures of George Wilson, a Foundation Scholar* (1854), by George Griffith, began as undiluted fiction, but its author was quickly overcome by his concern over the perversion of funds belonging to the endowed schools of England and the iniquitous ties, encouraged by founders' statutes, between these schools and the colleges of Oxford and Cambridge; this, and his feeling that the educational system neglected the middle and working classes while it deprived the wealthy of a practical curriculum, resulted in considerably more exposition than narrative. The same fault, though in a lesser degree, mars an autobiography by "a Member of the Middle Temple" entitled *The Tutor and the Student* (1858). The author attributed all his troubles in life to the wrong choice of a tutor made when he entered Trinity College, Dublin, and he intended his book to be a guide to rescue others from the same fate. What he had to say would, he declared, humiliate the Board of Trinity College for its preoccupation with money misappropriated for its own benefit. Specifically, he made the charge that his tutor, Dr. L——, was a villain of the old stamp, a "hog in the sty of Epicurus...a grovelling voluptuary."[8] The crisis arrived when the author could not pay Dr. L——'s quarterly bill, and was for that reason expelled from the college. He was able in time to return and graduate, but only after the tutor had cruelly extorted a large bonus for approving his work, and the financial ruin thus occasioned left him in poverty, one gathers, for the rest of his life.

These works all share the handicap of allowing their didacticism to distract whatever interest the reader might otherwise feel in narratives that are at best feeble vehicles for more serious matters. But the emergence of appeals for reform which could lay better claim to the name of novel was not long delayed. The first of these was a spectacularly bad book by no less a person than Dean Frederick William Farrar. *Julian Home: A Tale of College Life* (1859) narrates the college career of a youth of stupefying virtue, in a "Camford" (clearly Farrar's own Cambridge) quite given over to the reign of Satan; so isolated, in fact, is Julian's great soul, that the effect is more often that of low comedy rather than of the struggle of right with wrong which the author surely intended. Julian, eldest son of a poor widow, won while still at school a scholarship to "St. Werner's" College, where he matriculated as a sizar. He encountered at once the sneers of young noblemen and fellow commoners, but when his flashing eyes proved too much for them they learned to leave him alone. His career was marked by hard work and virtuous deeds (e.g., though a frail boy, he routed a mob of university roughs who had insulted a boatload of bargemen), and success met him at every turn until a cad one day screwed shut his door just before he was to try for the Clerkland scholarship, thus depriving him of certain victory. The issue between Julian and the college scoundrels was now drawn, but his warfare against these men, successful in the end, was not so preoccupying that his studies suffered, or that he lacked a little spare time in which to woo the sister of his friend Kennedy (who in turn sought the hand of Julian's sister). The conclusion of the tale saw the triumph of justice coupled with a matrimonial exchange of sisters.

As a reformer, Farrar's theses were that the snobbery and contempt encountered by sizars was a damnable shame; debts were an evil which only the blessed poor could escape; only Anglican orthodoxy could pull a man through college; and above all, the undergraduate world was a nest of unbelievable vice which only the influence of a sound reading man could restore to virtue. These could perhaps (but only perhaps) have passed unchallenged had it not been for the absurdity of Farrar's presentation. His world was one of black and white, so black and so white that it was afflicted with the unreality of melodrama. On the one side stood Julian, with his "hectic rose-colour, and blue eyes, and soft hair," innocent himself and unyielding in his stand against wickedness, preaching virtue to his friends and quoting the Greek of Homer and Aeschylus to the girl of his heart. He arrived at Camford with his mother and sister Violet, who set about decorating his rooms to accord with his gentle spirit. Over the fireplace Julian insisted there be hung the picture of the clergyman Mr. Vere, whom he admired:

"... every time I look on that noble face, so full of strength and love, and so marked with those 'divine hieroglyphics of sorrow,' I shall learn fresh lessons of endurance and wisdom."

Growth of Realism

"People will certainly call you a heretic, if you do," laughed Violet.

"People!" said Julian scornfully; "'Of whom to be dispraised were no small praise;' Let them yelp."[9]

Violet had her way about the Fra Angelico: " 'Dear old Beato ... put him opposite the door, that he may give a sensation of peace and beauty to everyone who enters the room.' " And his mother settled the fate of a third picture:

"The Ribera will be a capital pendant to the Fra Angelico; won't it, Vi.?" said Julian, driving a nail into the wall on the other side of the window.

"Yes," said Mrs. Home; "there will be something suggestive to the thoughtful mind in the contrast of the Virgin Mother with the *bienheureuse pécheresse.*"[10]

And finally, disposing of "a photograph of Van Dyke's great painting of Jacob's Dream ... 'We must hang this in your bedroom, Julian,' said Mrs. Home. 'I shall love to think of you lying under the outstretched hand of this heavenly watcher.' "[11] In this room, dedicated to great thoughts, Julian studied and savored the " 'thunderous lilt' of Greek epic, the touching and voluptuous tenderness of Latin elegy, the regal pomp of history, the gorgeous and philosophic mystery of the old dramatic fables,"[12] while from time to time he donned the buckler of his virtue and moved against the coarse depravity of St. Werner's. It is obvious that some facets of his mind were left undeveloped even by the pomp of history and the picture of Mr. Vere. Preparing for his wedding, which found him faced with the prospect of supporting himself and his family on £200 a year, he confidently asserted that "God never sends a soul into the world, without providing ample means for its sustenance,"[13] an economic axiom whose truth he was fortunately spared from proving by the sudden arrival of an aunt's legacy. The fact is that Julian Home was a pedantic fool, a university hero created but six years after Verdant Green and Mr. Bouncer yet so effeminately righteous that no trace of their robustly healthy spirits is to be found in him. His depressing nobility became a byword among university novelists; fifty years later another undergraduate, after defending an unpopular man against some college bullies, was congratulated by a friend: "'Wants some doing. Not only because you are one to ten, but because you look such a damned fool—so like a Farrar hero.'"[14]

On the black side there was a corresponding excess of sin. The villain Brogten despised virtue as a matter of principle (though his dislike of Julian on personal grounds is not incomprehensible); it was he who deprived Julian of the Clerkland, and he who was the companion of a still more sinister man, Bruce. The latter was a tufthunter who, finding that nobility no longer smiled on him, turned to the diverting work of corrupting the only virtuous men he could find. With Brogten, he considered and rightly discarded the idea that Julian could be led astray. But a candidate was seen in the sanctimonious Hazlet, and a bet arranged that he could be made intoxicated. In his treatment of Hazlet, Farrar took every opportunity to make ridiculous the groveling evangelical who could speak nothing but the uncouth jargon of his sect. The satire he heaped on this man's head was an expression of his own contempt for the sectarianism which, among other ills, Julian was free of, but it was so ferociously applied that Hazlet's fate seems somewhat more just than was intended. His ruin was unbelievably sudden: one breakfast, one wine party, one supper—no more was needed to turn him into a habitual drunkard, applauded by the schemers amid "screams of irrepressible laughter, almost as ghastly (if the cause of them be considered) as those which might have sounded round a witches' cauldron over diabolical orgies..."[15] Tiring of this victim, Bruce and Brogten next attempted the same amusement with the brilliant and kindly Lord De Vayne, Julian's sympathetic friend. He was a more challenging target, though Bruce

Growth of Realism 99

saw to it that the wines were of "insidious strength"; but when Lord De Vayne declined more than one glass Bruce drugged that one, accidentally administering a whole bottle of laudanum with tragic results. These characters are no more credible than is Julian, nor is their ultimate fate: Bruce, bankrupt and repentant, sailed to New Zealand and a new life; Brogten, *mirabile dictu,* after he had been horsewhipped by Julian, was converted to the reading set by the grace and charm of the conversation he found in Julian's rooms.

The novel is quite wonderful in its way—not less so because it came from Frederick William Farrar, Scholar of Trinity College, Cambridge, 1852, Fellow of Trinity, 1856, M.A., 1857, and Master at Harrow, 1855-1870, who should have known better. That his own university life should have left him with memories like these seems unlikely, and yet his testimony concerning the villainy of Bruce and Brogten is unmistakable:

So it was; I could not invent facts like these. They never could float across my imagination, or if they did, I should reject them as the monstrous chimeras of a heated brain. I can conceive a man's private wickedness,—the wickedness which he confines within his own heart, and only brings to bear upon others so far as is demanded by his own fancied interests; I can imagine, too, an open and willing partnership in villainy, where hand joins in hand, and face answereth to face. But that any knowing the plague of their own hearts, should deliberately endeavor to lead others into sin, cooly and deliberately, without even the blinding mist of passion to hide the path which they are treading,—this, if I had not known that it was so, I could not have conceived.[16]

Farrar not only kept alive the traditional university scoundrel, but he also created the paragon-hero beside whom even Hewlett's Matthew Scrawler and the friends of *Truth Without Fiction* appear to be of only normal attainments. And more than this, Farrar established the division between good and bad undergraduates engaged in conflict and rivalry which supplied a plot motif that had been only dimly recognized in *Reginald Dalton,* before the good had risen to such heights. It was a motif that was to be used over and over again. The most unfortunate aspect of Farrar's novel is the extent to which his portrayals are exaggerated; *Julian Home* has not one natural or unaffected character. One is reminded of Tommy Atkins' word of caution:

> We ain't no thin red heroes, and we ain't no blackguards too,
> But single men in barracks, most remarkable like you.

The authors of both *Peter Priggins* and *Julian Home* had claimed a degree of realism in their descriptions of Oxford and Cambridge, but it is clear that Hewlett's was one-sided and Farrar's distorted beyond recognition. A successful attempt to give a detailed and yet unexaggerated picture, however, is to be found in a thoroughgoing effort at reform by William Winwood Reade, nephew of Charles Reade. In *Liberty Hall, Oxon* (1860) Reade noted that he was "writing a drama, and not a burlesque; I try to paint scenes of truth and life, and not to etch mere caricature of humour and exaggerations."[17] He did not avoid caricature altogether, but he did create a plausible university atmosphere in which the daily routine of early chapel, breakfast in rooms, study and lectures, afternoons on the river, dinner in Hall, gossip in the quad, and evenings of strong tea and hard work has a matter-of-factness which is welcome after the madcap drunkenness, the poisonings, horsewhippings, and rioting, in novels that show less restraint. Reade's point of view is expressed by a second-year man who explained to two freshmen that they would not have much spare time for idling:

> "So, you see, your forenoons will be quite taken up, besides which, you must read hard on your own hook as well, if you want a degree. It is the greatest farce on earth to suppose that Oxford men don't read, they *must* read now-a-days..."

Growth of Realism

"But surely," said Rauch, "there must be many wild spirits among you; your songs and your novels—"

"Clever young fellows take up their pens to describe Oxford as it once was, or as they think it ought to be. These give wrong impressions; here everyone has to work hard: a noisy man has really a great deal of trouble to find choice spirits to co-operate. Alma Mater has given up the bottle, and now brews her own tea; she has thrown off the ivy leaves of Bacchus, and sits down to her bread-and-jam in a pinafore."[18]

Liberty Hall affords a good illustration of the difficulty which even authors familiar with all the events of college life still found in making sustained use of this material. Reade (of Magdalen Hall, Oxford) worked his theme hard, and on the whole successfully, until in the middle of the second volume he apparently found he had said all he wanted to say about Oxford. The story concerns a very normal freshman, Ted Saxon, who with his classmate Rauch, a veteran of the Indian Service, spent his first year in finding out what the university expected of him. Reade observed that his life was not like that of the conventional freshman of fiction by contrasting him with another:

Tims, likewise freshman, was a contrast verdant and vivid. I cannot pretend to follow him through all the mishaps into which he was flung by his own folly, and by the childishness of others. His embarking in a canoe capped and gowned, and upset in front of the University Barge. His calling upon the Principal in a green baize waistcoat; his inviting the Senior Proctor to breakfast; his buying a box of Huntley and Palmer's Reading biscuits to assist him with his studies. Such incidents have been penned by a genius ["Cuthbert Bede," of course] whose brilliant versatility I should tremble to compete with.[19]

Rather, Saxon was busy enough pursuing his work and making acquaintances. The thread which ties together an otherwise rather disconnected series of events is the progress he made toward passing the midway examination known as Responsions, or the "Little-go." Saxon was a hard and conscientious worker, confident of success in the examination. But six chapters,[20] in which for perhaps the first and last time in university fiction the events of the Examination Schools are made effectively dramatic, tell how Saxon, because of the perverseness of one of the examiners, was "ploughed." This was the end of him. He began to drink, left Oxford, and after a love affair in which the reputation of his old inamorata was ruined, departed for a rather miserable life in the northerly Shetlands with his friend Rauch.

Reade was given to a curiously petulant form of criticism which bitterly condemned Oxford's failings. It fell on the curriculum, on the "solitary, lifeless reading; groping over obsolete, useless books through four mortal years; slaving for two letters to cap our names, and then having to start afresh in some other channel, to begin at the bottom of some other routine, having already wasted so much time, and having wasted it in so industrious and disagreeable a manner."[21] It fell on the snobbery at Oxford which prescribed so narrowly the conduct of its social classes and made it "good form" to avoid recognizing anyone on the street.[22] It described the afternoon on which Saxon declined to go riding because of the expense (7s. 6d.) and instead wandered about High Street where the harmful credit system encouraged him to spend £5 11s. 3d. on photographs, a stereoscope with twelve slides, a silk scarf, and a pair of slippers, none of which he had any use for.[23] Reade was particularly moved by the extravagance of youth, and addressed his readers directly on the subject:

> It makes my blood run cold when I look into our Universities and see how many young men are ruined every year....
>
> Young gentlemen, before you throw away your money upon billiards and wine, and horseflesh, just think if it is worth your while to drink off all your nectar at one gulp, and to spread all your jam upon one slice of bread. If you must spend your little riches upon

Growth of Realism

selfish pleasures, surely it would be better to wait until you are in a position to ruin yourself in a more agreeable manner."[24]

It was through Rauch, however, that Reade made his most vituperative speeches. Midway in his Oxford career this man became (we know not why) bitterly disillusioned: "... the veil of classical humbug is falling off, and I see Oxford in its brutal nakedness; the domineering pedantry of its old, and the vapid childishness of its young."[25] He saw, among other things, that the customary punishments for college offenses (confinement, fines, imposition of extra work or extra chapel services) accomplished no good, but could only "hammer down on the wrong nails altogether, or else drive the right ones in sideways."[26] He felt that undergraduates as a group were distressingly immature, and on no subject was he more harsh than on that of the dons:

"What men are these? Industrious ciphers, men who have ridden their hobbies a little longer and a little harder than the rest of the world; men who have always had time and money at their command, and fine libraries at their elbow bones. I give them credit for industry and perseverance, but I cannot reverence their motives; I cannot even allow them credit for the narrow reputations which they thus obtain. They have had few, if any rivals, to compete with, few if any difficulties to fight against. There are not many people who care about devoting their whole lives to find out the number of bones in a bluebottle, or the exact age of a rotten wall, still fewer who care to publish the fruits of their valuable labours. These men are compilers, I cannot call them great....

"If there is anything which I can at the same time hate and despise, it is an Oxford don; I despise him as a mean crawling worm compared with the rest of mankind; I hate him as a poisonous hissing serpent, in whose power so many destinies are thrown. Go to their Common rooms, and hear them talk after dinner, where they eat like swine, hear their vapid sentiments, bloated and sensual, or see them in their Lecture rooms, ignorant, stupid, cowardly and brutal; put yourselves in their power, and pray to their cold bare hearts for pity and forgiveness.... these men hold our fates in their hands; for a slight peccadillo they can debar us from entering the professions, they can keep the bread from our mouths, and mar our prospects for our whole life-times.... I have heard stories since I have been here, and you must have heard them too, which have made my blood turn cold in my veins, and then boil with anger and with shame."[27]

One such story was about to be told, in the catastrophe of Ted Saxon's examination. His confidence was great, though he felt that had he taken the examination while he was fresh from school he would have known more than he did after a year at Oxford:

> No wonder that Oxford and Cambridge profound,
> In learning and science so greatly abound,
> Since some carry thither a little each day,
> And we meet with so few that bring any away.[28]

And his actual performance was creditable. But he was weakest in Latin prose, a subject about which one of the examiners was demanding, and the result was the failure which drove him away from Oxford and changed his life. Reade took his parting cut at Oxford by describing Saxon's farewell party in words that have a familiar sound:

> When sober, these school-boys are bashful and silly, when drunk they become impudent and noisy. It was not long before the first crisis was past, their dear little soft heads soon yielded under the nectar a la Rauch, and their own real brutish natures peeped forth one after the other...
> It was two o'clock; they had drunk themselves mad; they dashed their fists through the windowpanes, they seized hold of glasses and bottles, flung them against the walls; they raised chairs high in the air, and dashed them to pieces on the ground. It was a loathesome scene: the crashing of the furniture, the jingling sound of the broken glass, the loud coarse laughs, the beastly language, and the oaths, and murmurs or half-audible moans of those who lying on the ground were trampled upon without being able to rise.[29]

Even Reade's often baffling sentence structure cannot conceal the fact that for all his good intentions he at times slipped into the trap which had been the undoing of *Julian Home*. But for all that, the novel is an important one among those of its kind, both for the vigor of its views and for the agreeable way in which it offers with very few slips a convincing picture of an Oxford peopled by undergraduates who are neither clowns, saints, nor for the most part, sinners.

It is obvious that Thomas Hughes did not show the same originality when he wrote *Tom Brown at Oxford* (1861) that he had displayed in the earlier *Tom Brown's School Days* (1857); the novel of public school life was the first of its kind, but so many had preceded Hughes in the field of university fiction that he found all his materials ready at hand. It is also true that *Tom Brown at Oxford* shares the affliction of so many sequel-novels, in that it fails to achieve the excellence of its predecessor. The earlier novel owed much of its very considerable popularity to the spontaneity which marks its glorification of Rugby, of healthy boyhood, and of certain ideals to which Hughes responded strongly throughout his life. The ideals were not profound: Christian manliness, sympathy for the downtrodden, bodily vigor, and the mind that lives in intimate communion with God—these could have been the goals of any good man, and were in fact the common property of so many that *Tom Brown's School Days* quickly found a sympathetic audience and was, as Hughes intended it should be, a guide to generations of schoolboys. Moreover, few readers could—or probably can—fail to respond to the almost passionate enthusiasm with which Hughes re-created the life he had known at Dr. Arnold's Rugby, which to him was itself an ideal. But both the spontaneity and the enthusiasm of this novel failed to reappear in *Tom Brown at Oxford,* and the reason is not far to seek.

The book's plot is a slender one: Tom Brown, fresh from

Rugby, arrived at Oxford where for a time he was somewhat uncomfortable for the purely Arnoldian reason that he no longer had the responsibility of supervising three hundred schoolboys. But Tom was too healthy a creature to stay depressed for long; he was a hearty, genial boy, by no means perfect and intellectually so naïve that he was capable of saying seriously that he had always been bred to respect St. Paul's.[30] His spirits were restored by an introduction first to a fast set led by the carefree Drysdale, then to the rowing set that thought only of the fortunes of the "St. Ambrose" boat, and finally to the hard-working servitor Hardy. Tom's scholarly attainments were for a time not great, while he enjoyed the escapades of his pleasure-loving friends—a violent battle with the town, sporting excursions, and a flirtation with the barmaid of "The Choughs" which nearly broke up his friendship with the virtuous Hardy. Tom's first love, however, was the college boat, in which he early won a place and which occupied both Tom and the narrative for a great part of the novel. The end of his first year was celebrated by a convivial Commemoration, in the course of which Tom met pretty Mary Porter, whose affairs became entangled with his in the Long Vacation that followed. The second and third years at Oxford are treated rather perfunctorily, but show a more mature Tom improving as much by the patient guidance of Hardy as anything else. In the end he became a model young man, full of enthusiasm still but with a sounder head, and happy as the husband of Mary.

Except for the scenes of boat racing, and Tom's love affair, there is little attempt to sustain the tale by incident. But this was not Hughes's chief concern. He wrote the novel with a number of serious problems in mind, and it was the exposition of these which claimed most of his attention. Probably first in importance is what he had to say about the progress of democratization in the university. Employing the contrasts between

Growth of Realism

rich and poor, between sporting men and reading men, which had been so outrageously exaggerated in *Julian Home,* Hughes established Tom as a sort of healthy animal in whom a love of fun and a set of sound if immature moral values combined to make him susceptible to the attractions of both sets, which strove to win him to their antipodal views of what the life of an undergraduate should be. On the one side were the men who had ruined the reputation of "St. Ambrose":

> The chief characteristic of this set was the most reckless extravagance of every kind. London wine merchants furnished them with liqueurs at a guinea a bottle, and wine at five guineas a dozen: Oxford and London tailors vied with one another in providing them with unheard of quantities of the most gorgeous clothing. They drove tandems in all directions, scattering their ample allowances, which they treated as pocket money, about roadside inns and Oxford taverns with an open hand, and "going tick" for everything which could by possibility be booked. Their cigars cost two guineas a pound; their furniture was the best that could be bought; pine apples [*sic*], forced fruit, and the most rare preserves figured at their wine parties; they hunted, rode steeple chases by day, played billiards until the gates closed, and then were ready for vingt-et-une [*sic*], unlimited loo, and hot drink in their own rooms, as long as anyone could be got to sit up and play.[31]

When Taine visited England, he was told that if he wished to know what English university life was like he should read *Pendennis, Verdant Green,* and *Tom Brown at Oxford,* which together must have given him an interesting impression indeed; he accepted quite literally the passage just quoted, at any rate, and expressed his amazement at the luxury of undergraduate existence.[32] Tom found all of this quite to his taste, and for a time was in very real danger of becoming, in the hands of Drysdale, not only a snob but a scoundrel. But he discovered in the servitor Hardy that there was another side of the coin, and it was through Hardy that Hughes expounded not only the perils of the fast life, but also the cruel inequality which the undergraduate social classes encouraged. When Tom in his naïve way asked Drysdale what a servitor was, his only answer was, "'How the deuce should I know?'"[33] Hardy, with a repressed self-pity which is not always pleasant, made it clear to Tom that Drysdale could never know what a servitor was, for the rich and the poor had nothing in common so long as the poor were treated as inferior beings. Hardy's anger broke out strongly when he described how the wealthy student Chanter insulted the junior servitor by offering him a bribe to mark him present at chapel, and he reflected bitterly on the privileges enjoyed by those who did not deserve them:

"... lords' sons are allowed to go out [i.e., win a degree] in two years, —I suppose because the authorities think they will do less harm here in two than in three years; but it is somewhat hard on poor men, who have to earn their bread, to see such a privilege given to those who want it least...."[34]

Tom's rescue from the fast men came about partly through the guidance of Hardy, who was Hughes's spokesman for the underdog, and partly through the growth of his own mind. In his third year he mixed with a set of wild-eyed young liberals who were filled with enthusiasm for a large number of very vaguely defined democratic ideas. "At their parties, instead of practical jokes, and boisterous mirth, and talk of boats, and bats, and guns, and horses, the highest and deepest questions of morals and politics and metaphysics, were discussed ... [he discovered] that it was a very fine thing to have all these feelings for, and sympathies with, 'the masses,' and to believe in democracy, and 'glorious humanity,' and 'a good time coming.'"[35] At this time, too, his Union speeches won him the name of Chartist Brown; in his rooms an engraving of George III was replaced by one of Milton, flanked by facsimiles of the Magna Charta and (to his father's horror) the death warrant of Charles I.

Growth of Realism 109

Ludicrous as Tom's youthful and platitudinous ideas were, there was growing in him a genuine core of "broad sympathy for men as men, and especially for poor men as poor men."[36]

But most of all Tom was saved by his love of boating, which acted as a safety valve for his enthusiastic nature and incidentally provided Hughes with his second gospel of reform, "muscular Christianity." The doctrine of *mens sana in corpore sano* became common in later university literature, but Hughes was among the first to urge athletics as a corrective for the unhealthy occupations that tempted young men. Hughes's own devotion to the college eights is certain,[37] and Tom's became almost a religion. The moral value of athletics was established in the distinction which Hughes drew between "musclemen" and "muscular Christians":

...the only point in common between the two being, that both hold it to be a good thing to have strong and well-exercised bodies, ready to be put at the shortest possible notice to any work of which bodies are capable, and to do it well. Here all likeness ends; for the "muscleman" seems to have no belief whatsoever as to the purposes for which his body has been given him, except some hazy idea that it is to go up and down the world with him, belabouring men and captivating women for his benefit or pleasure, at once the servent and fomenter of those fierce and brutal passions which he seems to think it a necessity, and rather a fine thing than otherwise, to indulge and obey. Whereas, so far as I know, the least of the muscular Christians has hold of the old chivalrous and Christian belief, that a man's body is given him to be trained and brought into subjection, and then used for the protection of the weak, and the advancement of all righteous causes, and the subduing of the earth which God has given to the children of men. He does not hold that mere strength or activity are themselves worthy of any respect or worship, or that one man is a bit better than another because he can knock him down, or carry a bigger sack of potatoes than he.[38]

For Tom Brown and Tom Hughes alike the sacrifice and backbreaking labor of the oarsman meant more than a place at the head of the river or the defeat of Cambridge; it represented total absorption in a purpose not mean, and one of the genuinely good things of life.

At the end of *Tom Brown* Hughes summarized his views as a reformer by picturing St. Ambrose College, once the fastest in Oxford, after Hardy had served a year as its newest tutor. Hardy's formula was simple: "'... taking a real interest in all that the men do, and living with them as much as I can.... The fact is, I find that just what I like best is the very best thing for the men. With very few exceptions they are glad to be stirred up, and meet me nearly half-way in reading, and three-quarters in everything else.' "[39] Hardy coached the college eight, and so effectively preached muscular Christianity to the nearly fossilized college President that the old man was to be seen, every afternoon, pacing down the river towpath in the wake of the practicing oarsmen. In addition to instilling this sort of enthusiasm for something more than "common-room Christianity" and "wine-party religion," Hardy revived the college rule that all undergraduates—gentlemen commoners included—should pass the same matriculation examinations and attend lectures regularly, a move which had the beneficial result of weeding out most of the rich young men. Not all, of course, was set straight in that year. "When one thinks what a great center of learning and faith like Oxford ought to be—that its highest educational work should be just the deliverance of us all from flunkeyism and money-worship—and then looks at matters here without rose-coloured spectacles, it gives one a sort of chilly, leaden despondency, which is very hard to struggle against."[40] But to Hardy the key to further reform was clear: it lay, as any good Rugbeian like Hughes very well knew, in making men aware of Christian manliness, and teaching them to live like Christians and gentlemen.

Clearly the same theme runs strongly through both *Tom*

Brown's School Days and *Tom Brown at Oxford*. But there is an important difference between the two. Between the time he took his degree at Oxford in 1845 and the appearance of *Tom Brown at Oxford* in 1861, Hughes had met the man who influenced his mature thinking more than any other, Frederick Denison Maurice. It was Maurice who, working in the slums of London, made Hughes aware of the hard world of poverty and suffering, and aroused in him the political and social consciousness that led him into the active practice of what he called "the noble side of democracy." Predisposed as Hughes already was to Rugbeian ideals, it was probably inevitable that he should have become a dedicated worker among Maurice's Christian socialists. And it was also probably inevitable that when he came to write the rest of Tom Brown's story he should have eyed Oxford critically, and found Oxford wanting. Hardy, speaking for Hughes, states the whole case against an Oxford education which bred snobs instead of Christian socialists. Hence much of the novel is an indictment, not a glorification, of Oxford, and insofar as it is an indictment, it is a far more self-conscious and even laboured effort than was its predecessor; the more exhortative of Hardy's speeches constitute, in fact, its most serious artistic defect. Critical notices which greeted the book reflect the disappointment many must have felt who looked for another exaltation of English youth. One reviewer went so far as to declare, "A worse novel, written by a gentleman of education and ability, we do not remember to have ever perused...."[1]

But at the same time Hughes was torn between his new world and the old, between the new democratic concepts and the sense of English tradition which suggested to him, among other things, the name Brown as "a sort of synonym for the middle classes of Great Britain," and the name Tom because it was "commoner in England than in any other country," and the use of the two names together because they "have gone together in

England for two hundred years.... the commonest name I could get."⁴² This sense of tradition appears to have made it impossible for him to sustain his lecture upon his old university's shortcomings without frequent exclamations of delight at what he had found there. As a result, *Tom Brown at Oxford* reveals Hughes's persistent awareness of Oxford's *genius loci,* an awareness much like that expressed by Lockhart, but more fully developed in its intenseness and certainly more genuine than the occasional effusions of earlier novelists who were either fascinated or repulsed by the waywardness of university life. Hughes's feeling was voiced nowhere better than in the beginning of his tenth chapter, "Summer Term," in which he painted the beauty of Oxford and the pleasure of life within its walls. The undergraduate, he said, was in a way like the old salt who, granted the fulfillment of three wishes, asked for "all the grog in the world," and "all the baccy in the world," and for his third wish could think only of "a little more baccy"; his cup was full in the home of all delights. "Surely, the lot of young Englishmen who frequent our universities is cast in pleasant places: the country has a right to expect something from those for whom she finds such a life as this in the years when enjoyment is keenest."⁴³ With this point of view Hughes developed a new ingredient, and a most important one, for university fiction; it was to reappear in the idealization of undergraduate life which was to lead to the most significant achievement of the university novel.

Tom Brown at Oxford is not a great novel, but it is without doubt one of the best university novels and one of the best known. In the history of the genre it is notable for uniting all the elements of those which had preceded it and establishing the character of most of those which were to follow. In it are the conventional undergraduate rakes and comedians. It avoided the crudeness of the earlier reforming novels and at the same time was dedicated to the progress of reform. And more important to the convention of the university novel, in it appeared the undergraduate who was also a normal youth working out his adjustment to the new world of men by making his way through the vicissitudes of extravagance and high living toward maturity. In this respect Tom was not quite the first of his kind. A half-comic, half-sentimental romance, *Frank Fairlegh* (1850), by Francis Smedley, contained some Cambridge scenes in which appeared an undergraduate much like Tom, filled with good intentions that were nearly overwhelmed by the temptations of college life; but Frank Fairlegh lacked the boyish qualities of enthusiasm and susceptibility to human frailty which became familiar in future novels and make Tom an appealing person. It is, in fact, the character of Tom which, by being so convincing, lends conviction and a sense of reality to the novel itself.

The remainder of the novels which aimed at reform by exposing the distressing truth are by no means of the quality of Hughes's work. *The Mysteries of Isis: or, The College Life of Paul Romaine* (1866), by H. J. W. Buxton, begins with the promise that the author's purpose was to paint an accurate picture that would be neither a mere caricature nor a gloomy religious piece, revealing students as neither saints nor sinners; "... if those to whom Oxford life and doings are as a sealed book," he said, "find their ideas enlightened and their views modified, I shall not have written in vain."[4] Buxton asserted that it was a foolish fashion to imagine that Oxford men were merely "incarnations of mischief" or "athletic machines," when they were actually of all kinds, and mostly good sound men. But he was not able to fulfill his plan in a book that is too seriously marred by Farrarisms to be very successful. Paul Romaine and his friend Frank Challoner were two noble young men who stood pretty much alone in a naughty world; the end of their unequal struggle came, for Frank, when he was carried off by brain fever induced by overwork; and for Paul, with the blight of all his hopes when he failed, for a reason that is not made clear, to marry Frank's sister Edith. Between their bright-eyed matriculation at "St. Chrysostom's" and the death of Frank they moved in the allotted round of a town-and-gown fight, hard-won successes in the Schools, a succession of somewhat spiritless boat races, the gaiety of Commemoration, Show Sunday, and all the rest. Buxton, like Hughes, was apt to grow bitter about the social disparity between the rich and the poor at Oxford, and Paul's "grim satisfaction" in his poverty was much like Hardy's.[45] As usual, the fast set was at fault. The author offered a great deal of advice about the intimate relationship between the Oxford credit system and life in the Fleet. And the dons came off rather poorly: the Rev. Richard Swade Swade, "an oily, fat man with a white face and a soft, moist hand," cared as little for undergraduates as did the offensively pious Rev. Peter Smee; as for the head of the College, Dr. Benison "did nothing, thereby fulfilling the regular duties of a Master."[46]

Curiously enough, in the next year appeared another criticism of Oxford which claimed that the Oxford servitors were so far from being subjected to an inferior status that it was a problem to find men with a social background consistent with the dignity of the position. The Rev. Frederick Arnold in *Christ Church Days* (1867) observed:

At the present day there is no visible distinction between the commoner and the servitor. The name still implies an odious distinction which probably will be soon abolished, and cannot be abolished too soon. A servitor, as a servitor, has ceased to be an object of contumely. According to what he really is in himself he finds or makes the society in which he moves... they have mixed freely among the best men of their time.[47]

This statement would seem to share in the rather pious optimism which fills a very moral tale about a prodigal son. Charles Dudley was an orphan who showed great promise at Oxford; he was a handsome, athletic, and intelligent scholar. His character was marred, however, by a weakness which led him into debt and lazy habits, a combination his guardian uncle found sufficiently displeasing to warrant disinheriting him when his days at Oxford were over. For three years Dudley struggled vainly with his inclination to follow the bloods of Christ Church. What he should have been is typified by the plodding servitor Percival, but what he was at heart is seen in his flirtation with an innocent girl who trusted his good intentions too far. At length the neglect of his work resulted in failure in the final examinations, which in turn led to the desperate expedient of becoming a tutor in a German school. Then, however, a renascence took place as he began to read seriously for the first time, and it is no surprise to find at the end of the novel that uncle repented. Oxford took him back, and he turned into the best of clergymen. In describing an Oxford in which reading men "could be reckoned up on one's finger ends," Arnold burdens the reader with ponderous exhortations to learning and industry, and with enthusiastic and minutely detailed descriptions of the service of the Church of England. This heavy fare is lightened by eye-witness accounts of the activities of the Union, Commemoration, and the like, in which Arnold seems to have been bent on documenting these Oxford traditions. But he seldom wandered far from the thesis that life at Oxford was full of temptations and honest intellectual toil had a reward greater than the favors of noblemen or the pleasures of indolence.

Just as conspicuously moral is the tale of *College Debts* (1870), by "an Oxford M.A." The author set forth to make the pitfalls of university life so vivid that young men would avoid them, but there seems to have been one pitfall that was worse than any other—once again, it was the Oxford credit system. The downward path was pursued by Edward Grantley, a young man who was so rapturously in love with a pretty neighbor that the prospect of long terms at Oxford away from her filled him with gloom. In this unstable condition he fell an easy victim to the profligate example of one Osborne who, though himself finally expelled, left Grantley entangled in debts he could not possibly repay. At last his position became so desperate that he fled Oxford, joined the army, and so distinguished himself in India that he returned a hero with enough in pocket to settle his accounts and marry the girl who had been sure he was a good sort from the beginning. This cheerful conclusion is the only bright note in a story that is otherwise filled with the nightmarish remorse of the man who finds himself paying interest at the rate of ten shillings to the pound.

The deliberate and explicit realism of Buxton's record of Oxford life is typical of the general truthfulness such accounts exhibit from this period onward. Similar documentary reporting is found in works designed exclusively to enlighten the public—and presumably prospective students in particular—as to the mysterious ways of college life. An anonymous revelation of this kind, for example, entitled *Boating Life at Oxford* (1868), set forth in a collection of short narratives a complete study of the conventions and codes of the oarsmen, with descriptions of the races and celebrations in which they took part. *Oxford Days: or, How Ross Got His Degree* (1879), by F. E. Weatherly, is a handbook, in narrative form, which according to its preface was intended as a practical guide to Oxford, and it takes the reader carefully through the peculiarities of Oxford terminology, customs, and traditions that had become familiar fare in fiction but were here offered more for instruction than for pleasure.

As for the voice of reform, which had done so much to induce accurate representation of college life, it was not stilled entirely in the nineteenth century, or for that matter in the twentieth. *The Massacre of the Innocents* (1907), by "An Oxford Scholar," is a melodramatic burlesque in which the traditional classical

Growth of Realism

education is represented as a two-hundred-year-old conspiracy against humanity. A satanic don, Mr. Tremlitt, defended the old curriculum only because he saw that it left men "with wills untrained and characters weaker even than they were in childhood,"[48] while he secretly planned a world revolution in which these incapacitated beings would be trampled by a band of supermen employing the advantages of science and psychology. His dream was defeated, however, by a few good men and true who believed that the millenium was to come not through either classical or scientific education, but through a reformed curriculum in which modern literature, the practical and ornamental arts, and the principles of statesmanship would predominate. The work is a curricular extravaganza, incongruous in its time both for its anachronistic belaboring of classical education and for its exaggerated misrepresentation, even in jest, of what life at Oxford could be.

CHAPTER VII

THE ROMANTIC CRICHTONS

IN THE NINETEENTH CENTURY and in the twentieth as well a number of novels dealt with the university theme not as the humorists or reformers had done, but simply as material for light romances and melodramatic tales. As early as 1845, Charles Lister in *The College Chums* presented a weary pilgrimage through a series of adventures which started at Oxford and ended in murder, suicide, and a scattering of illegitimate children. Frank Usher's *The Three Oxonians* (1873) alternates between light-hearted scenes in Oxford and the problems inherent in the poisoning of an elderly uncle and the untangling of the terms of his will. *John-a-Dreams* (1878), by Julian Sturgis, with some good characterizations such as that of the tutor Blogg, "who had read Voltaire and acquired a name for infidelity," tells of an unstable youth whose Oxford career was spoiled by his inability to choose between two attractive girls and by a rather nervous flirtation with the church. Even the penny-dreadfuls picked up the theme. Samuel Bracebridge Hemyng (who omitted the humble "Samuel" from his title pages) wrote two extravaganzas entitled *Jack Harkaway at Oxford* and *Jack Harkaway's Strange Adventures at Oxford* (1897–1898?),[1] both filled with an unrelenting succession of student escapades which if somewhat improbable are undoubtedly spectacular, and eminently well suited to the wide-eyed young audience to which they were addressed. Undiluted melodrama characterizes another such novel, the anonymous paper-bound thriller celebrating *The Oxford and Cambridge Eights* (1880?); here a villain by the name of Mainwaring tried to poison the Oxford crew and was pursued by angry Oxford and Cambridge coxswains

---

[1] For notes to chap. vii, see p. 210.

through a complicated tangle of murder and blackmail.² On a quieter level, *The Undergraduate* (1891), by Frederic Henry Balfour but published under the pseudonym of Ross George Dering, is a conversational marathon of teas and talks in which the tribulations of a liberal Church of England minister mingle with those of his son Guy, pursued by the amorous wife of an ancient "St. Mary's" (i.e., Oxford) professor. Much less interesting than this occasionally humorous fare is *The Inseparables* (1905), by James Baker, a meandering tale in which good and evil are represented by the students Guyst and Mord, and the qualities of body, mind, and soul by three girls of appropriate degrees of virtue; neither life at Oxford nor the excitement of a university exploration team in Egypt can overcome the burden of this clumsy symbolism. *The Hypocrite* (1898), by Cyril Arthur Edward Ranger Gull, tells of a young man in whom an air of innocence concealed an extraordinary skill at deceit and extortion; his father's displeasure ended his Oxford career, but London offered rich opportunities for him until suicide at last seemed desirable. Gull tried his hand, too, at light comedy in *His Grace's Grace* (1903), in which His Grace the Duke of Dover, unwilling idol of his college, vacationed incognito with a friend to find out what life without a title might be like. He found it agreeable, for after considerable confusion of identity he won the hand of his friend's lovely sister Grace, a girl who would have perished of a broken heart rather than have pursued a title. *Nigel Thomson* (1905) by Valentine F. Taubman-Goldie is a well-written novel about an undergraduate who, with wealth and a propitious marriage awaiting him, ends his undergraduate career abruptly and with tragic results after being seduced by a shopkeeper's daughter. In a story that could appeal only to honest lovers of horse flesh, *The Primrose Path* (1911), by West F. de Wend-Fenton, shows how the sport of kings can make college life (in Christ Church, at least) bearable, and how it is that honesty in racing, as in most things, is a very good policy. None of these novels has much value; all of them make a vigorous bustle about picturing university life, but most of them allow the attractions of romantic adventure to overpower the university theme.

Beginning about 1880, however, university fiction began to reveal tendencies toward a more specialized kind of romantic novel. At times melodramatic and sentimental, in the vein of those just mentioned, it nevertheless developed still another characteristic which set it apart from mere melodrama and sentimentality. This was its assumption of the view—supported ever since by enthusiastic old grads—that actually the days spent in the camaraderie of college life are the best a man is ever apt to see. And even more, it created a breed of undergraduate Crichtons qualified to populate the new utopia. It was now that the undergraduate stood forth, much like Tom Brown, as a healthy and usually pure young man with sound instincts which his love for clean fun could not pervert. The Rev. H. C. Adams' *Wilton of Cuthbert's: A Tale of Undergraduate Life Thirty Years Ago* (1878) was perhaps the first of the new novels, though it was by no means the best.[3] It describes the successful struggle of Gerard Wilton against adversity to win a brilliant first; his only shortcomings were those of youthful folly, and even these did not stand long in his way. The most surprising thing about the book is that there is so little of the old Oxford in a story of the 1840's. Adams exploited his own Oxford memories again in *Charlie Lucken at School and College* (1886) and *School and University: or, Dolph Woolward* (1896), and if in the latter he reverted to the familiar strains of melodrama, he nevertheless retained his original faith in the soundness of the undergraduate who worked hard, played hard, and emerged thereby a man.

A much better novel is *Hugh Heron, Ch.Ch.* (1880), by the Rev. R. St. John Tyrwhitt. Tyrwhitt recognized that there was "a certain amount of vice in these parts [i.e., in Oxford], small in proportion to the number of lads who are here assembled," but he pointed out that Hugh "had the advantage of starting in a good set.... Most the men he knew were clean livers.... there always seemed to be a standard of positive duty somewhere about. In a large college, with all its inconveniences, there is great social liberty; and it is wonderful how much fun a lad may have without being led, or even invited, into mischief."[4] Hugh was the new sort of undergraduate brought to perfection; he was hearty and of course a "clean liver," very definitely a rowing type, and the sort who would (and did) add distinction to country-house life; he was the embodiment of "conscience, and honour, and truth, and right, and sound morals and decent life."[5] It was not to his disadvantage that his virtues were those of instinct, that morally he was rather like a good retriever, or that his tutor found him "handsome and puzzled" in his academic work.[6] It was as needless for his mother to fear for his orthodoxy as it was for his tutor to warn him against "young gentlemen in the French style," "decorative furniture and sham picturesque," the danger of the fast set, of idleness, and of trying to have a fling at Oxford.[7] A man of some means, Hugh at once made a good social start at Christ Church. He was spotted as a rowing candidate, and distinguished himself on the river. If he indulged in fox hunts, he also assisted in charity-visiting about Oxford, and his "manly religiousness" was an ornament of reading parties as well as of his college. He would play nothing but whist, drank almost not at all, consistently "slid through various temptations—or things which are temptations to the doomed race— without being much the worse."[8] Tyrwhitt dealt seriously with some issues, but he did it with the comfortable assurance that he would have nothing very bad to report; thus his strongest complaint about Oxford was that it was infested with a new type of student who viewed education competitively, was interested in nothing but "class, scholarships and prizes, cram, tips, and money in one form or another," while ignoring the nobler aspiration for honor itself, care for the truth, and "the generous madness" of the days before the competitive system had been perfected.[9] Hugh was of the old school, and so was the admirable exhibitioner Broadbeans—"exactly the sort of person so sanguinely expected and contemplated by statutes and founders, as a scholar in want of money."[10] He was brilliant, aggressive, fond of athletics, full of humor, the winner of the Hertford and the Ireland, and perfectly able to get on well with the rich as well as the poor.

While ennobling the undergraduate, Tyrwhitt did much to take the university don out of the monster class by describing him as a hard-working, underpaid counselor of young men. The tutor Dayrell is a good example of the new type, as he reflects:

"Tutor's work in Oxford is living in a Goshen of one's own—at least, one's time belongs to other people; but it's an independent life, more so than the political or commercial lines, or if one was a doctor in practice, or anyhow on one's way to great prizes. One pays for riding one's own hobbies by ignorance of the world. But leisure or liberty come irregularly. We all have to take work when we can get it, or fall out of the market. Few men dare send a job away when it's offered them. Look, I go on with articles for classical dictionaries; it's tiresome hard work on the top of my lectures, and there's very little pay; but if I refused somebody else would come in, and I might lose some very interesting bits of writing."[11]

Dayrell, a "half-Liberal ... who really made [himself] felt in modern thought," was one of the "scholars desiring to think and to instruct."[12] He made his mark in Oxford by being genuinely concerned more with what the men thought than with the honors they might win, if in winning them they were thrown to extremes of radical irresponsibility. The danger, as he saw it, was the new thought that led to nonreligion, the abolition of creeds, and the substitution of negative Liberalism for what he called Liberality. He was, in short, a new sort of don to appear in fiction, more conscientious and more thoughtful than his predecessors. Nor was he alone. Even his friend Atticus of "St. Green's," not always so nice in his distinction between what his students wanted (usually quick cramming, money, and an easy first class) and what they needed (more honorable ambition and moral certainty), recognized the danger that accompanied the profession of "advanced thought" among the very young: "I am the fashion, and sharp school boys come to me—to get rid of their doubts, they say; and I often find they want to get rid of their consciences. Always negative—I must feel how they can't believe this and can't see that;—really, it's wonderful how many things a man can't see at twenty."[13]

Another expression of this kind of sympathy toward university people was *Faucit of Balliol* (1882), by Herman Merivale, a rather florid romance in two parts, the first of which is concerned with Oxford. Guy Faucit as an undergraduate had been a university Crichton: he had "got the Balliol before he came up, and the Hertford in his first year, and the Ireland in his second, and a double first in Mods., before you knew where you were." As an oarsman he had "the matchless stroke which kept such a clean and even swing for the whole length of the course, steady and strong as a pendulum, and never quickening up through loss of nerves or want of reserve power, till just the critical moment of the finish, when he launched out in the strong, sharp spurt which set all the ranks of Oxford cheering from the steamboats, and defied all the pluck and skill of the Light Blue to redress the balance or to score a victory. The 'Faucit spurt' was a proverb..."[14] Faucit was quickly appointed to a fellowship, kept up his coaching of the college boat, and according to one of his students was "the best lecturer and the jolliest don in the place, and as good a fellow with the men of other colleges as he is with his own."¹⁵ The novelty of seeing a don in rooms "furnished and improved with every evidence of scholarship and taste" is matched by the sight of an inspired teacher:

> ... The magnificent energy with which he did everything he put his hand to was part of the strong, sweet nature of the man. Pupils of his could never fail to catch the infection more or less.... it was a great sight to see Faucit, with his hands deep in his trousers pockets, and the short pipe clearing the mental atmosphere.... He had the whole thing at his fingers' ends, and could dress up Plato's Republic improvisedly, in sympathetic and attractive English of his own. At another time he could tell anecdotes from Herodotus in a familiar style, quite after the old gossip's manner; and even on the perplexing mysteries of Aristotle's ethics he could throw an original light, and moralize... on the dangers of the career of the apolaustic man.¹⁶

It is something of an anticlimax to find that upon meeting a charming Daisy this man relinquished his university career to study law in London that he might someday support a wife, and for the remainder of the novel lived as a recluse after a postoffice error caused an imagined rift in his romance which was not straightened out until the book's last four pages.

The portrayal of sweetness and light in the universities achieved new heights in two novels by W. E. W. Collins. *The Don and the Undergraduate* (1899) deals with the deep mutual affection between the tutor Charles Ingram and his students. Ingram was a paragon of virtue and industry, active in his college's affairs, and so filled with charitable intentions and the gifts of the true teacher that he spent his free time in teaching trades to boys, and literature to working men. His talents, happily, were not wasted on the brilliant George Ronald and honest Tom M'Gregor. The latter had to work hard to win academic renown, but Ronald had the gifts of one who succeeds at everything: "...a tall upstanding young fellow, with crisp curling hair and steel-grey eyes. The firm lines of the mouth seemed to tell a tale of strong will and perhaps latent temper. But frank and cordial manners, coupled with a general willingness to oblige, had won him golden opinions in the undergraduate community; nor could it be said that anything to his discredit had been recorded in the college books."[17] It is perhaps incidental that he was an orphan and very wealthy, but not that he was given to performing secretly good works such as paying for the sea voyage and a winter in Australia for an old college servant who was ill. The novel is little more than a collection of sentimental incidents, showing, among other things, how Ingram rescued his little pupils from the second floor of a burning building. And throughout, the nobility of Oxford scholars is almost oppressive —nowhere more so than at the end, when Ronald, warned of his weak heart, said farewell to this life by personally winning the Oxford-Cambridge boat race, and in his will left his fortune to his friends and his fiancée to Ingram, who had loved her silently for years. The high tone of *The Don and the Undergraduate* is fully sustained in *A Scholar of His College* (1900) a work built solely around the problem of whether Richard Loder, an exemplary student, a fine cricketer, on the eleven and a blue, was to be a success in love and life by winning a first class. The shock, to his friends, of discovering that he actually did not get his first was eased by the revelation that he had had influenza throughout the week of final examinations, so his reputation was saved. Perhaps even more than the earlier novel, this tale is burdened with sentimental goodness; scarcely a character does not at one time or another purse his lips, put a twinkle in his eye, and mutter to himself, "I like you, my young friend!"

The lives of the Crichtons were continued well into the twentieth century, all proving that he who rows may also read. Lionel Portman's *The Progress of Hugh Rendal* (1907) shows a humorous young man as sound in mind as in wind and limb. Portman himself was an Old Blue, and in no novel is the excitement of college and university racing more successfully communicated; Hughes had done this well, and Tyrwhitt had made the urgency of the oarsman's work wholly convincing, but neither had achieved the color and vigor of Portman's descriptions. Hugh Rendal did not wholly avoid scrapes, and he went through the customary Oxford functions of Commemoration parties and bump suppers with so light a heart that he was at times barely out of the Proctor's punitive hands. But his integrity was proved by his defense of the eccentric scholar MacTaggart and particularly by his devotion to the eights.

A variation of the theme of splendid British youth appears in Desmond F. T. Coke's *The Comedy of Age* (1906). It is a kindly story of the ancient don Radford's sudden realization that he had lost all touch with undergraduates, whom he could not view except as incomprehensible inconveniences intruding from time to time upon his scholarly solitude. Deciding to see if this deficiency in himself could be corrected, he tried first to rejuvenate his interests by attaching himself to a perfect specimen of a young man, the student Ernan Lane; but when he tried to take an interest in athletics and student celebrations he felt only an awkwardness which was not lessened by Lane's visible embarrassment. He tried next to make Lane more mature, but, after worrying himself unnecessarily over a harmless flirtation which the boy carried on with an Oxford shop girl, he saw Lane recover quite naturally by himself, and realized that growing pains have to take their own course. His conclusion was that although he could be no younger, and the boys would not be made older, he had better let sympathy bridge the gap between himself and them and enjoy the pleasures of being surrounded by youth. The book is a sincere study of the relationships between dons and undergraduates, unmarred by sentimentality, and built on the belief that for all their noise and high spirits undergraduates are a good lot whose youthful view of life deserves to be accepted and treated seriously.

The Romantic Crichtons

The same point of view pervades H. N. Dickinson's *Keddy: A Story of Oxford* (1907). Malcolm Forth, for some reason called Keddy, was another bright and attractive boy who was armed cap-à-pie with healthy instincts of morality and clean living. He had an enormous capacity for pleasure which at times got the better of his creator, who remarked that he was "an incandescent mass of unlaboured enjoyment."[18] But he had also, from novels and the counsels of the clergyman Mr. Carpenter, a headful of notions about sin at Oxford, and was curious to see what form it took. He was not long in finding out, for the undergraduate Bobby Wilton was a belligerent and truculent boy capable of a good deal of mischief. But whereas no one else at Oxford had a good word to say for Wilton, Keddy discovered in him what he called Vitality, and set out to redeem him. After a number of adventures in which Keddy was Wilton's partner, or rather his companion, Keddy's friends and advisers took alarm at the course he was following; he, however, persisted in trying to be Wilton's friend that he might save him, and in the end it was Keddy's wholesome nature that brought out the good in the errant Wilton.

Perhaps the last of the Crichtons is to be found in another Cambridge novel by E. F. Benson, written long after *The Babe* and reflecting a decided note of nostalgia not found in the earlier work. *David of King's* (1924) concludes a schoolboy trilogy that is still popular among the young audience to whom it is addressed (the other two novels are *David Blaize* [1916] and *David Blaize and the Blue Door* [1919]). David was a marvelous boy, full of manliness, good humor, and healthy instincts, who won his predictable first in a Cambridge somewhat overrun with jolly dons. As with his predecessors, his impregnable character was able to work forcefully against the evils of wine and women, and even to permit Benson to do a bit of preaching on these inescapable subjects. Benson's late offering of Crichtonism is somewhat tempered by its avoidance of the worst of past excesses, but the tone is unmistakably that of late-Victorian undergraduate purity.

The sense that goodness was at last finding a home in the universities did produce some dreadful books. Mrs. Nellie Cornwall's *The Little Don of Oxford* (1902) is a nauseous tale about the tiny son of a widower tutor, whose pleasure it was to roam about Oxford's "twadrangles" clothed in miniature academicals, asking questions like, "Do you fink God knows about little boys' hearts, and sees all their little finks and aches?"[19] The reader can scarcely question his description of himself as "God's little child and Christ's little soldier."[20] A more sane, but not much more satisfying, effort is Normandy Venning's *The Spider of St. Austin's* (1910), a story about virtuous adolescents growing into manhood under the kindly eye of the Bursar of St. Austin's, an early Mr. Chips. But fortunately the bulk of university fiction at the beginning of the twentieth century was more mature, and it was, as the other examples suggest, dominated by the point of view that the universities were eminently good places for a young man to be.

There can be no doubt about the sincerity of those authors who created university Crichtonism in fiction; they without exception wrote with forceful and often sensitive conviction. But obviously, when once an "incandescent mass of unlaboured enjoyment" had been offered as the hero of a novel, the way lay open for anyone with a sense of humor to remark that glorification of the undergraduate had gone far enough, perhaps too far. By 1900 the university Crichton had had time not only to flourish but to achieve almost unbelievable perfection, and it was probably inevitable that there should have been a reaction to his perfection as there had earlier been a reaction to the villainy of his forebears. At any rate, there now began, with the turn of the century, a period of debunking the romanticized version of university life that had become thoroughly entrenched in fiction. The novels in which the new and irreverent view is to be found form a series of *jeux d'esprit* which perhaps could be included with the rest of the comedies of university life, but their distinctive point of view sets them apart, and they are important chiefly for their relationship to the more serious works. The tone of what was to come had been intimated in Benson's *The Babe,* which, while repudiating the excesses of university fiction, did not contradict them with anything more than simple realism. Benson had noted that once an author leaves the realm of homely incident which is common to the experience of most men, "when you begin to deal with spiritualities, century-making captains of eleven, chess blues, and higher aspirations, you desert the normal plane for the super-normal, where people like you and me have no business to intrude."[21]

Deserting the normal plane had certainly become common enough in other novelists, but a sudden and abrupt return was accomplished by a series of stories entitled *A 'Varsity Man* (1901), by Inglis Allen. The hero of this amusing book, known only as the Youth, was an adolescent who, while fancying himself a man of the world well coated with an Oxford polish, met embarrassment and frustration in all his attempts at chivalry, bravado, and suave flirtation. In company with an eightsman and a rugger blue, for example, he tried, by affecting the air of a Don Juan, to make away with a yokel's girl at a country fair; his absurd behavior was tolerated so long as his strong-arm companions were with him, but when they disappeared on a Ferris wheel, the resulting row soon put the Youth in the hands of the Proctor. In a succession of similar incidents the abrupt deflation of his determination to achieve the worldly manner foreshadowed the early demise of the undergraduate of heroic stature. This demise was carried a step forward in Charles Turley's *Godfrey Marten, Undergraduate* (1904). Godfrey was a cheerful bungler—a thoroughly honest and good person, a fine cricketer and even a very modest scholar—but a bungler nevertheless. When his naïveté did not lead him into trouble of his own he was quite innocently made the victim of other people's: if a row occurred in his college quadrangle, it was he who was mistakenly apprehended; it was he, too, who at a horse auction sang out the winning bid merely to help the auctioneer over a period of silence. He had a native wit, however, which permitted him to make shrewd observations of folly worse than his. Of the serious men of his college he remarked:

> Perhaps serious is not quite the right word to apply to them, for one of this gang wrote a comic opera and another wrote a farce; but these were just thrown out in their spare time, and when I attended a reading of the libretto of the comic opera I went so fast asleep that I cannot say how comic it was. But if it had been very funny I should think some one would have laughed loud enough to wake me up. Generally speaking this set seemed bent on the reformation of England, a thing which has happened once and is rather a difficult matter for a college debating society to bring about again. The reformation which they were bent on was not, however, religious, for they thought very little of the religion which satisfies ordinary people. One of them told me that religion was merely emotional and sentimental, a crutch for the weak man, and a cry for a better life and against the oppression of the poor. That man bored me terribly, but since one of his own set had told me he was the cleverest man in Oxford I did not like to tell him what I thought.[22]

Godfrey's generally serious approach to life bars him from the company of university clowns, and yet the clownish quality of his seriousness bars him equally from the company of Crichtons. Virtue in the undergraduate is, in *Godfrey Marten,* reduced from the heroic plane and put squarely on the ground where walk the ordinary men who make mistakes of their best intentions. Nowhere is Godfrey's character better revealed than in the precarious relations which he maintained with his tutor, Mr. Gilbert Edwardes:

The Romantic Crichtons

He was even smaller than the Warden and quite the most primlooking man I have ever beheld. His face was colorless and smooth, and as I sat opposite him in his gloomy room he looked so tidy and sure of himself that I found a great difficulty in speaking to him. Having said the usual things he was very obviously waiting for me to go, but I did not want him to begin by thinking that I was a saint, though why I imagined that he was in any danger of thinking so I cannot explain. He had, however, said so much about work and the great care I must take in avoiding men who distracted me from my duty, that I thought I had better tell him that I was a very normal human being.... The idea of working for Mr. Gilbert Edwardes never had much attraction for me, and for the first two or three weeks at Oxford I found it very difficult to satisfy him. However, the excuse that I took a long time to settle down to a fresh place did not seem as reasonable to him as it did to me, so I had to abandon it and try to appease him. The worst of him was that I never knew whether he was pleased or not; he accepted my most determined efforts at scholarship as a matter of course, and reserved his eloquence for the occasions on which my work showed symptoms of haste. In less than a fortnight I felt that my tutor and I were watching each other; he took it for granted that I would do as little as possible, while I was searching for something which could tell me that he was human as well as learned.[23]

Godfrey Marten is one of the pleasantest of all the university novels, and not the least of its refreshing qualities is the presence of its agreeable hero, who almost wins the reader to the belief that it is impossible to take seriously the massed and redundant virtues of his predecessors.

A 'Varsity Man and *Godfrey Marten* employed understatemen and irony against the tide of Crichtonism, but an even more effective variation lay in the burlesque of Max Beerbohm's extraordinary *Zuleika Dobson* (1911), the story of how the Duke of Dorset, and all Oxford with him, came to a watery end for the love of a beautiful girl. The Duke was no ordinary creature: a brilliant dandy (he had been called "Peacock" at Eton), he was the winner of a first in Mods. and of the Stanhope, the Newdigate, the Lothian, and the Gaisford prizes. He was reading, "a little," for *Literae Humaniores;* he "played polo, cricket, racquets, chess and billiards ... was fluent in all modern languages, had a very real talent in water-colour, and was accounted by those who had had the privilege of hearing him the best amateur pianist on this side of the Tweed."[24] The Duke was idolized by the undergraduates of his day, though he in turn did not like them. Only in the direction of the poor scholar Noaks did he condescend to nod: "He saw in Noaks his own foil and antithesis, and made a point of walking up the High with him at least once in every term. Noaks, for his part, regarded the Duke with feelings mingled of idolatry and disapproval," and while he envied him his easy first (Noaks got a second) his envy was assuaged by the suspicion that the brilliant man would come to a bad end; "Noaks may have regarded the Duke as a rather pathetic figure, as a whole."[25] No one, however, thought lightly of the solitary member of the exclusive Junta, whose views were so exalted that he was obliged to blackball his own nominations for successors.

At the height of the Duke's Oxford career the beautiful Zuleika arrived to visit her grandfather, the Warden of Judas College. No man had ever been able to resist this wondrous orphan who was making a career of modest conjuring tricks, but her heart had never been touched by abject lovers; she longed for one who would spurn her, and it seemed for a time that the aristocratic Duke would be such a one. Yet even he, after a show of indifference, threw himself at her feet on the day after her arrival, only to find that his protestations of love reduced him in her eyes to the level of other men. The Duke, however, was not like other men, and swore that if he could not love her he would die for her—a suggestion that charmed Zuleika, who had never contemplated such a decisive proof of devotion. The course of true sacrifice was not smooth, however,

The Romantic Crichtons

for the Duke's importunity so wore on Zuleika that she was driven on one occasion to douse him with a bowlful of water, thereby arousing in him a hate that conflicted sharply with his word as a nobleman to do away with himself for her sake. But his sense of *noblesse oblige* made evasion impossible, and he set about to keep his word. In the meantime, all of Oxford had learned of Zuleika's unusual distaste for devotion, and all of Oxford had fallen in love with her: sensing the Duke's intention, the undergraduates as a body resolved to follow him in suicide. On the last day of the college boat races the Duke, arrayed in the robes of the Order of the Garter, arrived at the Judas barge. His plan to wait until Judas had triumphed over Magdalen was spoiled by a sudden downpour which threatened to destroy the effect of his costume, and so before the race was over, with Zuleika's name on his lips, he leaped from the barge; swimming under water for a time, he rose once to see the triumph of Judas, and then went below to drown. And with a chorus of "Zuleika!" the rest of Oxford (with the exception of Noaks, who threw himself out of a window) followed him. The bump supper that night was attended only by the dons, who had no heart to tell the Warden of Judas what had happened. As for Zuleika, after a momentary thought of taking the veil she found she had been so touched by the scene on the river that she ordered a special train for Cambridge.

All of this is delightful fantasy. Beerbohm, in a note to me, has declared that he had no intention of parodying anything, and certainly not the excesses of university fiction. And yet, falling where it does in the long line of university novels, *Zuleika Dobson* typifies the irreverent deflation of the myth of Crichtonism which was prevalent at the turn of the century, and will remain one of the most cheerful pieces of fancy in university literature, as well as one of the best of the university novels. Its success was never repeated, though the process of debunking continued. Hamilton Gibbs, in *The Compleat Oxford Man* (1911), reverted to the technique of painting the Oxford scene in the completely prosaic terms that had been utilized by Allen and Turley. In a series of slightly connected exposés of undergraduate life Gibbs showed how the bacchanalian celebrations that had been the cause of earlier expressions of horror were rituals that ended not in mayhem but in retirement after the college porter announced that midnight had struck; how the Union, instead of being a forum which set the pattern for Parliament, was marked chiefly by confusion, frivolity, and inattention; how the august president of the Oxford Boating Club had his own frailty as he filled the university boat with friends from Christ Church rather than with more able but less distinguished men from lesser colleges; and how the undergraduate, after four pleasant years, emerged into the world with not the slightest idea of what he was to do with himself.[26]

Chapter VIII

THE "DAMNED TRIBE OF SCRIBBLING WOMEN"

Discussing modern Oxford, Christopher Hobhouse has written of its women students with the instinctive, unyielding revulsion of the man who sees his ancient university overrun by a race of bedraggled intruders:

Though their numbers are so small, a casual visitor to Oxford might well gain the impression that the women form an actual majority. They are perpetually awheel. They bicycle in droves from lecture to lecture, capped and gowned, handle-bars laden with note-books, and note-books crammed with notes. Relatively few men go to lectures, the usefulness of which was superseded some while ago by the invention of the printing press. The women, docile and literal, continue to flock to every lecture with mediaeval zeal, and record in an hour of longhand scribbling what could have been assimilated in ten minutes in an armchair. Earnestly they debate the merits of their teachers—the magnetism of X, the eloquence of Y, the spirituality of Z—as though these insignificant pedants were so many Abelards.

The assiduity of women undergraduates is stupefying. After the long morning's round of lectures they swarm to the Bodleian. Radcliffe Square is dark with their bicycles. After dark, in their own college libraries or in their own comfortless little college rooms, they huddle for hours on end, stooping and peering over standard text books. They are tremendous sticklers for tradition and routine. Every rule and regulation of college or university is literally observed; the prescribed books are read from cover to cover; the stereotyped opinions are faithfully noted and dutifully believed.

The women undergraduates have a truly Teutonic respect for their own dons, who in their turn take full advantage of it. Spinsters almost to a woman, the female dons present a terrifying caricature of the mediaeval tutor. They estimate work by quantity rather than quality. The fact that there is very limited accommodation for the women at Oxford, and that many hundreds of aspirants are yearly turned away, constitutes in the hands of the female don a scourge with which to drive on her pupils to ever more exaggerated efforts. By nature as industrious as bees, the unhappy girls are perpetually goaded on to the inevitable breakdown.... Very few of the women take the least pains to be attractive or even mature. Fifty years have not mellowed them; they still care nothing for appearance or comfort. They run no bills in the High Street, but deck themselves in hairy woolens and shapeless tweeds.... Their domestic background is equally repellent. Instead of a quiet pair of rooms, guarded by an impenetrable "oak," upon a secluded staircase, each girl has a minute green-and-yellow bed-sitter opening off an echoing shiny corridor. Instead of deep sofas and coal fires, they have convertible divans and gas stoves. Instead of claret and port, they drink cocoa and Kia-Ora. Instead of the lordly breakfasts and lunches which a man can command in his own rooms, they are fed on warm cutlets and gravy off cold plates at a long table decked with daffodils.

In this setting the mind of the Oxford woman grows narrower day by day.[1]

Women, though they have been admitted to, have clearly never been fully assimilated by, the still predominantly male societies of Oxford and Cambridge. They have enjoyed at best a doubtful welcome there. The "undergraduette," though she has her own colleges, is nevertheless suspect as a collegienne and is rather cruelly assumed to belong to a group that is plainly unattractive and fearsome in its devotion to learning. "Mainly architectural," wrote Max Beerbohm, "the beauties of Oxford. True, the place is no longer one-sexed. There are the virguncules of Somerville and Lady Margaret's Hall; but beauty and the lust for learning have yet to be allied."[2] This fact of women's being to some extent alien to the university scene perhaps explains, more than anything else, why women novelists who have tried to portray the life of England's older universities stand apart as a group afflicted with peculiar and very real difficulties. Though biographical details concerning the Victorian ladies who wrote about Oxford and Cambridge are difficult to come by, available information

---

[1] For notes to chap. viii see pp. 210–211.

suggests that the strange quality of their work is not always the result simply of ignorance; Mrs. Frances Marshall, for example, who wrote fantastic things of Cambridge, spoke frequently in her novels of her intimate acquaintance with the university. But even when the authoress knew something of university life, and perhaps participated in it, her participation was remote and different from that of men; and her portrayal of it had a corresponding air of fantasy quite out of keeping with both the facts and better informed novels. Women began writing about Oxford and Cambridge in the 'eighties, at the time when they were admitted to the sacred groves. But while men had been abandoning both melodrama and derogation in their novels, it was precisely these to which women, with an almost uncanny instinct for reversion, turned with enthusiasm. And this tendency was accompanied by another, equally strong, in the direction of romance and sentimentality expressed through effeminate undergraduates who make Julian Home appear, by comparison, a hardened man of the world.

This is not to say that all women were disqualified by sex from writing sensibly of university life. Mrs. Annie Edwardes, in her *Girton Girl* (1885), while letting a taste for romance quite overpower what, one judges from the title, must have been at least an intention, does suggest sympathetically the problems of a girl new to the ways of Cambridge. Mrs. Humphrey Ward, who was herself instrumental in winning a place for women in Oxford, displayed in *Robert Elsmere* (1888) a rare sense of the effect of doctrinal conflicts on members of the university; one of her later works, *Lady Connie* (1916), is scarcely excelled in all university fiction for its sympathetic and thorough understanding of the day-to-day life of Oxford dons, and for its vigorous refutation of the opinion that the university was a provincial backwater. Margaret Woods's *The Invader* (1907), and Mrs. Oona Ball's *Barbara Goes to Oxford* (1907) and *Their Oxford*

Year (1909) are filled with so much knowing appreciation of the scenes and legends of Oxford that there is no ground for doubt that the thing could be done, and done well.

But these lights shine brightly in a darkened landscape. In 1887 there appeared a book called *Passages in the Life of an Undergraduate* by "Bee Bee" (i.e., Mrs. Beatrice Braithwaite-Batty). Falconer Madan, of the Bodleian, noted on the title page of his copy of the novel that Mrs. Batty lived at "14 Crick Road, Oxford,"[3] but propinquity alone did not empower her to write an even passable university novel. The book concerns the friends Lancelot Winthrop and Gerald Delane—the latter, "fair and pale, with a quantity of brown hair clustering over a broad forehead, looked almost as fragile as any girl himself. A little hectic glow was on his cheek, for he was tired."[4] Gerald's hectic glow lasted throughout an entire Commemoration period in which, when the violent activities of concerts, college balls, boat races, and Encaenia were not engaging them, the friends consumed poisonous amounts of lawn-tennis cake ("a new invention of old Toffin's") and spent a great deal of time in chapel, where "the soprano voice in the anthem . . . transported many a listener into a paradise of ecstasy."[5] This calamitous novel contrives somehow to end in Portugal, where Gerald's sister Geraldine, ill with consumption and "brain fever," was suddenly restored to health by the reappearance of a lover falsely suspected to have treacherously married a naughty woman. Mrs. Batty's writing did not improve with time. In 1912 she produced *Mrs. Fauntleroy's Nephew,* an equally lamentable exploit into Oxford's term-end celebrations. This time Harold Fauntleroy, another pale young man, allowed himself to be so carried away by the enticements of garden and tea parties, dances, concerts, and polite conversation that he came close to being corrupted. Worried by signs of dissipation in her brother, Edith Fauntleroy consulted her aunt, who had been keeping the terrible truth from her:

The "Damned Tribe of Scribbling Women"

"Well, I happen to know that his tutor is not satisfied with him," said her aunt. "He is not keeping his chapels well, and I can guess why. He wrapped up those tickets which he got for us for New College last Sunday in a double sheet of note-paper, caught up in a hurry, I suppose. It contained two lines from some chum of his, asking him to come and smoke with him and some friends in his rooms at 12 o'clock that night."

"Oh, aunt!" exclaimed Edith.

"Aye," said her aunt, "what time would he get to bed?"

"Harold was never used to late hours," said Edith.

"I am afraid that he is now," said her aunt. "But they won't do, as he will find out to his cost by and bye."[6]

Scattered through the university novels there are to be found a number of striking examples of undergraduate room decoration, ranging from the bare cells of poor men through the littered hangout of the sporting set to the elaborate chambers of the wealthy. But it was left for Mrs. Batty to introduce the ultimate in decorative splendor. The passage describing Edith's visit to the rooms of Harold's friend Robinson is perhaps a measure of her familiarity with the haunts of undergraduates:

Edith could not utter at first, from sheer wonderment. Was she in Fairyland? Or in Aladdin's palace? Coming in from the glare of the spring sunlight without to a semi-gloom, broken by star-like radiance, shed by many tiny coloured lamps over luxurious draperies, concealing doors, and overlaying fauteuils and couches, she knew not what to say, or what to think. Whichever way she turned, some fresh fancy met her bewildered gaze. Here was a palm, a rare orchid, there a fig tree, overshadowing a cage full of bright-plumaged foreign birds. Grotesque jars and outlandish figures occupied brackets on the walls, whilst pretty trifles and valuable objets d'art covered every stand, table and what-not.

"But you cannot work here, with all these beautiful things about you?" at length she remarked.

"Read, you mean, Miss Fauntleroy?" asked Robin. "Oh! they don't prevent my reading. Why should they? They ought to help me. Doesn't someone say 'A thing of beauty is a joy forever?'" He laughed at the application of the quotation, and so did Edith.[7]

And so does the reader, who perhaps cannot understand about that fig tree. To say that Mrs. Batty's picture of college life is merely unreal is to understate the splendid freedom with which she has given it the quality of life in Mayfair; there is nothing in either novel to suggest that university men do not find their moments of keenest enjoyment over a teacup, or that their thoughts and words are not unctuous to the point of being offensive.[8]

Whereas Mrs. Batty is given chiefly to sentimentality, Mrs. Frances Marshall, writing under the pseudonym of Alan St. Aubyn, dipped into the past to revive some richly scandalous goings-on. It is not clear why she did this, for, as noted above, she claimed to know the Cambridge scene of her day. It is always possible, of course, that her experiences were unusual, but it is doubtful if they could have included the events of which she wrote in *A Fellow of Trinity* (1890). These revolved around the sizar Herbert Flowers; sizars of flesh and blood had long since been relieved of embarrassment about their position, but not Herbert, who was snubbed by the unfeeling members of Trinity College. But he was possessed of the sort of virtue, extremely rare in undergraduates, which roused him from bed in the morning in time not only to attend chapel but also to run for half an hour before breakfast, and it was not long before he, one day, "in the—ahem!—very spare clothing worn by members of the C.U.A.C.," distinguished himself as a runner and jumper in a track meet marred for him only by the grief he felt for the men he had beaten. The new "lion of the athletic set" celebrated with a "coffee" rather than a "wine," but a thoughtless man introduced some beer which overpowered Herbert's senses.[9] His prowess later extended to rowing as well, when, though not in training, he was called upon to fill a vacancy in the college boat and by his own efforts won the ensuing race. And true to the tradition of Crichtonism, he ended with a double-first and a fellowship in Trinity—after a day of triumph in which he brought pretty blushes to the cheeks of the girls of Newnham and Girton as he read his prize-winning Latin hexameters. But this was not all. Mrs. Marshall apparently felt that the threat of evil, even to a man like Herbert Flowers, was as strong as it had ever been, and she revived the old campaign against snobbery and extravagance in the universities. To this end, she introduced some villains of the old school: Grinley, worn before his time with dissipation, and Spurway, who gambled, bet at Newmarket, and (we are told delicately) kept a mistress at Linton. Living in no such bastion of virtue as Herbert's, the amenable student Brown was led by these men into debts that overwhelmed him to the point of attempted suicide. Herbert himself, though introduced to a gambling den in Chesterton (at which most of Cambridge spent its evenings) where he found himself obliged to help spirit away the body of a patron killed by the proprietress, and induced to drink two cups of coffee so strong that he was unable to attend chapel the next morning, avoided further temptation by thoughts of home:

... [he] suddenly found his eyes full of tears. He had just remembered the little mother at home, who at that very moment was most likely on her knees praying for him with all her heart!—and he was wasting her poor little substance, the result of, oh! so much self-denial and economy, in riotous living.[10]

Little more need be said of this work, in which sentimentality runs uncontrolled among events so preposterous that not even the *deus ex machina* of a collision of college eights, killing a man about to make a foolish marriage, can further alienate the reader (though he is comforted to know that the college authorities ordered alteration in the razor-sharp prow that had skewered the unhappy lover).[11]

It is surprising to read reviews such as that in *The Spectator* of October 25, 1890, which declared that despite minor faults

A Fellow of Trinity was "certainly the best novel of university life which has appeared for many years." But evidently Mrs. Marshall was a popular writer, and she was without doubt a prolific one: she published over sixty novels between her fortieth and sixtieth years. Her next university novel was *The Junior Dean* (1891). If it is hard to overlook a sense of unreality in melodrama of this sort, one must confess that the tale is at least seldom dull. It tells of how one Keith Fellowes, Junior Dean of "St. Stephen's College," Cambridge, and a shy cripple, became engaged to Cambridge's loveliest undergraduette, Molly Gray. He, however, innocently mismanaged his affairs so thoroughly that before he ever won Molly he was shot by an actress traveling under the striking name of Mlle. Rose De l'Orme, burned in effigy by an angry mob of Cambridge students, and (unjustly) exiled from Cambridge for conduct unbecoming a college official. *The Junior Dean* offers some excellent examples of the peculiarities of Mrs. Marshall's style. She early mastered the cliché, and the self-evident assertion, and the trick of stopping the narrative by means of the unnecessary statement. Listen, for example, to her reflections on Molly's matriculation:

> There never was such a busy, happy time as that first week. There never was any life so delightful as life in a women's college. If anyone is disposed to ask that foolish question: "Is life worth living?" let her settle it at once by coming to live in a college for women.
> In the first place, if she is new to it, she will have to set her room in order, and oh! what occupation is more congenial to the female mind than hanging up plates and arranging aesthetic draperies?
> This occupation will take a long time; it may be prolonged over the whole three years—*ten* terms, one should say—of residence. Meanwhile, there is always the serious work of lectures. These may be taken *ad libitum,* and afford unfailing sources of delight to the intelligent and thirsty mind. To fly about Cambridge with a big notebook, and elbow the meek and unresisting undergraduate out of all the best seats at lectures; to come out above him in the examinations; to take the highest places in the class lists; to beat him on his own

ground—surely, to the most jaded, this would give a new zest to life.
Add to all these delightful possibilities the possession of a lover—a real accepted lover, living in the same University, engaged in kindred work, and the picture is complete. The cup is full to the brim. Life worth living, indeed![12]

Passages like this are somewhat difficult to deal with, for it is not always possible to say that no irony is intended; at times it seems impossible that it is not. Yet there is in Mrs. Marshall's writing a complete lack of self-consciousness which seems to preclude even the suspicion of irony. Here, for example, is how she sets the scene for introducing her villain, the college stroke, as he heats water for tea:

> The kettle took a very long time to boil. It took longer to boil than any other kettle on the staircase, and it had a habit of singing on the smallest provocation without the slightest intention of boiling. It was a mendacious, untrustworthy kettle, but if any man on the staircase was up to it, it was stroke.
>
> He put the tea in the teapot with the same liberal hand that he had spread the potted shrimp, and he waited upon the kettle, ready to seize it the moment it boiled. It was singing in the most cheerful way, and steaming like a locomotive, but it couldn't take Mr. Brackenbury in.
>
> While he watched that shifty, untrustable [*sic*] kettle with a sly twinkle in his eyes, a sort of "you-don't-take-me-in-old-fellow" kind of look, Molly had an opportunity of watching him.[13]

It is only too probable that the woman who wrote that (and only a woman could have written it) could also write the following and still remain quite unaware of the humor in her work; here she is describing the performance of a Greek play:

> Never was there a performance so absorbing; it is not too much to say that not a single word of the play was lost. Sometimes to have heard a pin drop would not have adequately conveyed the situation. To have heard the echo of a dropped pin go travelling around the house would have been nearer the truth.

Perhaps this breathless attention was not wholly due to the charm of the Greek play itself, the ability of the actors, the delightful costumes, the artistic beauty of the scenery, or even the well-trained voices of the Chorus.

Everybody in the front was interested in somebody on the stage. There were plenty of people to be interested in.

There were men of Trinity, St. John's, King's, Pembroke, and nearly every other college in the 'Varsity. There were citizens and attendants without number in the play, besides the Chorus. Everybody that could be got on to the limited stage was lugged in by the heels—at least, he was beautifully dressed, and armed with a crook or some ridiculous weapon, and desired to stand at ease and look pretty.

The men performed this part of the programme perfectly. They stood very much at ease, and they looked lovely! And, oh, the way the Greek came out! There never was such a public exhibition of manly limbs as the scanty Greek draperies revealed. Such legs! such arms! such chests!

Oh, it was splendid!

It brought tears into the girls' eyes—at least, into the eyes of the girls of higher culture.[14]

Similar delights are to be found throughout Mrs. Marshall's novels. *The Master of St. Benedict's* (1893) tells of the troubles brought to the Newnham girl Lucy Rae by her fascination for an undergraduate who slit his own throat in a fit of delirium tremens. In this work the author explored more fully the life of Cambridge girls, their *"attaques des nerfs"* brought on by overwork, their triumphs in debate ("Oh, it was beautiful to hear the girls speak ... garrulity is not the sin of students of colleges for women..."), and their impassioned rivalry for scholastic honors with the incompetents of Trinity and St. John's. *The Proctor's Wooing* (1897), *The Senior Tutor* (1904), these and others—some of which, like *The Dean's Little Daughter* (1891) are frankly juvenile tales—rolled from her pen with ease which is not even deceptive. The works of "Alan St. Aubyn" stand as a monument to the facile degradation of the university theme. The chimeras of Mrs. Marshall's Cambridge and Mrs. Batty's Oxford did not deter others from similar attempts. *Some Married Fellows* (1893), by Suzannah Venn (but published anonymously), reveals a strong preoccupation with marriage. (Indeed, this is a trait which characterizes most of these novels; Mrs. Marshall, reviewing the life of the old Master of St. Benedict's, revealed his rewards in their ascending order of importance: "honor, riches, distinction, love.") The story is a wildly improbable tale about a handsome don who married but whose life was ruined by the sudden death of his wife, and a lonely, proud, crippled wreck of a don (his trouble: he had never known the love of either mother or sister) who married but made himself miserable by jealousy. A distinctly feminine touch is the author's apparent conviction that Cambridge was controlled chiefly by the socially minded women who as wives of the dons wielded their astonishing power with a sure sense of what was best for the university. *Within Sound of Great Tom* (1897), an anonymous work needlessly described by Madan as "by a lady," explores the problems of marriage encountered by both dons and undergraduates; its violent action includes the near-blinding (by firecrackers, of all things) of an oarsman who was unjustly suspected of trifling with the affections of his best friend's fiancée; the marriage of a Fellow to a flighty girl who, bored with Oxford, ran away with his brother only to meet sudden death in a train wreck; the marriage of another Fellow to his landlady's daughter who was herself distinctly not a lady and who brought him to a sad end; thus the world of collegiate tragedy unfolds. Adeline Sergeant wrote a less distasteful novel in *Blake of Oriel* (1899), but does not quite convince the reader that Oxford was really the home of fiends. *The Little Don of Oxford* (1902), by Nellie Cornwall, has already been mentioned, and its sentimentality remains unsurpassed by even the most competent sentimentalists. Mrs. David Ritchie wrote what is on the whole an acceptable work, *The New Warden* (1918), but her eyes were fixed, ladylike, on marriage as she told the story of how the elderly Warden of King's was nearly trapped by an ignorant little schemer.

The catalogue of these works is happily not large, but the point of view they reveal is unmistakable for its total disregard of reality. And it invited obvious parody, which appeared in *Sandford of Merton: A Story of Oxford Life* (1903),[15] by Desmond F. T. Coke, a good-humored protest against the oddly distorted picture of university life provided by Bee Bee, Mrs. Marshall, and the rest. With ruthless humor Coke assumed the role of "editor" of the work of "Belinda Blinders," stating in his preface:

No doubt the spurious astuteness of the modern youth, while admiring the characterization and tragic dénoûment of the story, will seize on various inaccuracies with regard to Oxford. It had of course been possible for me to remedy such, but I have chosen rather to leave the work untouched, the record of a clever woman's view of Oxford and its ways....

At the same time it must not, indeed it cannot be thought that Miss Blinders wrote without having gained a thorough knowledge of the City and the University. She spent a whole week in Oxford for that very purpose.[16]

And he quotes from a letter of Belinda's:

"...All has passed *delightfully*. Oxford is a simply charming old place, and I wore a dress of the quite new *vigogne* material.... Almost everywhere I met with civility, though never with more, and *often* with less. But that is only to say that I met chiefly *men*! Still my thanks are due to Messrs. Cook and Son, of Ludgate Circus, London, who managed my stay; to the college doorkeepers, who showed me the colleges; and to the many collegians who afforded me information as to Oxford life contained in my romance: the last named seemed to derive positive amusement from providing me with interesting details. At *some* colleges I met with rudeness, and *was refused ad-*

mittance. I was wearing a becoming motor-cap, but the college doors were slammed in my face. This is a scandal. I shall write to *Motoring Illustrated....*"¹⁷

The amusement of the collegians is explained by the hoard of misinformation which Belinda gathered, such as the notion that the Sheldonian Theater was the scene of music-hall performances. At the same time, she was already well prepared, without any advice, to misinterpret Oxford. With the confidence born of ignorance she described a football game, and noted: "My familiarity with the technical terms and rules of football must not be taken to show any acquaintance with, or approval of, the brutal pastime itself. I have *never* seen a game, nor have I sunk to reading newspaper reports. One knows all about *Bull Fighting*. Knowledge like this one acquires one knows not how; but still one has it."¹⁸ She was completely predisposed to find wickedness in great quantities, and refused to be disappointed. As she started Ralph Sandford on his college career, she remarked on the surroundings in which he found himself:

Who does not know the Oxford type? Of small stature, with clear cut features, clean shaven, displaying a mouth whose sternness shows its lack of strength: weak-faced, of a colour and contour almost feminine, but marred by a betraying light of cruelty and vice that brightens the eyes as with bella-donna; the costume loud and ill-assorted, but neat to the pitch of affectation. Ralph was almost a contrast: each was the antithesis of the other. His eyes were tender with innocence and universal love, his features soft yet not ill-defined, his figure large without being burly, his dress, though not untidy, yet failed to be affected, while he escaped the effeminacy of his fellows by a slight moustache and by small side-whiskers, good enough for our fathers, but, alas! too seldom seen on the weak faces of the *jeunesse dorée* of today!¹⁹

Ralph thought and behaved as one might expect. The first cocoa party to which he was invited he found frivolous, but it was far better than the party given by Ronald Dashgross:

Ralph was disillusioned as soon as he opened the door. Round a table sat some eight or nine young men, each inhaling the deadly fumes of nicotine, and in the centre of the table, surrounded by various fruits, there stood—a bottle! At once the full significance of the situation struck the lad. *He had been enticed into an orgie!* But he was of sterling merit, and steadfastly refused either to smoke or drink. Not so his comrades. As the bottle of strongest claret circulated, they became more and more riotous. Ralph sought an excuse to make his departure; but scarce had he determined that the most tactful method would be to say that he had a letter to write, when songs were called for. Ralph had ever loved music, and resolved to stay. Ah, Ralph! had you known the nature of those songs, you would have fled the swifter! All the latest productions of the gilded gin-palaces were bellowed out—"Two Lovely Black Eyes," "Ting-a-Ling," "The Bogey Man," and "Daisy"—each worse than the last, and all sung with relish. Ralph had never heard them before, nor had he ever imagined such depravity....

Such was the atmosphere in which Ralph was to learn to be a man! Masculine asceticism is intuitively hedonistic. [Belinda's footnote: I owe this sentiment to Ouida. The method of expressing it is my own. B.B.] And now the large bottle was almost empty. "Come Sandford," said Dashgross, already husky, "just a drop for the toast of the evening." Ralph complied—oh! perilous first step!—thinking they would toast the King.

"To Bacchus!" cried the host, and all drained their cups. All except Ralph.

"This is how I drink to a heathen deity," he cried, and shivering the tumbler upon the floor, he strode from the room. In that moment he looked almost like a god himself. [Belinda's footnote: It must not be thought that the above constitutes any attack on Oxford morals. Of the vicious side of a young man's life I have no personal experience: I derive my knowledge from Dean Farrar's "Eric" and like sources. Let us hope Oxford life is not so immoral. It was necessary to paint vice in its blackest colours, so as to show in relief the virtue of Ralph.][20]

Ralph made a similar scene at the Union, where he interrupted a playful debate on the proposition "That this house considers woman to be man's equal" by delivering a shattering speech on the holiness of female virtue; at the Sheldonian, he harangued an audience about lewd plays; this speech put him in the hands of the Proctor, and when Rose, the girl he left behind him, heard he was in trouble, she flew to Oxford to lead him again into the paths of virtue. She arrived just in time to see Ralph win the college boat race all by himself (the other seven oarsmen were stodgy creatures who rowed in unison while Ralph went faster and faster) and to perform a similar miracle at the Cambridge football match. In this, however, he broke his neck, and while in the hospital his winning Newdigate poem was stolen—an affront he avenged by fighting, and fouling, the thief. If these exploits could have left any doubts in Rose's mind, they were dispelled when Ralph rescued her from a burning hotel.[21]

Most of the ladies' voices seem to have been stilled during the Edwardian years, though Mrs. Batty, as noted above, was still unreformed in 1912. It was a merciful silence. This quaint and preposterous bypath of university fiction could have led nowhere; it is indeed remarkable that it existed at all. And its existence seems only the more improbable in that it appeared at the very time the university novel, in its more distinguished form, was about to achieve the culmination of its long development.

Chapter IX

THE CULT OF OXFORD

Looking back over what has been observed so far about novels having to do with Oxford and Cambridge, one is inclined to pause momentarily to reflect on certain generalizations which suggest themselves. First, the number of these novels is impressive, given the fact of their highly restricted subject matter and the hazards that obviously so often stood between the author and the writing of a good novel. And their number indicates that these novels did represent a popular literary form. More important, they follow a clear course of progress from initial fragmentary accounts of university life through the full-scale libels of the eighteenth century, to the earnest novels of reform, to a well-developed comic literature, and finally to a series of romantic novels glorifying college life. That the several kinds of university fiction were frequently current and popular at the same time, or that the clock should sometimes apparently have been turned back, as it was by well-intentioned women novelists, should not obscure the growth and existence of these distinct patterns.

Also, the validity of a comment made in chapter i of this study appears to be substantiated. Clearly, up to this point there has been much talk about Oxford, little about Cambridge. Mention has been made, of course, of Cambridge novels (e.g., *The Cambridge Grisette*), but their scarcity has been evident. And, excluding the work of E. F. Benson, even the most ambitious have been of relatively little merit. Only recently, in the work of C. P. Snow (discussed at the end of this chapter), have novels about Cambridge been written without the distinctively grimy quality that has consistently characterized them. For example, *A Green Bay Tree* (1894), by "W. H. Wilkins" (i.e., W. H.

de Winton) and Herbert Vivian, describes the seamy side of Cambridge life, centered largely in Magdalene College. Here, amid orgies a little more sophisticated but no more refined than those of earlier days, the protagonist engaged in a campaign to wreck the happiness of his best friend; the hero of Cambridge society, an outspoken Tory and leader of the Union, this villain was nevertheless a liar and a cheat, and he flourished like the tree of the title throughout this cynical tour de force. *The Cantab* (1926), by Shane Leslie, relates the partially autobiographical story of Edward Stornington, son of the rector of Cherryumpton, an innocent youth who kept his innocence while all about him were losing theirs and blaming it on him. Leslie created, in Mr. Meleager, a Cambridge don as brilliant as, but more eccentric than, the Faucits of Oxford; and he gave a convincing picture of life in the King's College boat. But Edward ran aground of a brace of religious fanatics who led him into Anglo-Catholicism and East End missions, and thence, when he was convinced that Anglican orders were invalid, to Russia, where he bribed a priest to admit him to the Communion of the Orthodox Church. After some desultorily mystical conversations with Tolstoy, Edward returned to England thoroughly disillusioned: "Very humbly he surveyed himself. He had somehow steered clear of Sex, and now he had no particular Religion to bring into the East End of London. He must find his religion there. ...To Cambridge he had given three years, but she had given him no qualification except to vaunt himself a CANTAB." These closing words suggest how far this novel, at least, departs from the themes that had colored Oxford fiction in the years just before the First World War.

This departure suggests the clue to a far more important observation. The reader of the novels thus far examined will have noted the occasional awareness of certain authors of an ingredient in Oxford life which had nothing to do with shoddiness, or mere boisterousness, or even intellectual stimulus. It appeared embryonically as far back as *Reginald Dalton,* in which Lockhart expressed his love for the university. It was elaborated upon by Thomas Hughes, who sensed the *genius loci* of Oxford, the atmosphere which, if it was not spiritual itself, at least worked on Oxford undergraduates to produce a sense of well-being and of sharing in the best that life could offer. For a time, recognition of this atmosphere was more implicit than explicit. It lay behind the concept of the noble Crichtons, whose animal spirits and brilliant minds alike were nourished in the only surroundings that could have given them full play. But by the turn of the century it had begun to produce a new type of novel representing the final stage in the process of idealization which had been going on since the publication of *Tom Brown at Oxford.* Portman's *Hugh Rendal* reflects it, when the author considers:

> To plunge further into the new life was to wish each day double its normal length, so vast was the surge of new interests, so strong was their grip upon mind and imagination. There were new books to be read, new points of view to be formed, new characters to be studied; Oxford itself was to be explored and revered, the charm of its quiet buildings absorbed, the throb of its active life enjoyed. There were exquisite choirs to be heard, excellent lectures to be attended; every kind of man, opinion, taste, and attitude to be met and weighed in the balance.[1]

A dramatic statement of the new feeling appears amid the mock heroics of *Zuleika Dobson,* in the form of a passionate outburst of affection for Oxford. Here the author imagines himself on the eve of Oxford's greatest tragedy sailing disembodied over the loved scene:

> I floated out into the untenanted meadows. Over them was the usual coverlet of white vapour, trailed from the Isis right up to Merton Wall. The scents of these meadows' moisture is the scent of Oxford. Even in hottest noon, one feels that the sun has not dried *them.*

---

[1] For notes to chap. ix, see pp. 211–212.

The Cult of Oxford 153

Always there is moisture drifting across them, drifting into the Colleges. It, one suspects, must have had much to do with the evocation of what is called the Oxford spirit—that gentlest spirit, so lingering and searching, so dear to them who as youths were brought into the ken of it, so exasperating to them who were not. Yes, certainly, it is this mild, miasmal air, not less that the grey beauty and gravity of the buildings, that has helped Oxford to produce, and foster eternally, her peculiar race of artist-scholars, scholar-artists. The undergraduate, in his brief periods of residence, is too buoyant to be mastered by the spirit of the place. He does but salute it, and catch the manner. It is on him who stays to spend his maturity here that the spirit will in its fulness gradually descend. The buildings and their traditions keep astir in his mind whatsoever is gracious; the climate, enfolding him and enfeebling him, lulling him, keeps him careless of the sharp, harsh, exigent realities of the outer world. Careless? Not utterly. These realities may be seen by him. He may study them, be amused or touched by them. But they cannot fire him. Oxford is too damp for that. The "movements" made there have been no more than protests against the mobility of others. They have been without the dynamic quality implied in their name. They have been no more than the sighs of men gazing at what other men have left behind them; faint, impossible appeals to the god of retrogression, uttered for their own sake and ritual, rather than with any intent that they should be heard. Oxford, that lotus-land, saps the will-power, the power of action. But, in doing so, it clarifies the mind, makes larger the vision, gives, above all, that playful and caressing suavity of manner which comes of a conviction that nothing matters, except ideas, and that not even ideas are worth dying for, inasmuch as the ghosts of them slain seem worthy of yet more piously elaborate homage than can be given to them in their hey-day. If the Colleges could be transferred to the dry and bracing top of some hill, doubtless they would be more evidently useful to the nation. But let us be glad there is no engineer or enchanter to compass that task. *Egomet,* I would liefer have the rest of England subside into the sea than have Oxford set on a salubrious level. For there is nothing in England to be matched with what lurks in the vapours of these meadows, and in the shadows of these spires—that mysterious, inenubilable spirit, spirit of Oxford. Oxford! The very sight of the word printed, or sound of it spoken, is fraught for me with most actual magic.[2]

In Oxford fiction this attitude produced what one can only call the cult of Oxford, dedicated to a belief in the efficacy of the university atmosphere itself as an educating force. Simply to submerge one's self in the traditions, the dignified culture, and the stimulating friendships of university life was to get the best out of an Oxford that had more important things to give its students than were to be found in books. The cult matured rapidly, and was soon given its most felicitous expression in what is in almost every way the best of all university novels, Compton Mackenzie's *Sinister Street* (1913–1914). In the second half of this long novel, Michael Fane began what he called "the adventure of Oxford"[3] as a sensitive, impressionable youth who, coming from a London school, found greater novelty in college life than did his friends from public schools. But he quickly adapted himself to it, and the first stage in his Oxford education consisted of his personal adjustment to a small circle of friends carefully chosen by him for both the variety and the value of their views of life. There was the sensible, serious scholar and cricketer Alan Merivale, a thorough conservative in whom any deviation from sound common sense was unthinkable; the serenely self-confident little humorist Lord Lonsdale, to whom an Oxford education was a lark and anyone who thought otherwise was an ass; the pompous Wedderburn, whose judicial manner usually obtained the last word in the criticism of art, literature, and wines; Maurice Avery, slightly aesthetic, often immature, but versatile and sincere in his radicalism; and Guy Hazelwood, poet and critic, "the most brilliant man in the university." Michael epitomized the results of his first term at Oxford by giving a dinner for this select group who, gathered together, represented for him Oxford itself, "the dream of youth's domination set against the gray background of time's endurance."[4] It was in their company that the spirit of Oxford became tangible and concrete. In Hazelwood's rooms one night he listened to the poet read a paper on the sonnet:

The Cult of Oxford

He heard in half-a-dream the level voice of Hazelwood enunciating his theories in graceful singing sentences, and the occasional fizz of a replenished glass. The tobacco smoke grew thicker and thicker, curling in spirals about the emaciated loveliness of an ivory saint. The paper was over: and before the discussion was started somebody rose and drew back the dull green curtains sown with golden fleur-de-lys. Moonbeams came slanting in and with them the freshness of the May night: more richly blue gathered the tobacco smoke: more magical became the room, and more perfectly the decorative expression of all Oxford stood for.[5]

The personal adjustment to Oxford was accompanied by intellectual growth. This significantly did not come at the hands of the dons, however. Rather, it took place through the youthful extravagances of liberal thought founded on the conviction that the world could be set straight by the younger generation which was, as Ibsen had said, knocking at the door. "The Oxford Looking Glass," fathered by Avery, was, with its articles on "Socrates at Balliol," "The Failure of the Modern Illustrator," and "Oxford Liberalism," a "curious compound of priggishness and brilliance and perspicacity and wit," and yet it achieved a "verisimilitude of the image of Oxford."[6] This image, dedicated to the future, nevertheless reflected the past as well. Back of the modernity of "The Looking Glass" and invisibly supporting it stood Oxford's Academic Muse, which Michael fancied might well be Pallas Athena, "the personification of the spirit of the university":

Well enough might the owl and the olive serve as symbols of Oxford. The owl could stand for all the grotesque pendantry, all the dismal hootings of age, all the slow deliberate sweep of the don's mind, the seclusions, the blinkings in the daylight and the unerring destruction of intellectual vermin; while the olive would speak of age and the grace and grayness of age, of age each year made young again by its harvest of youth, of sobriety sun-kindled to a radiancy of silver joy, of wisdom, peace, and shelter, and Attic glories.[7]

It was by participating in the informal intellectual life of undergraduates that Michael felt his development taking place, rather than in the set studies of philosophy and history which he at last, after absorbing the profit of the other, brought himself conscientiously to perform.

And finally, Michael's conscious effort to absorb the spirit of Oxford resulted in an emotional response which colored all his other impressions. This took the form of seeking out precisely what Oxford meant to him, what the vitality of Oxford's past meant as a force in the development of man's spirit. The answer was found in curiously out-of-the-way places, but in all cases it grew from the realization that Michael Fane, here and now, shared in the past; that the spiritual force of Oxford so worked upon his struggle for self-realization that what he did in the present was significant in even the smallest details because it was the product of the fusion of Oxford with the entity of Michael Fane. "Oxford seemed to him to provide an opportunity, and more than an opportunity—an inexpugnable command to wave with most reluctant hands farewell to the backward of time, around whose brink rose up more truthful dreams than those that floated undeterminate, beckoning through the mist, across the wan mountains of the future."[8] So thinking, he refused to give up his rooms in St. Mary's for better because he had labored, through his collection of books and pictures, to create an atmosphere of permanence, and of continuity with the past, and he had "a sentimental objection to denying them the full period of their participation in his own advance along the lines he had marked out for himself."[9] Most of all he found the heart of Oxford in the rooms of John Venable, "Venner," the steward of the Junior Common Room of St. Mary's for more than three decades.

Most people, seeking the imaginative reward of their sensibility, would obtain the finest thrill that Oxford could offer from the sud-

The Cult of Oxford

den sight of St. Mary's tower against a green April afterglow, or of the moon-parched High Street in frost. Michael, however, found in Venner's office, just as he had found in that old print of St. Mary's tower rather than in the tower itself, the innermost shrine of Oxford, the profoundest revelation of the shining truth round which the mysterious material of Oxford had grown through the Middle Ages.[10]

Here, amid the account books and memories of bygone years, and in the company of the wise and benign old man, gathered those undergraduates who had achieved the privilege of admission to the shrine.

There was no formal election to Venner's: there simply happened a moment when the St. Mary's man entered unembarrassed that mellow office and basked in that sunny effluence. In this ripe old room, generous and dry as sherry wine, how pleasant it was to sit and listen to Venner's ripe old stories: how amazingly important seemed the trivial gossip of the college in this historic atmosphere: how much time was apparently wasted here between eight and ten at night, and what a thrill it always was to come into college about half-past nine of a murky evening and stroll round the Cloisters to see if there was anybody at Venner's. It could after all scarcely be accounted a waste of time to sit and slowly mature in Venner's, and sometimes about half-past nine the old man would be alone, the fire would be dying down and during the half-hour that remained of his duty, it would be possible to peel a large apple very slowly and extract from him more of the essence of social history than could be gained from a term's reading of great historians even with all the extra lucidity imparted by a course of Mr. So-and-So's lectures.[11]

Shortly before leaving Oxford, Michael expressed his feeling that these emanations of the Oxford spirit had prepared him for a life of service to others:

"...I'm so positive that the best of Oxford is the best of England, and that the best of England is the best of humanity that I long to apply to the world the same standards we tacitly respect—we undergraduates. I believe every problem of life can be solved by the transcendency of the spirit which has transcended us up here."

"I think you have a great capacity for idealization," said Mrs. Ross gravely. "I wonder how you are going to express it practically."[12]

It was Michael's misfortune that he tried to express it impractically, devoting himself to the hopeless task of reforming a trollop with whom he had once been in love. Setting out to find her, he decided that in this deed there "lay easily discernible the true corollary to the four years at Oxford. They had been years of rest and refreshment, years of armament with wise and academic and well observed theories of behavior that would defeat the victory of evil."[13] At first, disillusionment overwhelmed him when he realized the disparity between his ideals and reality. But further reflection showed him that failure in his first venture beyond Oxford had not been due to any deficiency in the preparation Oxford had given him. Rather, it had been due to his own misunderstanding of what a life of service should mean, his own failure to serve disinterestedly. "I have been given knowledge and I fancied I was given disillusion. If now I offer myself to God very humbly, I give myself to the service of men. Man for man standing in his own might is a blind and arrogant leader.... God has only offered to the individual the chance to perfect himself."[14] And Oxford, offering its hours of profitable leisure, its lessons of what becomes the gentleman, its secret of companionship with the past, and its serene contemplation of the future, is at once the creation and creator of man's perfection.[15]

The richness of life at Oxford which *Sinister Street* explored so effectively found further expression in a novel by Ivor Brown. *Years of Plenty* (1915) is a strange and rambling book which takes its hero, Martin Leigh, through his days as a schoolboy and undergraduate, following no very clearly defined course other than the progress from boyhood to manhood. Like Michael Fane, Leigh was surrounded at Oxford by a group of widely differing personalities, all of whom contributed to an intellectual atmosphere that in turn reacted upon each individually.

The Cult of Oxford

Most of the Oxford scenes are devoted to the conversations of these young men, who called themselves "the Push," and who by uttering a great deal of nonsense effected a sort of catharsis of the intellect which in the end matured them. The years of plenty are those in which young men are free of responsibility and free to try their wings in the world of men. At Oxford, life was largely experimental—flights of oratory in the Union, weighty discussions in literary and political clubs, and clumsy experiments with love, were all part of the process of growing up. Like *Sinister Street,* this novel suggests that it is through contact with minds as young and inquiring as their own that undergraduates are educated, rather than through the formal procedures of the lecture room.

Incredibly the Push were blind to their own amazing superficiality. Even had they suffered from an inclination to be serious, life came so easily and so rapidly that it would have been impossible to do anything but play with it. So they trifled with wisdom and trifled rightly. For when a man is only nineteen and has enough to eat and drink, and more than enough to read and say, it was a crime to stop in thought and laboriously dam the pleasant shallows of an easy-going stream.[16]

Martin Leigh concluded at the end of his university career that "Oxford had been so generous and had given him so much to think and feel and say"[17] that he was not seriously disappointed to have to turn to a career in India for which he felt no enthusiasm, and his thinking is summarized in the verses of Hilaire Belloc which appear opposite the title page:

> The wealth of youth, we spent it well
> And decently, as very few can.
> And is it lost? I cannot tell:
> And what is more I doubt if you can.

The same feeling for Oxford as a kind of greenhouse for maturing young men is evident in Michael Sadleir's *Hyssop*

(1915), in which the undergraduate Philip Murray had a career very much like Michael Fane's, devoted to catching the mood of Oxford and responding to its influence through the medium of undergraduate activities that otherwise would have been trivial enough. *Hyssop* affords a good example of the peculiarities of undergraduate characterization which were coming more and more to be employed in these novels. Like Michael Fane's carefully chosen specimens, these are deliberately created to provide a suitable company among whom Philip Murray "found his level and could absorb the multitude of ideas and hopes with which the air of Oxford was alive."[18] But observe the author's attentive effort to emphasize eccentricities: there was Ian Macallister, for example, "Laddie" to his friends, "a slim dark-haired and rather beautiful youth with lilac socks and a tie to match ... indolent, rather affected and possessed of a curious taste for erotic simile and anecdote."[19] And Douglas Field, of Magdalen, "a frail, girlish-looking boy with a very fair skin and odd flail-like legs that never seemed controllable. He was a Roman Catholic, collected Missals and adored every manifestation of Gothic."[20] And "Pumblechook"—"He read Latin authors as easily as the ordinary man reads a modern novel, dabbled in witchcraft and was always bankrupt." It was this man's ambition to buy " 'an absurd little castle in the Apennines and wander about the country thieving and wenching till I am hung or until all my money is spent, whichever comes soonest. If the latter I shall save exactly enough to buy a third-class ticket to Amiens, climb to the topmost pinnacle of the cathedral and there sit, chanting the Ballad of Dead Ladies until I die of starvation.' "[21] Then there was Vardon: "He affected ruthless 'arrivisme,' wore a tortoiseshell monocle and straps."[22] And Tamworth: "He had a smooth round face with large tortoiseshell spectacles behind which unsmiling and sleepy eyes roved from face to face.... He read immense quantities of philosophy in a ruminative manner and with little apparent re-

The Cult of Oxford 161

sult, except a tendency to use long words and make puns.... When not reading philosophy he would contemplate Ibsen's plays gloomily in Norwegian (a language of which he was entirely ignorant) or play on a piano with two fingers the only tunes he knew, which were 'All the Little Pansy Faces' and 'Abide With Me.' He kept a large yellow tomcat in his rooms, who shared his sombre disposition and was suspected of being a familiar spirit."[23] These portraits, coming one on top of the other in the space of a very few pages, suggest that the air of Oxford was alive with some very odd ideas and hopes, but their function in the novel is clear enough. When Philip's tutor Trafford set forth his "theory of community-value in the undergraduate" he was only providing a prefatory remark for this unusual cast of characters, but he was making explicit an idea that had come to dominate serious fiction about Oxford.

A slight variation of this point of view appears in *A City in the Foreground* (1921), by Gerard Hopkins. Hugh Kenyon, a sensitive, shy, and very serious young man, was troubled because he was incapable of grasping what he knew was in Oxford.

"Look at Oxford down there, how beautiful she is. Listen to her bells, the very towers and roofs are talking. I *know* what they're saying, and I'd give everything in life if they'd speak to me, but they won't.... That's where the real modernity is, because life and spirit is [*sic*] essentially modern, and that valley city is where life thrills and germinates. It doesn't matter what the professors teach, it's what the *place* teaches, it's the young spirit that breathes in the hearts of those who are taught. They come here to grow up, and that, after all, is the only teaching worth anything.... I lose all patience with people who talk of Oxford and systems of education as though the two had anything to do with one another. *It's just because Oxford teaches nothing in particular that she is such a priceless possession. She has all the treasures of the world hidden in the folds of her garments, and he who is lucky enough to be able to search for them and find them has the greatest education that the world can give.*... I have found nothing except the knowledge that the treasure is there, and that I can never reach it."[24]

Hugh Kenyon was afflicted with a bad case of intellectual drift, never sure of himself or of the direction he was taking, and though he came to Oxford with an attitude of "surrender and adoration," looking for "the old ideal of male companionship and the intensity of life," he was pretty certain not to find it until his own ideas stiffened a bit. When the war came he thought for a time that he had found a purpose and a goal, but even this could not really move him, and he was left at the end as much at sea as ever. But *A City in the Foreground* is one of the most painstaking examinations of the state of Oxford to appear in fiction; in this respect it quite dwarfs anything produced in the nineteenth century. Hopkins' tendency is to wish back the old days, the days when all life in Oxford was limited to the colleges and halls, before the arrival of the hordes of bespectacled, complacent students living out on the Iffley Road who wanted "a good degree," who neither knew nor cared what Oxford should have meant to them, who

declaimed against the teaching of classics, questioned the value of college loyalties, waxed eloquent in the condemnation of youthful extravagance and eccentricities which, as a matter of fact, far more than bulging notebooks and regular attendance at lectures, show the vitality of the growing mind.... These men, who claimed as their right a share in the treasures of culture and education, were, by the very clamor which they raised, deafening their ears to the softer sound they sought to hear. What they wanted was not Oxford, but a new thing made in their own image. They wished, not to fling wide the city gates, but to demolish her very walls, to tear down her buildings stone by stone that they might build they knew not what.[25]

The postwar life of Oxford, Hugh Kenyon knew, was more democratic, more commercialized, than it had been before, and was on the whole more shabby as well. The less distracted youths who were his friends felt that perhaps as veterans of the war they were too mature to indulge in the prewar undergraduate life with its lack of little responsibilities and its concentration on

The Cult of Oxford

the one great responsibility, and so they contentedly let the old ideal fade away. But it would not disappear from the mind of one like Hugh Kenyon, who, though he did not say so, was wishing back the days of *Sinister Street*.

The ultimate expression of the note of longing for things past is without doubt Beverly Nichols' *Patchwork* (1921), and here the lost ideal is very explicitly identified with Mackenzie's Oxford. *Patchwork*, moreover, affords perhaps the clearest indication of how deeply the university novel had finally penetrated the vital problem of what a university could and should mean to its scholars; it fails to rise to the heights of *Sinister Street*, but in its failures is revealed how greatly its predecessor had succeeded. Its protagonist, Raymond Sheldon, had returned from the war to find a disastrous change in Oxford: the university lacked the spontaneity and charm of earlier days, and suffered from an air of reserve and self-consciousness—the students were determined to work, and everything was devoted to sordid and practical ends. Ray Sheldon had an artist's temperament, and with it a great longing for the days when Oxford was the home of youth where the demands of the outside world could be rejected for the luxury of surrender to frivolities that were really not frivolous, where it was not thought a waste of time for one like Michael Fane to collect editions of *Don Quixote,* proclaim liberalism to the world, and dwell in satisfied contemplation of surroundings rich with intrinsic values that were no less real because they contributed to the extravagances of youth. His ideal was the Oxford of *Sinister Street,* and he tried to live up to it:

He'd read *Sinister Street,* and he'd made up his mind he was going to live that sort of life again. And when he came up, he found he couldn't. Everything was different—you know how different it was yourself. Ray really belonged to the past. And instead of accepting things as they were, like most of us, he just sat down and said, "I'm going to make Oxford again myself. I'm going to change everything, or rather to make everything what it once was." Of course, it was absolutely impossible. But, as a matter of fact, he nearly did succeed. He influenced Oxford more than anybody else since the war.[26]

His first move was to revive *The Isis,* an undergraduate publication that had been dormant throughout the war; he succeeded in so filling his first number with brilliant epigrammatic wit that its success was ensured. This was followed by the appearance of a creation of his own, *The Oxford Mercury,* devoted to the liberalism of young men who have Something to Say—after the manner of *The Oxford Looking Glass,* of course. Liberal thought at war against "the wisdom and experience of age" was given still another support in his Star Club, established to rival the Union. But the hostility created by Ray Sheldon's determination to take nothing seriously except his war against serious and plodding undergraduates finally drove him to reform the Union itself, which he won to his cause by his own wit and brilliance. His unsuccessful campaign for its presidency, however, proved that though Oxford could still be charmed by the light-hearted effervescence of its own past, its past could not be revived. Disheartened, Ray was nevertheless determined to try again, until word of his mother's death so shocked him that he had no further heart for a lost cause, and left Oxford. We see him next in New York, a brilliant and successful playwright, ostensibly disillusioned about what he now called the "false softness" of life before the war and the inappropriateness of Oxford's past in a world that was grown accustomed to death and tragedy, a world that was best expressed by the sharp, hard lines of New York's skyscrapers. But at the end of a speech in which he discussed his new ideas and his love for the modernity of America, he suddenly broke off:

He felt terribly as though he might cry. Everything was so lonely, his listeners so cruel, so far away....
 Oxford—how he longed again for Oxford! It would be spring now at Oxford, and the larches would be green over the Cherwell. Boar's

Hill was ripe with bluebells now, and there would be primroses in Chorley Wood. The very names of these places were sweet. Oxford!—the city that belonged to youth, to enthusiasm, to impulse, and to laughter....

Through the bright gilded windows he looked out wistfully to the drifting clouds.[27]

The Oxford of *Sinister Street* and of *Patchwork*'s reminiscing mood dedicated to youth and enthusiasm and impulse, represented the height of the ideal which the university fiction writers had succeeded in creating. It may be worthwhile to quote a rather long passage from Beverly Nichols which points indirectly to the past by showing how great was the change that had taken place since the early days of university fiction, and directly to the future by its recognition of the demise of Victorian and Edwardian Oxford that had been foreseen by Tyrwhitt and lamented by Hopkins. Ray Sheldon is reflecting on the state of postwar Oxford:

... there is evidence enough of a spirit which now seems to have vanished forever—the spirit which a distinguished son of Magdalen caught so perfectly when he wrote of "days of lyrical ardour and of studious sonnet-writing; days when one loved the exquisite intricacy and musical repetitions of the ballade, and the villanelle with its linked long-drawn echoes and its curious completeness; days when one solemnly sought to discover the proper temper in which a triolet should be written; delightful days, in which, I am glad to say, there was far more rhyme than reason."

It was days like that, days when Oxford had really been Oxford, days when one could abandon oneself without interruption to a mood, days such as Michael Fane had known in his primrose passage through Sinister Street, which Raymond longed above all things to recapture. He opened the second volume of "Sinister Street" at random: "Michael wandered on in meditation. From lighted windows in the High came a noise of laughter and voices that seemed to make more grave and more perdurable the spires and towers of Oxford, deepening somehow the solemnity of the black entries and the empty silver spaces before them. Michael pondered the freshmen's chatter and apprehended dimly how this magical sublunary city would convert all that effusion of naïve intolerance to her own renown..."

Would Oxford ever again be like that? Had it ever been like that, or had it only existed, a silver city of dream and shadow, in the mind of a novelist? Everything seemed to have been so easy in those days— the channels so well worn. Ray had loved even the evidence which he had found of intolerance, of effete and unique tradition, in the same way in which he loved the mottled corbels and gargoyles which dreamed their twisted dreams above the dim cloisters of Magdalen. He had loved the superstitious veneration which had clustered round a fourth-year man, the particular and meticulous social grades represented by the President of the Union, a Blue, an editor of *The 'Varsity,* the head of a political club. He had loved the evidence he had found of wit and laughter, the epigrams scattered like hard crystals through the pages of college magazines. He had loved the superficiality because it was superficial, and as such, an evidence of light-heartedness, an evidence of youth untarnished. He had loved all this comedy of manners in the same way he had loved the fripperies, the patches and the powder of some painted Macaroni from the coloured pages of a history that had passed.

All these things, as he began to discover sadly, were gone. Blackwell no longer published precious sonnets in which monstrous linnets sang unearthly melodies in the golden fume of impossible September mornings. Instead, he published "Wheels," the quintessence of modernity, poems in which there was no rhyme, and for which there was too much reason. "Wheels," with its harsh angular covers, its black lines and its brick-red curves, seemed symbolical, in some ways, of the Oxford that was to be. Poems inspired by bitterness, by hatred, by a vision of the sham and rottenness which lay behind the faded pomp and circumstance of war. And the damnable part of it all was that the poems were *right*. They were right because they were disillusioned, because they were harsh, because they had swept away, with a gesture, the fabric of dreams which Oxford had once built with so superb an unconsciousness.

There is nothing more sad than the renunciation of a symbol, the surrender of a flag. Oxford seemed to have capitulated, to have realized that she too was beaten. It was not merely the outward signs and sordid symbols of defeat which were most striking. It was most

The Cult of Oxford

of all, thought Ray, the astonishing commercialization of the undergraduates themselves. He had managed to discover, and to lead, a small set which was either too well bred or too insensitive to show any marked effects of the war. But the rest of the College, and the rest of the university, seemed to be talking of nothing but work. And then, some men even imported to the J.C.R. something of the atmosphere of a mess and talked in loud voices, from behind pipes, about such things as "Boches," and "Black Marias" and "spinning nose-dives"—atrocities which in Oxford should never have been mentioned as even existent. . . .

Was it, however, impossible that the old Oxford should return? Were things always to be so sordid, so practical, so commercial? Was the time never to return when one could wander into the J.C.R. and inform the assembly there that one had been in travail all the afternoon with a triolet, and not be regarded as mad? It was not merely the somewhat narrow, but not unpraiseworthy, attitude of the aesthete. It was something infinitely deeper than that—the exaltation of culture for the sake of culture, the praise of folly for the sake of folly. And more, the love of living for the sake of life—life irresponsible, full-blooded, triumphant.[28]

The old Oxford did not, however, come back—at least not in fiction. It probably could not have done so in the prosaic years following the war, when the university was crowded with businesslike and determined students old beyond their years. But still another reason lay behind Ray Sheldon's failure to recapture the wonder that had passed: despite his awareness of the ideal that had brought *Sinister Street* into being, despite his wistful longing to reclaim the past, Ray Sheldon seriously misinterpreted Michael Fane's Oxford days. Perhaps it was the sense of contrast between the apparent frivolities of prewar Oxford and the earnest "commercialization" of his own time which led him —and, one suspects, Beverly Nichols as well—to confuse the cult of Oxford with its surface phenomena. At any rate, his error is clear: he mistook the effusions of the dilettante for the ideal of leisured culture which was the very foundation of the cult of

Oxford. Confusion between the two was complete in the effort Ray Sheldon made to revive the Oxford of *Sinister Street* by trying to make it a place " 'where you can wear any damned thing you like and do any damned thing you like too,' " where the undergraduate could be "a delightful, inconsequent, brilliant individual."[29] Michael Fane aspired to no such freedom; if he savored brilliance, he certainly did not admire inconsequence for its own sake. The difference between the two could hardly be greater: the ideal of *Sinister Street* was that of the individual's submission to the magical influence of Oxford; in *Patchwork* this was twisted, no doubt unconsciously, to an ideal of the individual's uninhibited self-expression in an atmosphere that would permit him to play the fool or the wise man with equal impunity. Michael Fane experimented freely with the emotions and ideas Oxford thrust upon him, but he never struck a pose while doing so. Ray Sheldon posed interminably, with his taste for Beardsley and *The Yellow Book,* his frustrated desire to wear a black cloak and a green carnation, and his longing for rooms with "windows giving onto a slow river; deep bookshelves, in which reverently he might have placed rare editions of Walter Pater and exquisitely bound copies of the Decameron," where "all that was superb and splendid in Oxford would have passed, shadowy and shod with silver, before him."[30] In an "Author's Note," Nichols explained that he "endeavored to give as faithful a picture as possible of the New Oxford, the Oxford which has emerged from the chaos of war, and which has even yet to recover her ancient tranquility and many of her most precious traditions."[31] Although he succeeded in showing that Oxford had suffered a loss, he mistook the nature of that loss when he identified it in terms of Ray's aesthetic tastes. For Ray was an aesthete, and he was a dilettante; and the fact that he should have also been meant as a latter-day Michael Fane requires some explanation, for Michael Fane was neither of these.

The Cult of Oxford

The reason for this confusion perhaps lies in the very aestheticism that colored most of Ray Sheldon's actions. Now aestheticism and the cult of Oxford were by no means the same things, but they bore a curious external relationship to one another which was strong enough, after the meaning of the cult had been lost, to lead to their being identified as the same. An integral part of the cult of Oxford was the manner which Beerbohm described as a mixture of the casual and the gracious; it was defined more fully in *A City in the Foreground* as one that "amuses, provokes and decorates. It may have no greater depth than a stream, but it is a stream that occasionally 'maketh music with the enamelled stones,' rushing over miniature waterfalls with noise and many rainbow colours."[32] It appeared in glittering conversation, an effect of brilliance, a suave politeness, and an essential decency. These surface phenomena did indeed belong to prewar Oxford, which polished and refined while it also matured the undergraduate; but if the outward evidences of Oxford culture were permitted to represent all that *Sinister Street* implied, then there would be a danger that they might be taken as ends in themselves; and it was this danger that Ray Sheldon failed to avoid. The Oxford manner had, in fact, early been recognized in a very primitive form in the aesthetes of the undergraduate world, and as *Patchwork* so clearly shows, it never quite lost this unfortunate association.

The beginnings of aestheticism in the university novels go back to the early recognition of a class of effete young men who led expensive but profitless lives amid luxurious surroundings. Hewlett's Singleton Slipslop was an outstanding example of the early breed, and so was his Byron Scott Montgomery Wilks, "reclining gracefully on his sofa, dressed in an elegant silk reading gown, with a guitar suspended to his neck by a broad scarlet ribbon."[33] But the type did not become common in university fiction until the vogue of aestheticism spread through England at the end of the nineteenth century. Perhaps the first real university aesthete appeared in Julian Sturgis' *John-a-Dreams* (1878) in the person of Osman Belgrave, living in musk-scented rooms graced with a bowl of dried rose leaves, chairs covered with Japanese silk, and engravings both saintly and sensuous.[34] After this, examples are plentiful. Hugh Heron observed men who furnished their rooms according to a period, and he wondered "what made all the most effeminate men in Oxford go on about gymnastics and manly beauty."[35] Dickinson's Keddy was warned to avoid "men who use scent and dress too well, and wear green ties and write poetry."[36]

But it is notable that during the height of nineteenth-century aestheticism, even while Oscar Wilde (Oxford, B.A. 1878) was luridly distinguishing himself and Magdalen College with his aesthetic cult, the university novels appear to have done little more than note the presence of these men. It was left to the twentieth-century novelists to bring them out of their relative obscurity, and in the process the aesthetes, receiving kinder treatment than one might expect, emerged somewhat transformed. Their eccentricities were analyzed with good humor and not a little real affection, and at times the label of aesthete was deliberately removed. A good example is the character of Charles Dallas in *A City in the Foreground* who, despite his pretentions, his affected speech, and his effeminate perfection of dress, was in his way a sincere and amiable person. There were many such men, remarked Hopkins, in the Oxford of that time:

> There had been, for years past, a constant succession of young men at All Saints of the species of Charles Dallas. They formed a set within the college, recognizable by those of an older generation as the true children of parents whom they had themselves known, admired, or ridiculed. It was not only a definite attitude of life that made of these young men a distinct society. There seemed to be with them a tradition of personal appearance which, though it varied sufficiently to escape monotony, possessed that truth to the original

The Cult of Oxford

which marked them out as the undoubted heirs of their prototypes. They were all good looking, with the smoothness of skin which escapes the razor through adolescence with an almost uncanny persistence. Without exception they spoke in what, for want of a happier description, may be termed 'fat' voices. They dwelt long and lovingly over their sentences, stressing unduly the last syllables of words and ostentatiously employing a vocabulary of affected choiceness. Most of them were in the habit of quoting French which, as a rule, they spoke, if not with fluency, with a purity of accent which compensated for the gaps in their grammatical knowledge, and lent distinction to their conversation. No one of them had ever been seen dressed otherwise than perfectly. Even their negligée was a thing to wonder at, and it was whispered that the trousers of their pyjamas were creased, not down the sides, as with less precise people is usually the case, but unerringly down the front. This, as a matter of fact, was untrue, for almost without exception they remained loyal, with a refinement of elegance incomprehensible to baser minds, to the tradition of the night-shirt. In their tastes they were dilettante, preferring the sweetness of the boudoir to the brutal comforts of the study. Their knowledge of old china, furniture, eighteenth century "Belles Lettres," and the more esoteric forms of cookery attained, in certain cases, a notable eminence. With regard to the deeper problems of existence, they found consolation, without exception, in the ritual and vestments of the most extreme branch of the Anglican Church. As a rule they eschewed the Roman Communion on the ground that it tended to cheapen what they chose to invest with an almost ethereal refinement. One or two, however, had wrestled with the Scarlet Woman, and in their final overthrow found sanctuary in the bosom of St. Peter. For all this, Dallas and his contemporaries, though true to the spirit of their past, were not aesthetes in the sense given to that term in the "eighties.' They liked to profess a degree of masculinity, and even adopted certain vulgarities, which, however, they cloaked delicately until they were hardly recognizable as elements alien to the general choiceness of their lives.[87]

There is very little difference between the dilettantism of Charles Dallas and that of Ray Sheldon, both of whom stopped far short of the goal that had been reached by Michael Fane. The cult of

Oxford fell, after the war, into the partial decadence typified by both Dallas and Sheldon, and the extent of its fall may be measured by a brilliant work of burlesque which brings abruptly into focus *Patchwork*'s erroneous and insufficient interpretation of *Sinister Street*. *The Oxford Circus* (1922), by Hamish Miles and Raymond Mortimer, creates in the person of Gaveston ffoulis a character in whom the Oxford manner is carried to delightfully improbable extremes. Gaveston was the son of a delicate wanton who was married to her fourth husband but was respondent in the divorce case of "Penhaligon v. Penhaligon, Rosenbaum, Litovski, du Val, Spirella, van Houton, Casabianca, and Mahmoud Pasha." Like Ray Sheldon, he had *Sinister Street* in mind when he arrived in Oxford, and he telegraphed his mother that "The Spires are still dreaming."[38] Gaveston was a striking figure. Surrounded by his sixteen suitcases, he spent his first evening in Oxford standing before his cheval glass:

Was it so, he wondered, that Oxford would see him—a svelte, willowy figure, with fair hair and fair skin and fair eyes, whose every trait bore the subtle handwriting of race and breeding, and on whose lips played the most infectious of enigmatic smiles.

"*Quel hors d'oeuvre!*" he exclaimed in involuntary admiration. He was indeed a masterpiece.[39]

With tongue in cheek the playful authors parade Gaveston through a succession of violent posturings—mimicking the stages of development through which both Michael Fane and Ray Sheldon had passed. Gaveston went through a political phase, a Roman Catholic phase, a pagan phase, and most spectacularly through an aesthetic phase, undertaken deliberately after an adventure in "Bohemian living" in the form of his first 'bus ride through London. Back at Oxford,

Sipping in carefully calculated rotation glasses of *crème de cacao* and *vodka* and *mavrodaphne*—somehow the interblend of their hues and aromas seemed that night to chime in with the interplay of his own

The Cult of Oxford 173

emotions—Galeston was planning the redecoration of his rooms and his personality. "Each mirrors the other," he reflected sagaciously [as had Michael and Ray]. And a becoming blush illuminated his cheeks as he realized how insular and barbarian his life had been so far, despite that long childhood of foreign *table d'hôtes*—how English and ingenuous, despite the many stories long current in Society of his authentic artistic temperament.

"Myths!" he cried aloud. "Myths!"⁴⁰

To equip himself for his new life he bought pictures and books, including

obscure texts from the Silver Age of every tongue, and the declining decades of every century yielded him their rich harvests of perverse and curious fruits. He delighted, for instance, to pore over the Forty-seven Books of the Eroticks of Kottabos the Syracusan. Recumbent upon a score of Liberty cushions, and meshed in the twining and thuriferal fumes of musk and attar and patchouli, Gaveston would ponder upon the corrupt and fetid beauty of the Sicilian's style...⁴¹

This life lasted for a full term, at the conclusion of which Gaveston determined to sum up his experiences at Oxford by celebrating (like Michael Fane) with his friends, six Roman Catholics and six aesthetes.

The *decor* of Gaveston's room, of course, was a technical masterpiece that an S. Diaghilev or a B. Dean might have envied. The richly figured curtains were closely drawn. The air was pregnant with frankincense and chypre. The apartment was delicately illuminated, partly by a score of night-lights floating in tall Venetian glasses abrim with many-hued liqueurs, partly too by the votive tapers that always burned before Gav's private altar of St. Symphorosa and his veiled image of Astarte Mammifera of the Kabbalists.⁴²

Each guest was offered a choice between a kimono and a cowl, and after "seven finely modulated courses," a second choice between "caramels and *coco*."

When the merriment was at its height, Gaveston rose abruptly and recited in poignant *tremolo* tones two litanies of his own composition, both of haunting beauty and addressed to Satanas Athanatos and the Blessed Curé d'Ars respectively. The severed heads of vermilion poppies were thrown lavishly over the recumbent guests, who, chewing them appreciatively, were soon transformed into new De Quincies. And suddenly, from the curtained recess, stole out the sombre, blood-curdling strains of Sibelius' Valse Triste and Rachmaninov's Prelude. The eerie witchcraft of the concealed gramophone, exacerbating their nerves, made repose intolerable, and soon half the party was afoot, swinging in frantic rhythms between the voluptuous divans in the mad inebriation of the dance.

"*Après nous le déluge!*" cried the host, in a tone that seemed to defy both Paradise and Limbo, and ecstasy followed ecstasy in orgiastic sequence.[43]

No further word could be said about the transformation which had turned the ideal of *Sinister Street* into the cult of aesthetic self-expression portrayed in *Patchwork*. But neither the well-intentioned mistakes of *Patchwork*, nor the parody of those mistakes, can destroy the validity and worth of what had been the cult of Oxford; they only show that in the war years between 1914 and 1918 it disappeared from fiction. And they show also that it was in *Sinister Street* that the university novel completed its growth from its discreditable beginnings to the point where it made a genuine and successful effort to express the meaning of the university's contribution to the mind and spirit of youth.

◇   ◇   ◇

Succeeding representations of English university life have been so plentiful, and occasionally so vigorous, that it is clear the theme is far from exhausted; it is not quite so clear, however, that much has been added to the achievement of the novels just examined. For example, Louis Golding's *Seacoast of Bohemia* (1924) is an amusing protest against fadism which in its third chapter gives an extended account of a set of excitable and art-conscious undergraduates; the warblings of its aesthetes have an authentic ring, but no new notes. James Saxon Childers, an American Rhodes Scholar, expressed convincingly in *Laurel and Straw* (1927) his attachment to an Oxford not, one would gather, unlike Michael Fane's; the book is a somewhat sentimental resurrection of the Oxford ideal. *The Age of Reason* (1928), by Philip Gibbs, is a lugubrious tale about the marriage of a young Oxford undergraduate to her middle-aged biology professor, but it treats the Oxford scene only slightly. Much more of an Oxford novel is Joanna Cannan's *High Table* (1931). Certainly a lady's hand is evident in this story of an utter misfit who fled the world to live out his life at the university; by the time he was maneuvered into the wardenship of his college he had become a ludicrous caricature of the academic recluse, whose subsequent misfortunes cannot possibly seem other than a fit reward for a life ill spent. A far more effective reworking of traditional materials is to be found in the extensive portion of Evelyn Waugh's *Brideshead Revisited* (1945) that is set in Oxford. Here is a vivid and witty evocation of the familiar aesthetic motif, together with a reaffirmation, of sorts, of the benefits inherent in youth's wildest extravagances:

... all the wickedness of that time was like the spirit they mix with the pure grape of the douro, heady stuff full of dark ingredients; it at once enriched and retarded the whole process of adolescence as the spirit checks the fermentation of the wine, renders it undrinkable, so that it must lie in the dark, year in, year out, until it is brought up at last fit for the table."

But, for Waugh the Oxford setting remains only a setting, which exists chiefly to set the stage for the subsequent and somewhat tortured study of neurosis induced by family and church.

One of the most grotesquely remarkable of the recent books about English universities is Kingsley Amis' *Lucky Jim* (1954), which depicts life at a provincial "redbrick" university in a mood of uproarious hatred. Through the eyes of a dreadfully clear-sighted young jokester suffering out his short and disastrous career as an instructor in medieval history, Amis surveys the problems of the junior lecturer: at the bottom of the academic ladder, he endures with a ghastly smile the whims and crotchets of pedantic eccentrics who, as his superiors, know that he may be tolerated only if in agony he produces and peddles his sterile scrap of scholarship, the "telling" article, with "its funereal parade of yawn-enforcing facts, the pseudo-light it [throws] upon non-problems." The focus upon the shams of academic life at its worst is clear, merciless, and very funny. Amis is a blunt and violent writer, impatient with subtleties, but his iconoclastic bludgeoning has been governed by a sure ear for professorial gibberish that leaves the reader with the sense that higher education may after all be simply a matter of comic lunacy. The tone of *Lucky Jim* would be unique in university fiction were it not for a less well-known but equally amusing predecessor, *The Struggles of Albert Woods* (1953), by William Cooper, the story of an academic Napoleon making his way through the hierarchy of Oxford's chemists.

A much more placid novel is *The Guardians* (1955), by J. I. M. Stewart, of Christ Church, Oxford. Writing under his pseudonym of "Michael Innes," Stewart is best known as the author of mystery thrillers (some of which are referred to below), but he has here taken respite from crime to describe the brisk competition among a group of Oxford's learned men for the literary remains of a nineteenth-century man of letters. The predominant tone of the book is provided by the odd academic personalities that inhabit it. Exploring the academic temperament has, in fact, been the common pursuit of a number of contemporary writers. One of the most distinguished of these, Angus Wilson, has written an extended study of academic integrity in *Anglo-Saxon Attitudes* (1956); the scholarly issue at stake is at times obscured by domestic problems more colorful than those granted to most men, however learned, but the book makes convincing the efforts of a very troubled historian to set straight an archaeological hoax.

The universities have given rise to a number of mystery novels. This is not at first glance a development one might readily anticipate, but reflection suggests that the juxtaposition of murder and great learning is perhaps a natural one. For one thing, the fictional college may, with little effort, be made to contain enough neurotic personalities to support crime on a fairly massive scale. The tensions within its group of ambitious and overworked Fellows need hardly be exaggerated to provide occasion for abundant shootings, bashings, and knifings. Better-than-ordinary surprising motives for murder come quickly to mind if one considers the pursuits to which the academic mind can dedicate itself. Any academician knows these truths; it is only surprising that the writers of detective stories discovered them so late, together with the Gothic college setting, and the amateur intellectual sleuth (occasionally a professor of English, of all things) ready to hand. The earliest such novel I have found is *An Oxford Tragedy* (1933), by John Cecil Masterman, now Provost of Worcester College, Oxford. Like so many that have followed, its action springs from the rivalries and jealousies of its community of dons. One of the best known of all university novels is Dorothy Sayers' *Gaudy Night* (1935), a finished piece of suspense and in addition a remarkable portrayal of the least desirable aspects of life in the women's colleges. The list further includes *The Cambridge Murders* (1945), by "Dilwyn Rees" (i.e., Dr. Glyn E. Daniel, a Fellow of St. John's College, Cambridge); *The Case of the Gilded Fly* (1944; American title: *Obsequies at Oxford*), by "Edmund Crispin" (i.e., Robert Bruce Montgomery); *Don Among the Dead Men* (1952), by C. E. Vulliamy; *The Missing Link* (1955), by Katharine Farrer; and *Landscape With Dead Dons* (1956), by Robert Robinson.

Apparently more dedicated than any of these to university crime fiction is "Michael Innes," already referred to above by his own name of Stewart. His *Death at the President's Lodging* (1936; American title: *Seven Suspects*, 1937) offers the complicated and gruesome murder of the President of a college in a mythical university lying midway between Oxford and Cambridge; most of the Fellows of the college are such odd types that suspicion falls easily upon the lot of them. *Operation Pax* (1951; American title: *The Paper Thunderbolt*) makes fantastic scenes of violence, including a mad chase through the subterranean chambers of the Bodleian, seem quite a part of the Oxford scene. And finally, his *Old Hall, New Hall* (1956) moves to a provincial university for a tale of buried treasure.

These seem rather substantial works if compared with some recent novels which have returned to the light vein of Oxford comedy. A piece of froth called *Oxford Marmalade* (1946), by Paul Harrison, opens with the claim that it is meant to be farcical, but its hodgepodge of stereotyped incident (e.g., drinking bouts, a rendezvous hoax, etc.), together with the satisfying removal of a number of its noxious scholars as wartime casualties, makes very doubtful its publisher's claim that it is "... as funny as anything written about Oxford since the far-off days of Mr. Verdant Green." A much better bit of humor is Dacre Balsdon's *An Oxford Comedy* (1952). It is a knowing and witty novel, in some ways suggesting what *Tom Brown at Oxford* might have been if Hughes had possessed a more reliable sense of humor. *Oxford Folly* (1956), by Louis MacIntosh, is a first novel which perhaps need not have been written, but it rather skillfully sets forth a hoax within a hoax as it lures the unwary reader into conceiving of the modern Oxford undergraduate as dressed in black jeans and spending his effete energies on an unbroken round of intramural parties.

Two books require particular attention here, both by Charles

The Cult of Oxford

Percy Snow, a scientist, civil service commissioner, and novelist, and for twenty years a Fellow of Corpus Christi College, Cambridge. *The Light and the Dark* (1947) is the story of a brilliant young scholar who became one of the world's leading orientalists but was so stricken by attacks of melancholy that he sought a violent death as a wartime pilot. Insofar as the book deals with this situation, it is adequate; insofar as it moves beyond it, it is very good indeed. The young man is proposed for election to a fellowship in his Cambridge college, but it is not an easy election, and the resulting political and personal clashes between the Fellows who must vote on the issue are spectacular. It is in this struggle that the merit of the novel lies, for the author speaks with sure and devastating knowledge of the phenomena of donnishness. Fortunately he seems to have recognized his strength, for *The Masters* (1951) is given over wholly to the study of these same college inmates. The central and whole problem of the novel is the election of a new Master for the college, but this becomes an enormously complex matter. Snow has contrived to create a strong awareness of the college as a unit at the same time he makes painfully apparent the lack of unity between its members. The range of divergence is great: the Fellows include the very young and the very old, the generous and the mean, the adroit and the inept. And the movement of the narrative, which commences with an air of professorial calm, reaches a frantic climax as the in-fighting between parties of the rival candidates becomes bitter with hatred and exhaustion. Somehow this should be a bitter novel, too, but it is not. The author is too aware that the college has been performing this unhappy ceremony for three hundred years, and will be obliged to continue to do so—that the hatreds will pass, while what remains is the group of scholars, some brilliant and many quite impossible, that constitutes the thing cherished by them all, the college itself. There is in this novel scarcely a mention of what has traditionally been the material of university fiction, the undergraduate world. But it would be difficult to find a comparable revelation of the governors of that world. Snow's attentiveness to their thoughts and speech renders them mercilessly exposed without demolishing them, though demolition would not have been difficult in most instances, as when a sturdy 70-year-old delivers his opinion of an incredible and long-sought gift to the college of £120,000: "I foresee grave difficulties.... I am positive that it will need the most serious consideration before the college could possibly decide to accept." These are men of many skills, of which the obstructionist committee technique is only one. For its thoughtful and often brilliant re-creation of a world that must seem strange to the outsider but yet has many delights, *The Masters* is a distinguished novel, without doubt the finest that Cambridge has yet produced.

Of this body of more or less recent fiction it may be said that at worst it is entertaining, and at best it is comparable in quality to the achievements of the most successful university novelists. But it is different in kind from the novels produced immediately before and after the First World War. The dedicated fervor which so moved Beerbohm, Mackenzie, and their followers has disappeared from English university fiction; no longer does one find novels extolling the beneficent effects of existence among the dreaming spires. But a sense of the mystery of Oxford is not quite lost. J. C. Masterman (author of *An Oxford Tragedy*) published in 1952 his book *To Teach the Senators Wisdom: or, An Oxford Guide Book,* certainly a significant Oxford work though I am not at all sure it is a novel. It purports to be a series of conversations among the dons of "St. Thomas's College" engaged in preparing a guide book which will enable them to interpret Oxford to some American visitors. The subject matter of their talks is broad—the University, the function of the colleges, examinations, student life, athletics, architecture, tradi-

The Cult of Oxford

tional anecdotes, history, colorful personalities—all, in fact, that might help to explain what they recognize as a fascinating enigma, the secret of Oxford. In the discussion, the participants emerge as skillfully drawn characters who, one feels, hold within themselves part of the answer. But to them the secret remains undefinable. And it is difficult not to recall the mood of *Sinister Street,* with its almost mystical faith in the beauty and efficacy of the spirit of Oxford, as they search in vain for the words that might illumine themselves as well as their American guests. As one of them concludes:

The great age for us was the age of our youth, but it seems to me that every October, when the freshmen arrive, the great age dawns for them and the golden years begin. We're here to help them and if we can, not to impose our standards and our views and our rules of conduct upon them. Your famous secret cannot be told because for each individual it is a different secret—and each must find it for himself.

Chapter X

CONCLUSION

Toward the end of chapter i in the present work, the question was raised as to why so few major Victorian novelists contributed to what was obviously a popular literary fad. It was suggested that one reason lay in the fact that so few of them knew the universities firsthand; this remains a valid reason, but it is only one of those which by now may have occurred to the reader. Another is more complex. Insofar as nineteenth-century fiction shows any clear phases of development or change, the university novel was out of step with almost all of them. Certainly it is bold speculation to ponder the novels that have not been written, but it does seem unlikely, for example, that unreformed Oxford and Cambridge should have supplied material for the romantic fiction popular early in the century. As realism, and the novel of reform, came into vogue, the university novel of the mid-century seems to have been more nearly in step with popular taste; but one recalls the pitfalls that beset even the most dedicated university "realists," and the grotesque posturings of most of the reformers. Subsequently, in the 'eighties, the English novel moved in two diametrically opposed directions: toward the naturalism of George Gissing and George Moore, and toward the revival of romanticism typified by Stevenson and Kipling. Clearly the university novel, with its host of Crichtons, stayed firmly with the romantics and quite away from the later experiments of more modern fiction. These are admittedly very broad generalizations, vulnerable to the extent that all such generalizations must be. But familiarity with the English novel in general and with the university novel in particular does, I believe, substantiate them.

But still another reason was initially proposed, in the sugges-

Conclusion

tion that the university theme itself held inherent difficulties which made it uncongenial to serious fiction. These were most marked at the beginning, and diminished with the progress of reform (see chap. iv), but still they persisted. Certainly it is self-evident that some of these novels are not only juvenile but also trash, and not good trash at that. Yet even after dismissing this portion, there remains a substantial body of novels about which nothing very bad may be said, but which fall far short of great fiction. Their deficiencies may perhaps best be gotten at through a comment on university novelists made by Mark Pattison in an article published in 1875:

The novelist sets up his *camera lucida* in the middle of the High Street and lets the passing figures mirror themselves as they flit to and fro. He gives us what he sees. And he sees all from the student's side. And as the worst regulated student's life affords the most telling materials for fiction, it is the life of the idle and disorderly which is usually presented for our edification by the novelist. In all these drawings there is a level uniformity such as pervaded the new comedy at Athens. In that stage of dramatic development, the repertory of character was limited to the young scapegrace in the capital, and his severe governor from the country, the designing hetaera, and the saucy slave who abetted his young master's dissipations; and on this slender cast of parts the changes were rung to infinite variety without novelty. So in the university novel we have the stereotyped parts of the fast undergraduate, beset by duns, contrasted with the slow reading man in woollen socks and spectacles, who is his foil and butt—the deluded father, the inefficient proctor, a pompous and incapable tutor, a gyp thievish and patronizing, the breakfast and the wine party, the ruffian of the playground, who is the admired hero of the bevy of charming girls who come up to Commemoration in pink ribands. The fast young man is the first part, the reading student is only brought on the scene to be quizzed, and the senior part of the university become stage dons, who are only there to provoke our derision by various forms of the witty definition of 'donnism,' 'a mysterious carriage of the body intended to conceal the defects of the mind.'[1]

---

[1] For notes to chap. x, see p. 213.

Had he considered more carefully the accuracy of this judgment he would have seen that in some ways it was inadequate; by 1875 it should have been clear that university fiction was capable of getting somewhat beyond this simple formula. *Tom Brown at Oxford* had done so conspicuously and well. But even so, in 1875 the statement bore much truth, and it is interesting not only for its suggestion of the tenacity with which novelists continued to cling to the traditional representation of university figures. More than this, it points up the fact that the university novelist was still, after long experience, being driven to rely largely on roughhouse and stereotyped humor. It remained as true in the nineteenth as in the eighteenth century that good men often lead very dull lives. The universities no doubt produced, as time went on, a more desirable race of students, but authors had a hard time replacing adolescent bounders with characters of equal interest. If the trivialities of which Pattison complained were objectionable, substitutes drawn from the lives of sober youths were apt to be quite as unsatisfactory. A writer for *Blackwood's,* commenting on the charge that *Tom Brown at Oxford* made the life of idle men somewhat too enticing, saw this trouble very clearly:

... it is difficult to treat undergraduate life in any other way, in order to make a successful story. The career of the university student who is really in earnest is full of interest and delight; it has both its deep quiet enjoyment and its intense excitements; but they are not such as are well adapted for the purposes of fiction, or such as would do to present as their monthly dole to the readers of a magazine. It is of immense importance, and therefore full of the most lively interest, both to themselves and their friends, whether Smith gets his 'first' after all, or whether Jones or Robinson is the winner of the 'Ireland'; but it is beyond the power of man to spin out the facts of the case into a three-volume novel. If it be true of women and of nations that the happiest have a very dull history, it might also be said of the college undergraduate, that the story of his college years will not give him less pleasure in the retrospect, because it would have been im-

Conclusion

possible to weave out of its material either an exciting romance or a moral story.... the public would never have felt any very deep interest either in the plot or the catastrophe.... That first class which he was so proud to get—he is not quite sure that his country neighbors know what it means, even if they ever heard of his having got it; the squire of the next parish was plucked, yet he is an excellent magistrate, and rides well to hounds; and as for that open fellowship which he did not get, why, he has got a wife instead of it, which is probably a much better thing for him.[2]

Many university novelists, unless they were either insensitive to monotony or singularly determined to strike new chords from the few old notes of conventional university fiction, must have been aware that they were being forced to keep alive the old clichés primarily because in them lay the most obvious stuff of university fiction. It was a handicap most good novelists would scarcely have cared to face. And it must account for much of the mediocrity of the great majority of university novels.

This leads to a crucial question: what is the value of an extended study of the English university novel? That it touches upon some admirable flights of comedy is true, but insufficient. That it leads to a better understanding of at least a few extraordinarily good novels is true but also insufficient. Looking further for an answer, however, one recalls another significant fact about the works in question. It must be clear to the reader that the university novel, in the long course of its development, has been shaped more than anything else by the state of the English universities. As a literary genre, it has always reflected conditions within Oxford and Cambridge far more closely than it has followed any literary trends or movements. This is true of the often nasty novels written before reform began, of the urgently serious reforming novels, and of the romances which followed the hard-won salvation of both Oxford and Cambridge. It does not follow that the picture has always been accurate. Dean Farrar cared not for the literal truth, any more than did Joseph Hewlett and a host of others. There has been occasion in the pages above to remark on very knowing judgments pronounced upon the truthfulness with which college stories represented college life. Hewlett, it will be recalled, admitted his own flamboyant exaggerations; William Winwood Reade delivered a little lecture on the prosaic routine of Oxford life which belied the tales about its wild ways; Buxton, in *The Mysteries of Isis,* thought it time to correct the false impressions about Oxford created in the pages of novels; and Mark Pattison solemnly announced that it was not likely university fiction could ever be believed. One finds that all agree the university novel has been guilty of excesses. Oxford's Andrew Lang, in a reminiscent mood, once reflected that accounts in university novels were too often either idealized or uninformed, and their authors faced an insurmountable temptation to draw themselves and their friends "too large, too noisy, too bibulous, too learned, too extravagant, too pugnacious."[3] Even Cyril Arthur Edward Ranger Gull, himself guilty of more than one extravagance, perceived that the common weakness was to overdraw, exaggerate, and caricature reality.[4] Observing that these remarks were, except for the last, uttered before 1900, almost no one would disagree with them. Adventures in both virtue and villainy had by that time become so prevalent, and been provided in such strong doses, that it was possible for E. F. Benson in *The Babe* to effect a small literary revolution simply by avoiding "remarkable and stirring events." Now when events become as remarkable and stirring as they do in the tales of "Alan St. Aubyn," there is admittedly not much to be salvaged from the entire fabrication. And from time to time a reformer's zeal carried him along too enthusiastically, and produced a strange vision of college life such as that of Dean Farrar's. But if even reasonably temperate novels show symptoms of these conspicuous afflictions, the reader may profitably dispose himself to admit that no great harm has been done. Read in conjunction with any good history of Oxford or Cambridge, the novels come off remarkably well, and even enjoy a kind of success at producing a cheerfully careless effect of verisimilitude. Oxymel Classic's Oxford was by no means an unjustifiable slander, if we are to believe more sober witnesses; Reginald Dalton's was no better and no worse than the Oxford of prereform days; Tom Brown's was credible; the Babe's Cambridge was a deliberate copy of the real Cambridge; and the novels of Edwardian years mirror the good that had fallen to both universities. The majority of the novelists, excluding of course the few determined anachronists, wrote in the vein they felt to be warranted by the condition of the universities.

Thus the university novels have always had to a large extent the quality of the documentary about them. More often than not, this has kept them at a distance from the realm of more clearly belletristic literature, and must in some measure be still one more reason why they have so largely been the products of a very specialized group of writers. They have recorded, with surprising accuracy, the issues of reform, the temper of the reformers, and the astonishing changes they wrought, perhaps as accurately and certainly more vividly than could any memoir or official account of the most important era of university reform that England has known. How conscientiously fiction has attempted to follow fact when the subject matter of fiction has been English university life may be typified with an example drawn from outside the university novel itself. The 1862 edition of Charles Kingsley's *Alton Locke* contained a preface addressed to "The Undergraduates of Cambridge in which Kingsley stated that since the first edition of 1850 he had

... rewritten all that relates to Cambridge.
Those sketches were drawn from my own recollections of 1838-1842...
I am assured by men in whom I have the most thorough confi-

dence, that my sketches had by then at least become exaggerated and exceptional, and therefore, as a whole, untrue; that a process of purification was going on rapidly in the university; and that I must alter my words if I meant to give the working men a just picture of her."[5]

The early version of chapters 12 and 13 showed Cambridge to be the home of a great deal of filth and vulgarity: the towpath by the river swarmed with prostitutes; the language of the undergraduates was foul, their songs were indecent, and their entertainments disgustingly drunken. They thought the university, its dons and its studies, all humbug. As for the dons, their only anxiety was to avoid scandal; they had no influence over the students save as they connived at their ill-doings. And yet reform, complained Kingsley with more vigor than accuracy on the eve of the Royal Commissions, was impossible: if one change were made "the whole rotten house" would fall; for this reason the injustice of religious discrimination was perpetuated, the profligacy of undergraduates was countenanced, and the whole intent of college founders denied, while Cambridge remained a monopoly of the rich, and the poor, who should have benefited from the provisions made for them, were excluded from an education they could not afford. The palinode of 1862 included this statement: "I see at Cambridge nothing which does not gain my respect for her present and hope for her future"; everything, he said, was unbelievably improved. And in the revised chapters Cambridge undergraduates emerged as good-hearted young men blessed with an overwhelming number of enviable advantages. Kingsley's revision followed with diplomatic haste his appointment as Professor of Modern History at Cambridge (1860); clearly the scurrilities he removed would have proved embarrassing for a professorial incumbent to defend. But his concern about giving an accurate picture is otherwise in every way comparable to that felt by almost all who wrote of the universities either before, during, or after the great Victorian reform movement.

Conclusion

The English university novels, therefore, have a very considerable documentary value, recording as they do the story of the most critical century in the history of English universities. More than that, they contain the record of much that is elsewhere unrecorded. The portrayal they offer of English university life in the nineteenth century is monumental in scope, and it fills out the picture of the universities in a way that no history could possibly do, for it has re-created the world of the undergraduate. Special insight is needed to penetrate the lives of Pendennis and Harry Foker, Verdant Green and Mr. Bouncer, the Babe, Tom Brown, Keddy, Godfrey Marten, Samuel Golightly and Mr. Pokyr, Hugh Rendal, Ray Sheldon, Michael Fane, and all the rest. And as is customarily true, it is the novelist, not the historian, who possesses this special insight. Improbable some of their adventures may seem, but seldom their reality as characters. Here is the undergraduate himself—and fortunately he is still with us—capable of supreme indifference to authority, but essentially open and honest; bent usually on pleasure, but surprisingly aware that in the final reckoning he must not be found wanting; very foolish at the beginning, a little less so at the end. It is a rewarding portrait, and one is encouraged to think that when the many derogations about them have been uttered, Oxford's and Cambridge's young men testify through these novels that the Victorians, when they set out to save their universities, perhaps wrought better than they knew.

But then, there were also the rogues and the scoundrels, and more disturbing, there were the undergraduates who, like the hero of Hamilton Gibbs's *The Compleat Oxford Man,* emerged from their universities with no clear idea of what they had accomplished, and no notion at all of what was to follow next. Even the Crichtons, for the most part, merely drifted away from Oxford; the great Faucit himself, after staying on to become, one gathers, the best tutor in the university, suddenly chucked it all for the hand of a maiden and then was reduced to a most preposterous life of misanthropic seclusion. Now a documentary novel, however accurate, is at best of only limited value, whether it documents the good, the bad, or the simply aimless. And it is perhaps of least value when it documents the aimless. That so many university novels did just this is in some ways regrettable, so regrettable in fact that were there nothing else to be said for the genre beyond conceding its accurate portrayal of jolly young men, one would find it difficult to justify an extensive study of the university novel.

Fortunately there is more. For the university novel did ultimately overcome the handicaps and limitations inherent in its subject matter. It did ultimately become more than a documentary. It did, in fact, come to terms with the old and ever-new question, What are the ends of a university education? Or even more broadly, What is a university? In this, it seems clear, lies its chief claim to attention.

Passing reference has been made in chapter i to criticism by certain novelists of the traditional classical education; Bulwer-Lytton especially found it elaborately useless. But apart from bandying about this rather ancient chestnut, nineteenth-century novelists as a group were slow to deal with the question of what the universities should be teaching, or for what ends. Displays of scholarship, when they occur in the novels, are not contemptible, but it is difficult to see the maturing of a young mind, or detect a concept of education, in the writing of a Newdigate poem or in an examination triumph brought on by severe and painful cramming. It is defensible, even, to conclude that most nineteenth-century university fiction was given over to depicting a state of continuing war between undergraduates and their dons, a war in which the goal of the former was to elude the services of the latter in any way that would create sufficient merriment to make the effort worthwhile. The fact that a serious

Conclusion

idea of any kind would have been out of place in so many university novels cannot entirely account for this; even the most morbidly earnest of them failed for long to come to terms with the problem.

One reason for the deficiency is to be found in the universities themselves: for much of the Victorian period they continued as the domain chiefly of two groups, the clerical and the wealthy, and though it was much disputed, the question of what kind of education should be offered to either was perhaps never really an open one. For training the former, the curriculum was established and prescribed along traditional lines. For the latter, it was only too often irrelevant. Convention and conviviality drew titled sons, and elder sons of the common rich as well, whose lives as future heads-of-family were planned in advance along lines that seldom called for the exercise of learning. And large numbers who were not cast for so fixed a future role found themselves—if they were determined against taking religious orders—faced generally with a choice between a life of leisure (if they could afford it), a college fellowship (if they could arrange it), or a tour of duty in the Inns of Court or the Civil Service, for neither of which was the preliminary training very specialized. In spite of advances in broadening curricula, the classics at Oxford and mathematics at Cambridge were the staple academic fare, and if novels neglected the question of what a man might do with all that Latin and all that Greek (save as they complain about their uselessness), they did so in part because it was in a sense no question at all. But they neglected it also for a second and more immediate reason, by now familiar—the obstinate and persisting difficulty of portraying the academic side of university life in fiction. The most brilliant and the most energetic Victorian students seldom came to life in the novels until they turned to very extracurricular activities, a fact which, as much as anything else, gave to university fiction its frequent note of triviality. It does not follow that the subject of university education is not appropriate for fiction, as all the admirable comedies, burlesques, and romances demonstrate. But just so long as scenes of university life were limited to the tutor's lectures, the river, college quarters, and the green fields beyond, these formed its backgrounds in fiction—with the lectures more often forgotten than not. Something else was needed if fiction were to be empowered to explore the worth and purpose of the years spent at Oxford and Cambridge.

The answer was ultimately found in the twentieth rather than in the nineteenth century, but it echoes the great debate that had occupied Victorian educational theorists throughout one of the most lively discussions in all the history of English education. The central issue was, of course, the value of a liberal education as against a practical, or "useful," one. On the one side, proponents of useful and scientific training from Jeremy Bentham to Thomas Henry Huxley and Herbert Spencer had argued that the new world of material progress of which Victorians were so conscious and so proud required a new, specialized kind of education, a descent from the ivory tower, a thorough understanding of the great age of science which was already at hand. On the other, equally determined critics—notably Newman and Arnold—maintained that if education were left to the utilitarians and scientists man's noblest capabilities would be shrunken, even destroyed, through the neglect of that liberal learning which alone could nurture his mind while his body was being so amply cared for by the triumphs of science. Clearly, university fiction, when it belatedly entered the debate, took up the latter view; no single university novelist (Charles Reade is a bit outside the field) proposed that either Oxford or Cambridge was valuable for the useful knowledge to be found there, but many saw that the real value—of Oxford especially—lay in the power of the university to make its undergraduates better men, rather than merely more learned. It is probably no accident that their view was most forcefully enunciated by two men who today are associated with Oxford perhaps as closely as are any of the great Victorians: Newman and Arnold.

Compton Mackenzie has acknowledged, in a letter to me, the influence Matthew Arnold had on him as a youth, and it does seem clear that both men had felt deeply the force with which "Oxford, by her ineffable charm, keeps ever calling us nearer to the true goal of all of us, to the ideal, to perfection..."[6] This is the very conclusion Michael Fane reached at the end of his Oxford career, and it is the summation of the idea behind the cult of Oxford. Arnold, perturbed and perplexed by the disparity between his conviction that his fellow Englishmen could achieve a state of cultured enlightenment and the reality he saw about him, knew that "the home of lost causes, and forsaken beliefs, and unpopular names, and impossible loyalties" held the key that "could save us from the bondage to which we are all prone," the bondage of the Benthamism and Philistinism with which he was perpetually at war. In Oxford, as among the classical Greeks, he found his ideal. Its quiet peace held the serenity that gave immortality to the Scholar Gypsy, and could rescue the rest of England as well if England would but give it the chance. "Apparitions of a day, what is our puny warfare against the Philistines, compared with the warfare which this queen of romance has been waging against them for centuries, and will wage after we are gone?"[7] Characteristically, Arnold did not emphasize in detail the academic ends of a university education. For him, Oxford was an example of what had been done, and a promise, time-tested, perfect, and proven, of what could be done, toward the attainment of an ideal. And it was all this because it was devoted less to academic ends than to the perpetuation of an atmosphere that nourished the highest goals of liberal enlightenment, of "culture"—culture which "indefatigably tries, not to make what each raw person may like, the rule by which he fashions himself: but to draw ever nearer to a sense of what is indeed beautiful, graceful, and becoming, and to get the raw person to like that."[8] Arnold's concept of culture, like Mackenzie's concept of a university education, was "a study of perfection."[9]

Newman said almost the same thing. He was even more insistent, however—or perhaps simply more explicit—in stating that practical and useful knowledge was not the first end of a university at all. His defense of a liberal education is one of the noblest as well as one of the most vigorous set forth against the utilitarian view, and it threw some clear light on just what "liberality" in a liberal education meant. And if part of his protest against what he felt was a degradation of the ends of university education was based on an etymological error (that a university by definition was "a school of knowledge of every kind, consisting of teachers and learners from every quarter"),[10] the whole was founded on a high ideal: a liberal education that was indeed free, subservient to no end except the perfection of the intellect. He did not claim that such an education would by itself make a good man, but he was sure that it would make a gentleman, possessed of the "freedom, equitableness, calmness, moderation, and wisdom" that attend intellectual excellence:

> Liberal Education makes not the Christian, not the Catholic, but the gentleman. It is well to be a gentleman, it is well to have a cultivated intellect, a delicate taste, a candid, equitable, dispassionate mind, a noble and courteous bearing on the conduct of life;—these are the connatural qualities of a large knowledge; they are the objects of a University.[11]

Newman found that the universities of his day made, among others, one particularly deplorable error by emphasizing what he called "mere" knowledge, memorized and acquired so superficially, and in such quantities, that it could only encumber, not enlighten, the student. However wide the range of subjects, no enlargement of the intellect could follow from studies performed perfunctorily, in haste, without "the mind's energetic and simultaneous action" to transmute the ore to metal. And the university, unless it afforded the student the atmosphere of an enlightened and dispassionate search for truth in all fields of knowledge, denied the mind this vital power. Throughout *The Idea of a University* one finds Newman's insistence on the value of the university *community,* all the members thereof given over to this high pursuit, and it is the *community* that makes a university quite literally "an Alma Mater, knowing her children one by one, not a foundry, or a mint, or a treadmill."[12] This, he felt, was a *sine qua non* of a university education, and in behalf of its efficacy he made some rather extraordinary statements:

I protest to you, Gentlemen, that if I had to choose between a so-called University, which dispensed with residence and tutorial superintendence, and gave its degrees to any person who passed an examination in a wide range of subjects, and a University which had no professors or examinations at all, but merely brought a number of young men together for three or four years, and then sent them away as the University of Oxford is said to have done some sixty years since, if I were asked which of these two methods was the better discipline of the intellect—mind, I do not say which is *morally* the better, for it is plain that compulsory study must be a good and idleness an intolerable mischief,—but if I must determine which of the two courses was the more successful in training, moulding, enlarging the mind, which sent out men the more fitted for their secular duties, which produced better public men, men of the world, men whose names would descend to posterity, I have no hesitation in giving the preference to that University which did nothing, over that which exacted of its members an acquaintance with every science under the sun....

How is this to be explained? I suppose as follows: when a multitude of young men, keen, open-hearted, sympathetic, and observant, as young men are, come together and freely mix with each other, they are sure to learn one from another, even if there be no one to teach them; the conversation of all is a series of lectures to each, and they gain for themselves new ideas and views, fresh matter of thought, and distinct principles for judging and acting, day by day....

Let it be clearly understood, I repeat it, that I am not taking into account moral or religious considerations; I am but saying that that youthful community will constitute a whole, it will embody a specific idea, it will represent a doctrine, it will administer a code of conduct, and it will furnish principles of thought and action. It will give birth to a living teaching, which in course of time will take the shape of a self-perpetuating tradition, or a *genius loci,* as it is sometimes called; which haunts the home where it has been born, and which imbues and forms, more or less, and one by one, every individual who is successfully brought under its shadow.... Here then is a real teaching, whatever its standards and principles, true or false; and it at least tends toward cultivation of the intellect; it at least recognizes that knowledge is something more than a passive reception of scraps and details; it is a something, and it does a something, which never will issue from the most strenuous efforts of a set of teachers, with no mutual sympathies and no inter-communion, of a set of examiners with no opinions which they dare profess, and with no common principles, who are teaching and questioning a set of youths who do not know them, and do not know each other, on a large number of subjects, different in kind, and connected by no wide philosophy, three times a week, or three times a year, or once in three years, in chill lecture-rooms or on a pompous university.[13]

It is at least open to conjecture that *Verdant Green,* published a year after *The Idea of a University,* represents a waggish reply to the notion that one's college chums could in any way prove elevating. When it was being decided whether or not Verdant would go to college at all, his father at first opposed the plan with a what-was-good-for-his-father-and-grandfather-is-good-enough-for-him argument; but the neighboring rector, Mr. Larkyn, answered him with a Newmanesque speech: it was not so much, he said, the Latin and Greek he would learn that would be important, but the mixing with other young men and living under the tutor's able surveillance, for the atmosphere of the university was designed to create "refined thoughts and noble feelings." Just how refined and how noble Verdant's friends were, we know well; they did indeed teach him many things, not one of which was desirable. But Newman's idea was not to be destroyed by such irony. Thomas Hughes was another who thought about the problems of education, and his views coincided very nearly with the passage just quoted (except, of course, his ideas about muscular Christianity, which in many ways resembled a crotchet rather than a theory of education). It was his task—attempted for the first time in fiction—to show the transition from youth to manhood brought on by the years spent gaily but—in the end—profitably at Oxford. Hughes did not, however, try to add glamour to the lecture hall, which he neglected as enthusiastically as did the others. To make real the part played by Oxford as Tom was brought to put away childish things, he introduced that apparently magical formula of intellectual intercourse between students which resulted in their mutual profit. It was through the experiments of burning his fingers with the fast set, through the benevolent influence of Hardy, and through the vaporings of young liberals that Tom was brought to his new wisdom.

What Hughes began was not completed until the romantic period of university literature had produced its most important creation, the cult of Oxford. By 1911 this was so strong a force that it almost overwhelmed the farce of *Zuleika Dobson*. In a relatively short time it had become a legend, the strength of which was responsible for *Sinister Street, Years of Plenty,* and the postwar *Patchwork* and *A City in the Foreground;* and it was itself burlesqued in the outrageous extravagances of *The Oxford Circus*. It was the cult of Oxford which produced, in *Sinister Street,* what must be recognized as the first penetrating and comprehensive attempt in literature to evaluate the profoundly significant effects of university life upon the undergraduate. And more than that, it is in *Sinister Street* that the university novel at last emerged with its answer as to what a university should be. Here, convincingly at work, is Newman's idea of a university, its goal nothing short of perfection, and its instrument the wonder-working quality that dwelt "in the shadows of these spires—that mysterious, inenubilable spirit, spirit of Oxford!" That this achievement should have come so late was inevitable: it could not have happened while the universities were discredited, as they were in the first half of the nineteenth century; it could not have happened in the purely comic literature; it could not have happened in the romances which were content to stop at glorified externals of character and incident. Perhaps it was not likely to have happened at all before the universities were opened up to a broadly comprehensive body of undergraduates of all classes and were rescued from the exclusiveness that had made them important to relatively few. It did happen, however, when an idealized university atmosphere could be shown as it molded the thoughts and emotions of undergraduates. And this in turn was possible only after the predecessors of *Sinister Street* had created, from early crude attempts to paint a young man's fancies in the artificial world of the university, a heightened concept of what that world could give him that was not artificial. That *Sinister Street* should stand as proof that the university novel came to offer more than triviality is due to Mackenzie's fortunate possession of new matter with which to work, in an Oxford whose spiritual and emotional emanations played so visibly upon the minds of men that they all but supplanted its academic role and permitted the novelist for once to pause in the flight from the serious implications of university education while he exploited the fictional value of the cult of Oxford. The intractability of the university theme

Conclusion

in serious fiction disappeared when it became possible to portray university life in spiritual rather than in academic terms. The final success of the early twentieth-century novels arises from the debt they owe to the tradition of university fiction as it took form in the nineteenth century. It was in the cult of Oxford that they achieved the climax and serious justification of the whole literary tradition.

NOTES

Notes to Chapter I

Introduction
(Pages 1–10)

[1] Other English universities have been almost completely neglected by the novelist, for perhaps obvious reasons. For one, they were with few exceptions (London, 1836, Durham, 1837, and Manchester, 1851) not founded until late in the nineteenth century—Leeds, Bristol, Sheffield, Birmingham, Liverpool, and Reading all received their charters between 1874 and 1892; even when they were in existence, therefore, they lacked the aura of a long and colorful past which plays such a dominant part in novels about Oxford and Cambridge. In addition, they lacked the settings provided by the residential colleges of the older universities, where both the social and intellectual life of the undergraduate were drawn together in a way admirably suited to the purposes of fiction. A similar reason may account for the lack of novels about such venerable universities as those of Edinburgh and Glasgow.

[2] *A City in the Foreground* (London: Constable and Co., Ltd., 1921), p. 228. It was, however, probably an exaggeration to say, even at the end of the nineteenth century, that "for one novel written about Cambridge there are some twenty which deal with Oxford."—"Cambridge: by an Oxonian," *Blackwood's Magazine*, CLXIII (1898), 38.

[3] For convenience I am employing the term "major" as it has been used in the *Cambridge Bibliography of English Literature* to distinguish between the great and the not-quite-so-great.

[4] See below, p. 147.

[5] *The Young Duke*, 3 vols. (London: Henry Colburn and Richard Bentley, 1831), I, 18; *Contarini Fleming*, 4 vols. (London: John Murray, 1832), II, 5, 29, 130; IV, 114; *Coningsby: or, The New Generation*, 3 vols. (London: Henry Colburn, 1844), II, 102, 220, 234–235; III, 78; *Sybil: or, The Two Nations*, 3 vols. (London: Henry Colburn, 1845), I, 73; II, 194.

[6] *Contarini Fleming*, II, 29.

[7] *Lothair*, 3 vols. (London: Longmans, Green and Co., 1870), *passim*; *Endymion*, 3 vols. (London: Longmans, Green and Co., 1880), I, 18–19.

[8] *Pelham*, 3 vols. (London: Henry Colburn, 1828), I, 7 ff., 333; II, 266–267.

[9] *Ibid.*, II, 291.

[10] *Kenelm Chillingly*, 3 vols. (London: Blackwood, 1873), II, 377, and III, 50. Lytton repeated these opinions outside the novel in *England and the English* (2 vols. [London: Blackwood, 1833], Book III, chaps. 1 and 2), together with the obvious corollary that the English upper classes were being sadly put upon by an education that was at best useless, and at worst debilitating.

[11] *Doctor Thorne* (London: Oxford University Press, World's Classics edition, 1926), pp. 289–290; *The Warden* (London: Oxford University Press, World's Classics edition, 1942), pp. 73, 127, 159; *Barchester Towers* (London: Oxford University Press, World's Classics edition, 1932), chaps. 3, 5, 11, 20, 24, 32.

[12] *Hard Cash*, 3 vols. (London: Sampson Low, Son, and Marston, 1863), I, Prologue, chaps. 1, 2, 5; III, chaps. 6, 17, 20; *Foul Play*, 3 vols. (London: Bradbury, Evans and Co., 1868), I, 8, 38, 72; *A Simpleton*, 3 vols. (London: Chapman and Hall, 1873), II, 143.

[13] *The Way of All Flesh*, chaps. 45–50.

[14] By the time *Jude the Obscure* was published in 1896, however, Hardy's complaint that the universities were still the strongholds of the rich seemed just a little old-fashioned, and it is not surprising that a reviewer should have accused him of scolding

and of injustice. (*The Athenaeum*, no. 3552, November 23, 1895). When Jude first reached "Christminster" (i.e., Oxford), he felt keenly what he called "the sentiment" of the university, but he soon experienced, as Hardy himself had done, enough rebuffs to alter his view.

Notes to Chapter II

Early Literary Portraits

(Pages 11–32)

[1] Samuel F. Hulton, *The Clerk of Oxford in Fiction* (London: Methuen and Co., 1909). Though this work places too much emphasis on a tenuous vein of didacticism traced through centuries of Oxford scholars in literature, it is most useful bibliographically for its study of university fiction exclusive of the novel before 1800.

[2] Ed. by Thomas Wright (London: J. B. Nichols and Sons, 1860), p. 189.

[3] *The History and Antiquities of the University of Oxford*, ed. in three parts by John Gutch (Oxford: The Clarendon Press, 1786), Part II, p. 81, as quoted by Charles Edward Mallet in *A History of the University of Oxford*, 3 vols. (New York: Longmans, Green and Co., 1924–1928), II, 79.

[4] *Ibid.*, Part II, p. 114, as quoted in Mallet, *op. cit.*, II, 94.

[5] Reprinted in *Shakespeare Jest Books*, 3 vols., ed. by William Carew Hazlitt (London: Willis and Sotheran, 1864), II, 3–36.

[6] *Ibid.*, pp. 10–15.

[7] Also reprinted in *Shakespeare Jest Books*, II, 52–161.

[8] *Ibid.*, p. 84.

[9] *Ibid.*, pp. 68–69.

[10] *Ibid.*, p. 68.

[11] *The Second Part of the Anatomie of Abuses*, ed. by J. J. Furnivall (London: The New Shakespeare Society, 1882), ser. 6, no. 12, p. 20.

[12] Jo[hn]. La[ne]., *Tom Tel-Troths Message, and His Pens Complaint*, ed. by F. J. Furnivall. (London: The New Shakespeare Society, 1876), ser. 6, no. 2, p. 115.

[13] *Euphues: The Anatomy of Wit*, in *Works*, 3 vols., ed. by R. Warwick Bond (Oxford: The Clarendon Press, 1902), I, 274–276. That Lyly meant Oxford, and specifically his own college, Magdalen, is attested by the "Address to my good friends, the Gentlemen Scholars of Oxford" affixed to the second edition of the work (1581), in which he tried to soften his criticism while denying none of it.

[14] W. S., *The Puritan: or, The Widow of Watling-Street*, ed. by C. F. Tucker Brooke in *Shakespeare Apocrypha* (Oxford: The Clarendon Press, 1908).

[15] *The Overburian Characters*, ed. by W. J. Paylor (Oxford: B. Blackwell, 1936), pp. 33–34.

[16] *Ibid.*

[17] *Ibid.*, pp. 18–19, 93–95. The latter was written by John Donne.

[18] *Ibid.*, pp. 46–47.

[19] John Earle, *Microcosmographie*, ed. by Gwendolyn Murphy (London: The Golden Cockerel Press, 1928), pp. 33–34.

[20] *Ibid.*, p. 34.

[21] *Ibid.*, p. 58.

[22] *Ibid.*, p. 64.

[23] *Ibid.*, pp. 42–43.

[24] *Ibid.*, pp. 28–29.

[25] *Ibid.*, p. 71.

[25] Wye Saltonstall, *Picturae Loquentes* (1631 and 1635), Luttrell Reprints No. 1 (Oxford: Printed for the Luttrell Society by B. Blackwell, 1946), pp. 36–37. This collection of characters also includes "A Scholler in the University," describing another poor young man living in the shadow of Aristotle.

[27] See *The Leviathan*, Part IV, chap. 46.

Notes to Chapter III

Decline of the Universities

(Pages 33–50)

[1] More than adequate documentation of their objectionable aspects may be found in the works of antiquarians and historians. See, for example, Thomas Hearne's *Remarks and Collections*, 11 vols., ed. by C. E. Doble and others (Oxford: Printed for the Oxford Historical Society at the Clarendon Press, 1885–1921); George Valentine Cox's *Recollections of Oxford, 1789–1860* (London: Macmillan and Co., 1868); C. H. Cooper's *Annals of Cambridge*, 5 vols. (Cambridge: Printed by Warwick and Co.[etc.], 1842–1856); and Henry Gunning's *Reminiscences of the University, Town, and County of Cambridge from 1780*, 2 vols. (London: G. Bell [etc.], 1854).

[2] This distinction should, by the way, throw emphasis upon the conjunction of today's cliché of praise.

[3] Quoted in Hulton, p. 269.

[4] In *The British Essayists*, 45 vols. (London: Nichols, Son, and Bentley [etc.], 1817), XVII, 209.

[5] *Ibid.*, XVI, 124.

[6] *Ibid.*, XXI, 276.

[7] *Ibid.*, XXII, 100.

[8] *Ibid.*, XXXIII, 112–115.

[9] Quoted in Hulton, p. 120.

[10] Henry Fielding, *The History of Tom Jones, a Foundling*, 6 vols. (London: A. Millar, 1749), III, Bk. VIII, chap. 11.

[11] *Ibid.*, p. 240.

[12] In the first edition (London: M. Cooper, 1751), Bk. II, chaps. 12–15. This university section was ultimately altered: it became chaps. 10–12, and was revised to give an even more damning picture of undergraduate life.

[13] *Ibid.*, p. 231.

[14] In the later version the old recluse was inexplicably removed, and a pointless story about a college physician who wanted to dissect Pompey was added.

[15] Bk. V, chap. 14.

[16] *The Adventures of Oxymel Classic, Esq.: Once an Oxford Scholar*, 2 vols. (London: W. Flexney, 1768), I, 27.

[17] *Ibid.*, p. 32.

[18] *Ibid.*, p. 34.

[19] *Ibid.*, p. 101.

[20] *Ibid.*, pp. 133–137.

[21] *Ibid.*, chap. 8.

[22] *Ibid.*, p. 141.

[23] *Ibid.*, p. 152.

[24] *Ibid.*, p. 154.

[25] Full title: *Memoirs of an Oxford Scholar. Containing His Amour with the Beau-*

tiful Miss L——, of Essex; and Interspersed with Several Entertaining Incidents. Written by Himself... (London: W. Reeve, 1756).

[26] *Ibid.*, p. 40.

[27] "By a Member of the University." 2 vols. (London: J. Roson, 1771).

NOTES TO CHAPTER IV

REFORM AND THE UNIVERSITY NOVEL

(Pages 51–65)

[1] Mark Pattison, *Memoirs* (London: Macmillan and Co., 1885), p. 244.

[2] For reference to some of the arguments proposed by educational theorists in this matter, see pp. 192–196.

[3] The index volumes of the *Edinburgh Review* reveal how persistently this criticism was heaped upon Oxford and Cambridge. Much of it was merely captious, but much of it too was motivated by the comparisons any knowledgeable Scot could have made between the Scottish universities, which were employing professorial lectures to further scientific research and encourage contributions to learning, and the English universities, which favored tutorial instruction to impart a limited and well-defined body of traditional learning. Sir Alexander Grant, in *The Story of the University of Edinburgh,* 2 vols. (London: Longmans, Green and Co., 1884), develops the principle of university education in Scotland.

[4] Though it turned out that this was in fact the only way in which the universities tried seriously to help themselves, their achievements were commendable. Examination reforms had the effect, during the first half of the nineteenth century, of both broadening the curricula and raising the standards of scholarship. Cambridge retained the emphasis it had long placed on mathematics, but in 1824 it initiated the Classical Tripos and in 1836 began to provide separate examinations for honors and pass men. Similarly, Oxford, maintaining its traditional emphasis on literature and philology, added in 1810 the school of mathematics to that of Literae Humaniores; in each the pass and class men were rated according to their examinations, and great honor went to a "double first," or a first class in both schools (Robert Peel was the first to win this distinction). By 1850 Cambridge had further enlarged its program to include the Moral Science Tripos and the Natural History Tripos, and at Oxford the two schools of law and modern history, and natural sciences, were functioning by 1853. The existence of these examinations did not mean that academic achievements suddenly became impressive, but they were certainly improved, and by the 1830's the class lists contained the names of most of England's distinguished Victorians.

[5] Wellington concurred in Tory Oxford's protest against interference in its affairs by the Liberal government of Lord John Russell; Prince Albert, aware of the delicacy of his position as the new chancellor (he had been installed in 1847) of a university about which he still had much to learn, and hesitant, as prince consort, to involve the throne in a contest with its members, sided with the majority of Cambridge who felt that the university should be allowed to work out its own reforms.

[6] See n. 4, above.

[7] Albert Mansbridge, *The Older Universities of England* (London: Longmans, Green and Co., 1923), p. 160.

[8] Vicesimus Knox, *Liberal Education,* in *Works,* 7 vols. (London: J. Mawman, 1824), IV, 163.

[9] *Hugh Trevor,* 4 vols. (3d ed.; London: G. G. and J. Robinson, 1801), I, 143.

[10] *Fleetwood,* 3 vols. (London: R. Phillips, 1805), I, 45–99.

[11] *Frederick,* 2 vols. (London: W. Miller; and Oxford: J. Parker, 1811), II, 181.
[12] *Ibid.,* I, 233.
[13] *Ibid.,* p. 264.
[14] *Reginald Dalton* has been described as the first university novel. George Saintsbury, in "Novels of University Life," *Macmillan's Magazine,* LXXVII (March, 1898), 335–336, remarked, "I cannot think of any novel mainly, or in large part, devoted to university life before Lockhart's *Reginald Dalton* . . ." And W. S. Knickerbocker's *Creative Oxford* (Syracuse, 1925), p. 14, discussing Oxford's place in literature generally, concludes that *"Reginald Dalton* . . . was the first novel of Oxford life." The claim is probably defensible if the university novel is conceded to be one that is "mainly, or in large part, devoted to university life," and indeed, as noted above, a more exact definition is difficult to come by.
[15] Andrew Lang, *The Life and Letters of John Gibson Lockhart,* 2 vols. (London: J. C. Nimmo; New York: Charles Scribner's Sons, 1897), I, 59.
[16] Robert Plumer Ward, *De Clifford: or, The Constant Man,* 4 vols. (London: Henry Colburn, 1841), II, 46. Ward also wrote of Oxford in *Tremaine: or, The Man of Retirement* (London: Henry Colburn, 1825), a rambling novel that ascribes to the university an unusually monastic atmosphere in telling how its cloistered retreats provided the life of study and meditation which purged the hero of an unfortunate attachment to deistic thought.

NOTES TO CHAPTER V

PERSISTENCE OF THE ROWDY TRADITION

(Pages 66–87)

[1] *Confessions of an Oxonian,* 3 vols. (London: J. J. Stockdale, 1826), II, 88.
[2] *Charles O'Malley,* 2 vols. (Dublin: Wm. Curry, Jun. and Co., 1841), I, 78.
[3] Review, "Charles O'Malley," *The Athenaeum,* no. 696 (February 27, 1841), p. 167.
[4] *Charles O'Malley,* I, 87.
[5] Lionel Stevenson, *The Showman of Vanity Fair* (New York: Charles Scribner's Sons, 1947), p. 180.
[6] *The History of Pendennis,* in *Works,* 24 vols. (London: Smith, Elder, and Co., 1878), III, 189–190.
[7] *Ibid.,* p. 194.
[8] *Ibid.,* p. 205.
[9] *Ibid.,* p. xi.
[10] *The Book of Snobs,* in *Works,* XIV, chaps. 11–13.
[11] *Ibid.,* chap. 14.
[12] *Ibid.,* chap. 15.
[13] *Ibid.,* p. 64.
[14] *Ibid.,* p. 65.
[15] *Pendennis,* loc. cit., 174–175.
[16] Joseph Hewlett, *Peter Priggins, the College Scout,* 3 vols., ed by Theodore Hook (London: Henry Colburn, 1841), I, 3.
[17] *Ibid.,* p. 183.
[18] *Ibid.,* pp. 82 ff.
[19] *Ibid.,* p. 130.
[20] *Ibid.,* chap. 4
[21] *Ibid.,* pp. 146–147.
[22] *Ibid.,* pp. 79–80.

[23] *College Life: or, The Proctor's Notebook*, 3 vols. (London: Henry Colburn, 1843), II, chaps. 22–23.

[24] First published in three parts entitled, respectively, *The Adventures of Mr. Verdant Green: An Oxford Freshman* (London: Nathaniel Cook, Milford House, 1853), *The Further Adventures of Mr. Verdant Green: An Oxford Undergraduate* (London: H. Ingram and Co., Milford House, 1854), and *Mr. Verdant Green Married and Done For* (London: James Blackwood, 1857). An account of the book's history, in part in Bradley's own words, may be found in an article by Carroll A. Wilson, "Verdant Green," in *The American Oxonian*, XX (January, 1933), 27–33.

[25] Robert Bowes, in his *Catalogue of Books Printed at or Relating to the University Town and County of Cambridge* . . . (Cambridge: Macmillan and Bowes, 1894), describes (Item no. 2594) a copy of *The Cambridge Freshman* in which the following note is inscribed on the title page, after the name "Martin Legrand": "Mr. James Rice—literary partner of Messrs. Besant and Rice—from 'London Society.' The title was suggested to Mr. Rice by me—Cuthbert Bede."

[26] *The Babe* (London: Putnam, 1896), pp. iv–v.

[27] *Ibid.*, chap. 5.

[28] *Peter Binney* (New York: Dodd, Mead and Co., 1921), p. 38.

[29] *Ibid.*, p. 76.

[30] *Lambkin's Remains* (Oxford: J. Vincent, 1900), pp. 88–89.

[31] *Ibid.*, pp. 14–16.

[32] It may seem strange that the novel is dated in the year preceding the first Rhodes Scholarships, but the contents of Rhodes's will had been published in early April, 1902, less than two weeks after his death.

[33] *The Adventures of Downy V. Green* (London: Smith, Elder, and Co., 1902), p. 75.

Notes to Chapter VI

Growth of Realism
(Pages 88–117)

[1] *Truth Without Fiction* (3d ed.; London: W. Emans, 1838), p. 6.

[2] *Ibid.*, p. 13.

[3] *Ibid.*, p. 253.

[4] *Ibid.*, p. ix.

[5] *Godfrey Davenant at College* (London: Masters, 1849), p. ix.

[6] So far as Oxford is concerned, "official" Oxford is referred to here. The effect Newman had on individual members of the university was profound and lasting. In addition to countless journals and memoirs which attest to his influence, one might well cite the tribute paid to him by Matthew Arnold in the opening of his lecture on Emerson.

[7] An almost complete catalogue of reform issues is to be found in a work which is hardly a novel but is nevertheless fiction of a sort. *Oxford in 1888: A Fragmentary Dream by a Sub-Utopian* (Oxford: H. Slatter, 1838), by Richard Walker, describes a vision of the Oxford scene after fifty years of self-imposed reform have made the university a haven of the useful arts and sciences, rich in piety, and adorned by a faculty of the most able men in England.

[8] *The Tutor and the Student* (London: Longman, Brown, Green, Longmans, and Roberts, 1858), chap. 6.

[9] *Julian Home* (Edinburgh: Adam and Charles Black, 1859), p. 64.

[10] *Ibid.*, pp. 65–66.

Notes

[11] *Ibid.*, p. 67.
[12] *Ibid.*, p. 97.
[13] *Ibid.*, p. 432.
[14] Lionel Portman, *The Progress of Hugh Rendal* (London: W. Heinemann, 1907), p. 44.
[15] *Julian Home*, p. 265.
[16] *Ibid.*, p. 280.
[17] *Liberty Hall, Oxon.*, 3 vols. (London: Skeet, 1860), I, 91.
[18] *Ibid.*, pp. 58–59.
[19] *Ibid.*, p. 91.
[20] *Ibid.*, II, chaps. 3–8.
[21] *Ibid.*, I, 59–60.
[22] *Ibid.*, pp. 85–90.
[23] *Ibid.*, pp. 332–344.
[24] *Ibid.*, pp. 347–350. It is probable that Rauch's opinions were Reade's as well. He too left Oxford without a degree. F. Legge, in an introduction to a late edition of Reade's *The Martyrdom of Man* (New York: E. P. Dutton and Co., 1924, pp. v–vii) suggests that the author ran into trouble there for lack of "mental discipline" which might have saved him from "a somewhat dissipated set."
[25] *Liberty Hall, Oxon.*, I, 301.
[26] *Ibid.*, p. 304.
[27] *Ibid.*, II, 26–29.
[28] *Ibid.*, I, 312.
[29] *Ibid.*, II, 95–96.
[30] *Tom Brown at Oxford*, 3 vols. (London and Cambridge: Macmillan and Co., 1861), I, 152.
[31] *Ibid.*, pp. 4–5.
[32] Hippolyte Taine, *Notes on England*, trans. by W. F. Rae (New York: Holt and Williams, 1872), pp. 141–142.
[33] *Tom Brown at Oxford*, I, 90.
[34] *Ibid.*, p. 147.
[35] *Ibid.*, III, 152.
[36] *Ibid.*, p. 153.
[37] Thomas Hughes, *Memoirs of a Brother* (London: Macmillan and Co., 1873), pp. 62–79.
[38] *Tom Brown at Oxford*, I, 199.
[39] *Ibid.*, III, 221–222.
[40] *Ibid.*, pp. 227–228.
[41] Review, "Tom Brown at Oxford," *The Athenaeum*, no. 1779 (November 30, 1861), pp. 720–721.
[42] *Tom Brown at Oxford*, I, xi–xii.
[43] *Ibid.*, I, 162–164.
[44] *The Mysteries of Isis* (London: T. and G. Shrimpton, 1866), p. vii.
[45] *Ibid.*, p. 26.
[46] *Ibid.*, p. 185.
[47] *Christ Church Days*, 2 vols. (London: Bentley, 1867), I, 18.
[48] *The Massacre of the Innocents: An Oxford Conspiracy and Romance* (London: Simpkin, 1907), p. 188.

Notes to Chapter VII

The Romantic Crichtons
(Pages 118–134)

[1] Parts 4 and 5 of the Harkaway Series, published by E. J. Brett, "Boys of England" Office, Hogarth House, London.
[2] Also published by Brett's Hogarth House.
[3] It was published again in 1880 as *College Days at Oxford*.
[4] *Hugh Heron, Ch. Ch.* (London: Strahan and Co., Ltd., 1880), pp. 51–52.
[5] *Ibid.*, p. 122.
[6] *Ibid.*, p. 50.
[7] *Ibid.*, p. 44.
[8] *Ibid.*, p. 52.
[9] *Ibid.*, p. 57.
[10] *Ibid.*, p. 193.
[11] *Ibid.*, p. 88.
[12] *Ibid.*, p. 56.
[13] *Ibid.*, p. 59.
[14] *Faucit of Balliol*, 3 vols. (3d ed.; London: Chapman and Hall, 1882), I, 4.
[15] *Ibid.*, p. 16.
[16] *Ibid.*, pp. 95–97.
[17] *The Don and the Undergraduate* (Edinburgh and London: W. Blackwood and Sons, 1899), p. 5.
[18] *Keddy: A Story of Oxford* (London: W. Heinemann, 1907), p. 122.
[19] *The Little Don of Oxford* (London: J. F. Shaw and Co., 1902), p. 55.
[20] *Ibid.*, p. 70.
[21] *The Babe*, p. v.
[22] *Godfrey Marten, Undergraduate* (London: W. Heinemann, 1904), p. 21.
[23] *Ibid.*, pp. 12 and 29.
[24] *Zuleika Dobson* (London: W. Heinemann, 1911), p. 30.
[25] *Ibid.*, pp. 40–41.
[26] *The Compleat Oxford Man* (London: Skeffington, 1911), chaps. 2, 3, 4, and 40.

Notes to Chapter VIII

The "Damned Tribe of Scribbling Women"
(Pages 135–149)

[1] Christopher Hobhouse, *Oxford* (New York: Oxford University Press, 1946), pp. 101–103.
[2] *Zuleika Dobson* (London: W. Heinemann, 1911), pp. 94–95.
[3] The Yale University Library now owns Madan's collection of Oxford books, of which this is one.
[4] *Passages in the Life of an Undergraduate* (London: Swan Sonnenschein, Lowrey and Co., 1887), p. 6.
[5] *Ibid.*, p. 21.
[6] *Mrs. Fauntleroy's Nephew* (London: J. Ouseley, 1912), p. 183.
[7] *Ibid.*, p. 75.
[8] Mrs. Batty also wrote a little book called *Some Oxford Customs* (London: Swan Sonnenschein, Lowrey and Co., 1888), in which she tells of her familiarity with the university, but the book, with its three consecutive chapters on May Day, and its tend-

ency to gossip and wander from the subject, leaves much to be desired as a source of either pleasure or profit.

[9] *A Fellow of Trinity*, 3 vols. (London: Chatto and Windus, 1890), I, 135–136.

[10] Ibid., pp. 93–94.

[11] Extraordinary as many of the incidents in Mrs. Marshall's novels appear to be, testimony does exist to support her claims of realism. Her son, the Rev. Paul Marshall, has stated in a letter to me that during her residence in Cambridge from the late 1880's to sometime in 1897 he himself, a Cambridge undergraduate, was able to supply her with details of undergraduate life of that period. An oarsman, he says, actually was killed in one of the eights during the May races.

[12] *The Junior Dean* (London: Chatto and Windus, 1893), pp. 20–21.

[13] Ibid., p. 29.

[14] Ibid., p. 190.

[15] The title is of course a play on Thomas Day's unutterably moral children's tale of *Sandford and Merton* (1783–1789), a parody of which, *The New History of Sandford and Merton*, by F. C. Burnand, had been published in 1872.

[16] *Sandford of Merton: A Story of Oxford Life*, by Belinda Blinders [pseud.], ed. by Desmond F. T. Coke (Oxford: Alden and Co., Ltd., Bocardo Press; London: Simpkin, Marshall, Hamilton, Kent, and Co., 1903), pp. viii–ix.

[17] Ibid., pp. ix–x.

[18] Ibid., a footnote on p. 110.

[19] Ibid., pp. 8–9.

[20] Ibid., pp. 15–17. The reference to Farrar's *Eric* is another Blinders error. This novel is a moral tale of little boys at school from which she could have learned nothing about "the vicious side of a young man's life."

[21] *Sandford of Merton* parodies not only the priggishness of Thomas Day's work, but also the flamboyance of "Ouida," and in so doing represents something of a literary tour de force. "Ouida" afforded, with her penchant for somewhat naughty and dissolute elegance, a most useful pattern for the burlesque of university "shockers." Her splendid heroes, too, had much in common with the Crichtons; Beerbohm surely recognized the similarity when he pointed out that the Duke of Dorset had been known as "Peacock" at Eton, where The Honourable Bertie Cecil (*Under Two Flags*) had earlier paraded as "Beauty."

NOTES TO CHAPTER IX

THE CULT OF OXFORD

(Pages 150–181)

[1] *The Progress of Hugh Rendal* (London: W. Heinemann, 1907), p. 24.

[2] *Zuleika Dobson* (London: W. Heinemann, 1911), pp. 189–191.

[3] *Sinister Street* (New York: D. Appleton and Co., 1914), p. 1. The American title is referred to here as distinguishing what was published in England as *Sinister Street*, Part II. Part I had appeared in 1913, and was published in the United States as *Youth's Encounter*.

[4] Ibid., p. 97.

[5] Ibid., p. 91.

[6] Ibid., p. 167.

[7] Ibid., p. 168.

[8] Ibid., pp. 145–146.

[9] Ibid., p. 144.

[10] Ibid., p. 147.

[11] *Ibid.*, pp. 149–150.
[12] *Ibid.*, p. 222.
[13] *Ibid.*, p. 378.
[14] *Ibid.*, p. 653.
[15] A reviewer in the *Times Literary Supplement* (November 12, 1914, p. 506) petulantly demanded a sequel to the novel: "He [Michael Fane] comes out of Oxford as devoid of purpose as when he entered it; he finds the problem of vice and misery more than his unaided strength can solve; he is deceived by a woman who every one told him was born to deceive; and then—off to Rome! We want to know what Michael Fane was at forty . . ." It is true that at the novel's close Michael Fane presumably was about to become a priest, but it is not true that he was ever devoid of purpose. Years later, in 1932, on the occasion of his installation as Rector of St. Andrew's Hall, University of Glasgow, Compton Mackenzie delivered an address in which he enunciated that the purpose of "every contemporary system of education . . . [is] to educate a man to be of service not to himself but to others." (*Address by Compton Mackenzie . . .*, Glasgow: Jackson, Wylie and Co., 1932, p. 18.) The hero of *Sinister Street*, as well as the author, understood this perfectly, and the fact that Michael Fane found himself not yet fully prepared did not invalidate the lessons that Oxford had taught him, all of which pointed to an understanding of the nobility of man.
[16] *Years of Plenty* (London: M. Secker, 1915), p. 214.
[17] *Ibid.*, p. 334.
[18] *Hyssop* (London: Constable and Co., Ltd., 1915), p. 52.
[19] *Ibid.*, p. 31.
[20] *Ibid.*, p. 52.
[21] *Ibid.*, pp. 53–54.
[22] *Ibid.*, p. 55.
[23] *Ibid.*, pp. 56–57.
[24] *A City in the Foreground* (London: Constable and Co., Ltd., 1921), pp. 182–183. The last italics are mine.
[25] *Ibid.*, pp. 275–276.
[26] *Patchwork* (London: Chatto and Windus, 1921), pp. 299–300.
[27] *Ibid.*, p. 305.
[28] *Ibid.*, pp. 38–41.
[29] *Ibid.*, p. 164.
[30] *Ibid.*, p. 22.
[31] *Ibid.*, p. viii.
[32] *A City in the Foreground*, p. 137.
[33] *Peter Priggins, the College Scout*, 3 vols., ed. by Theodore Hook (London: Henry Colburn, 1841), III, 241.
[34] *John-a-Dreams* (London: Blackwood, 1878), p. 155.
[35] *Hugh Heron, Ch. Ch.* (London: Strahan and Co., Ltd., 1880), p. 266.
[36] *Keddy: A Story of Oxford* (London: W. Heinemann and Co., 1902), p. 8.
[37] *A City in the Foreground*, pp. 54–56.
[38] *The Oxford Circus: A Novel of Oxford and Youth* (London: John Lane, Ltd., 1922), p. 27. Cf. the title of Bk. I of *Sinister Street*, "Dreaming Spires."
[39] *Ibid.*, pp. 18–19.
[40] *Ibid.*, pp. 100–101.
[41] *Ibid.*, pp. 104–105.
[42] *Ibid.*, pp. 116–117.
[43] *Ibid.*, p. 118.
[44] *Brideshead Revisited* (Boston: Little, Brown and Co., 1945), p. 45.

Notes to Chapter X

Conclusion
(Pages 182–199)

[1] Mark Pattison, "A Chapter of University History," *Macmillan's Magazine*, XXXII (July–August, 1875), 237–246, 308–313.

[2] "School and College Life: Its Romance and Reality," *Blackwood's Magazine*, LXXXIX (February, 1861), 143.

[3] *Oxford: Historical and Picturesque Notes* (London: Seely and Co., Ltd., 1890), p. 256.

[4] *His Grace's Grace* (London: Greening and Co., Ltd., 1903), pp. 64–66.

[5] *Alton Locke* (London: Macmillan and Co., Ltd., 1862), p. v.

[6] Matthew Arnold, *Essays in Criticism, First Series* (London: Macmillan and Co., Ltd., 1907), p. xi.

[7] *Ibid.*

[8] Arnold, *Culture and Anarchy* (New York: Macmillan and Co., 1895), p. 14. Compton Mackenzie has suggested to me in the letter cited above that this atmosphere of "culture" represents still another reason why Oxford novels have so overwhelmingly taken over the field of university fiction. I quote: "I think the reason why Cambridge has produced so few novels has been its greater devotion to academic education."

[9] *Ibid.*, p. 7.

[10] *The Rise and Progress of Universities*, in *Works*, 41 vols. (London: Longmans, Green and Co., 1914–1927), XV, 6.

[11] *The Idea of a University* (London: Longmans, Green and Co., 1898), pp. 120–121.

[12] *Ibid.*, pp. 144–145.

[13] *Ibid.*, Discourse VI, sec. 9.

BIBLIOGRAPHY OF ENGLISH UNIVERSITY FICTION

BIBLIOGRAPHY OF ENGLISH UNIVERSITY FICTION

The following titles, listed chronologically, represent the English novels which have dealt, either wholly or in significant part, with the theme of English university life. The few entries not referred to in the text or notes are accompanied by a brief comment or description.

Fielding, Henry. *The History of Tom Jones, a Foundling.* 6 vols. London, 1749.
Coventry, Francis. *The History of Pompey the Little.* London, 1751.
Smollett, Tobias. *The Adventures of Peregrine Pickle.* 4 vols. London, 1751.
Amory, Sir Thomas. *The Life of John Buncle.* 2 vols. London, 1756–1766.
Memoirs of an Oxford Scholar, Containing His Amour with the Beautiful Miss L——, of Essex; and Interspersed with Several Entertaining Incidents. Written by Himself. ...London, 1756.
The Adventures of Oxymel Classic, Esq.: Once an Oxford Scholar. 2 vols. London, 1768.
The Oxonian: or, The Adventures of Mr. G. Edmunds, Student of Brazen-Nose College, Oxford. By a Member of the University. 2 vols. London, 1771.
Graves, Richard. *The Spiritual Quixote.* London, 1773.
Holcroft, Thomas. *Hugh Trevor.* 6 vols., London, 1794.
Godwin, William. *Fleetwood.* 3 vols. London, 1805.
Austen, Jane. *Sense and Sensibility.* 3 vols. London, 1811.
Frederick: or, The Memoirs of My Youth. 2 vols. London and Oxford, 1811.
Austen, Jane. *Pride and Prejudice.* 3 vols. London, 1813.
———. *Mansfield Park.* 3 vols. London, 1814.
———. *Northanger Abbey* (with *Persuasion*). 4 vols. London, 1818.
Lockhart, John Gibson. *Reginald Dalton: A Story of English University Life.* 3 vols. Edinburgh, 1823.
[Ward, Robert Plumer]. *Tremaine: or, The Man of Retirement.* 3 vols. London, 1825.
[Little, Thomas]. *Confessions of an Oxonian.* 3 vols. London, 1826.
[Bulwer-Lytton, E. L.]. *Pelham.* 3 vols. London, 1828.
[Beazley, Samuel]. *The Oxonians: A Glance at Society.* By the Author of The Roué. London, 1830.
Disraeli, Benjamin. *The Young Duke.* 3 vols. London, 1831.
———. *Contarini Fleming.* 4 vols. London, 1832.
Truth Without Fiction, and Religion Without Disguise: or, The Two Oxford Students in College, London, and the Country; A True Tale of Characters and Occurrences in Real Life. By a Country Rector. London, 1838.
[Walker, Richard]. *Oxford in 1888: A Fragmentary Dream by a Sub-Utopian.* Oxford, 1838.
Thackeray, William Makepeace. "A Shabby Genteel Story," *Fraser's Magazine*, June–October, 1840. Reprinted in New York, 1852, and in *Miscellanies: Prose and Verse*, Vol. IV, London, 1857. Chapter 2 contains a stinging condemnation of the degrading influences of an English university education.
[Hewlett, Joseph]. *Peter Priggins, the College Scout.* Ed. by Theodore Hook. 3 vols. London, 1841.
Lever, Charles. *Charles O'Malley.* 2 vols. Dublin, 1841.
[Ward, Robert Plumer]. *De Clifford: or, The Constant Man.* By the author of "Tremaine," "De Vere," etc. 4 vols. London, 1841.
Hewlett, Joseph. *College Life: or, The Proctor's Notebook.* By J. Hewlett, M.A. 3 vols. London, 1843.
Disraeli, Benjamin. *Coningsby: or, The New Generation.* 3 vols. London, 1844.

———. *Sybil: or, The Two Nations.* 3 vols. London, 1845.
Lister, Charles. *The College Chums.* 2 vols. London, 1845.
[Hewlett, Joseph]. *Great Tom of Oxford.* By the Author of "Peter Priggins." 3 vols. London, 1846.
[Froude, James Anthony]. *Shadows of the Cloud.* By Zeta (pseud.). London, 1847.
Thackeray, William Makepeace. "Codlingsby," in "Punch's Prize Novelists," *Punch,* April–October, 1847. "Punch's Prize Novelists" was reprinted in *Miscellanies: Prose and Verse,* Vol. II, London, 1856, as *Novels by Eminent Hands.*
Collins, Edward M. *Colleges and Collegians.* Bristol, 1848. This book was omitted from discussion in the text because it is hardly a novel, or even fiction. It consists of a series of conversational essays uttered by a group of unbelievably witty and learned Oxford undergraduates. The thread of plot which holds it together is not strong enough to sustain this stream of epigrams and pretty wisdom.
Froude, James Anthony. *Nemesis of Faith.* London, 1848.
[Newman, John Henry]. *Loss and Gain.* London, 1848.
Thackeray, William Makepeace. *The Book of Snobs.* London, 1848. Appeared first as "The Snobs of England" in *Punch,* February, 1846–February, 1847, with the chapters (xvii–xxiii) which were omitted from the first edition of the book.
Heygate, the Rev. William Edward. *Godfrey Davenant at College.* London, 1849.
Thackeray, William Makepeace. *The History of Pendennis.* 2 vols. London, 1849–1850. The novel originally appeared in 24 monthly parts, November, 1848–December, 1850.
Kingsley, Charles. *Alton Locke.* London, 1850. Rev. ed., 1862.
Smedley, Francis. *Frank Fairlegh.* London, 1850.
[Bradley, Edward]. *The Adventures of Mr. Verdant Green.* By Cuthbert Bede (pseud.). Published in three parts entitled, respectively, *The Adventures of Mr. Verdant Green: An Oxford Freshman,* London, 1853; *The Further Adventures of Mr. Verdant Green: An Oxford Undergraduate,* London, 1854; and *Mr. Verdant Green Married and Done For,* London, 1857.
Griffith, George. *The Life and Adventures of George Wilson, a Foundation Scholar.* London, 1854.
[Bradley, Edward]. *Tales of College Life.* By Cuthbert Bede (pseud.). London, 1856.
Conybeare, the Rev. William John. *Perversion: or, The Causes and Consequences of Infidelity. A Tale for the Times.* London, 1856.
Trollope, Anthony. *Barchester Towers.* 3 vols. London, 1857.
Heygate, the Rev. William Edward. *The Scholar and the Trooper: or, Oxford During the Great Rebellion.* Oxford and London, 1858.
Trollope, Anthony. *Doctor Thorne.* 3 vols. London, 1858.
The Tutor and the Student. By a Member of the Middle Temple. London, 1858.
Farrar, Frederick William. *Julian Home: A Tale of College Life.* Edinburgh, 1859.
Reade, William Winwood. *Liberty Hall, Oxon.* 3 vols. London, 1860.
[Hughes, Thomas]. *Tom Brown at Oxford.* By the Author of "Tom Brown's Schooldays." 3 vols. London, 1861.
Peacock, Thomas Love. *Gryll Grange.* London, 1861.
Kingsley, Henry. *Ravenshoe.* 3 vols. Cambridge, 1862. Chapters 7 and 8 deal briefly but vividly with the Oxford scene. Kingsley describes chiefly the reprehensible aspects of undergraduate life, but has added a highly realistic account of a boat race, based, he says, on his recollections of the race of 1852.
[Morgan, Vaughan]. *The Cambridge Grisette.* By Herbert Vaughan (pseud.). London, 1862.
Thackeray, William Makepeace. *The Adventures of Philip.* 3 vols. London, 1862. The

novel was published first serially in *Cornhill Magazine,* January, 1861–August, 1862. Chapter 5 gives a lively and facetious account of the "awful radicalism and republicanism" that marked Philip's career at an unspecified university.

Reade, Charles. *Hard Cash.* 3 vols. London, 1863.

[Buxton, Harry John Wilmot]. *The Mysteries of Isis: or, The College Life of Paul Romaine.* Oxford and London, 1866.

Arnold, the Rev. Frederick. *Christ Church Days: An Oxford Story.* London, 1867.

Kingsley, Henry. *Silcote of Silcotes.* 3 vols. London, 1867. Insofar as this novel touches upon Oxford, it is notable for its portrait of Arthur Silcotes, a don at the university. In many ways a prig, he is nevertheless characterized chiefly by his integrity and devotion to hard work.

[Jackson, T. W.]. *Boating Life at Oxford. With Notes on Oxford Training and Rowing at the Universities.* London, 1868. The author is identified by Madan.

Reade, Charles. *Foul Play.* 3 vols. London, 1868.

College Debts. By an Oxford M.A. 2 vols. London, 1870.

Disraeli, Benjamin. *Lothair.* 3 vols. London, 1870.

[Rice, James]. *The Cambridge Freshman: or, Memoirs of Mr. Golightly.* By Martin Legrand (pseud.). London, 1871.

[Bradley, Edward]. *Little Mr. Bouncer.* By Cuthbert Bede (pseud.). London, 1873.

Bulwer-Lytton, E. L. *Kenelm Chillingly.* 3 vols. London, 1873.

Reade, Charles. *A Simpleton.* 3 vols. London, 1873.

Usher, Frank. *The Three Oxonians.* London, 1873.

Adams, Henry Cadwallader. *Wilton of Cuthbert's: A Tale of Undergraduate Life Thirty Years Ago.* London, 1878. The novel was republished in 1880 as *College Days at Oxford.*

Sturgis, Julian. *John-a-Dreams.* Edinburgh and London, 1878.

[Weatherly, Frederick Edward]. *Oxford Days: or, How Ross Got His Degree.* By a Resident M.A. London, 1879. Also published in the same year with the title *Frank Ross at Oxford,* in *Cassell's Family Magazine.*

Disraeli, Benjamin. *Endymion.* 3 vols. London, 1880.

The Oxford and Cambridge Eights: or, The Young Coxswain's Career. London, [1880?].

Tyrwhitt, the Rev. Richard St. John. *Hugh Heron, Ch. Ch.* London, [1880].

Shorthouse, Joseph Henry. *John Inglesant.* London, 1881.

Merivale, Herman. *Faucit of Balliol.* 3 vols. London, 1882.

[Traill, William Frederick]. *Tales of Modern Oxford.* By the Author of "Lays of Modern Oxford." London, 1882.

[Cook, Charles Henry]. *With the Best Intentions: A Tale of Undergraduate Life at Cambridge.* By John Bickerdyke, M.A. (pseud.). London, 1884. Reprinted in 1888 with the title *Undergraduate Frolic.*

Church, the Rev. Alfred John. *The Chantry Priest of Barnet: A Tale of the Two Roses.* London, 1885. A historical novel of the mid-fifteenth century, with some credible scenes of Eton and Oxford.

Edwardes, Mrs. Annie. *A Girton Girl.* 3 vols. London, 1885.

[James, Gavin F.]. *The Undergraduate: or, College Life in Five Phases.* By B. A., Cantab. Cambridge, [1885]. I have been unable to find a copy of this book.

Adams, Henry Cadwallader. *Charlie Lucken at School and College.* London, 1886.

Church, the Rev. Alfred John. *With the King at Oxford: A Tale of the Great Rebellion.* London, 1886.

[Braithwaite-Batty, Mrs. Beatrice]. *Passages in the Life of an Undergraduate.* By Bee Bee (pseud.). London, 1887.

[Braithwaite-Batty, Mrs. Beatrice]. *Some Oxford Customs.* By Bee Bee (pseud.). London, 1888. This is not fiction. Its only interest lies in its demonstration of the extent of Mrs. Braithwaite-Batty's familiarity with the Oxford scene.

Ward, Mrs. Humphrey. *Robert Elsmere.* 3 vols. London, 1888.

[Keddie, Henrietta]. *A Young Oxford Maid in the Days of the King and the Parliament.* By Sarah Tytler (pseud.). London, [1890].

[Marshall, Mrs. Frances]. *A Fellow of Trinity.* By Alan St. Aubyn (pseud.) and Walt Wheeler. 3 vols. London, 1890. I can find no information regarding the identity of "Walt Wheeler."

[Balfour, Frederic Henry]. *The Undergraduate.* By George Ross Dering (pseud.). London, 1891.

[Marshall, Mrs. Frances]. *The Dean's Little Daughter.* By Alan St. Aubyn (pseud.). London, 1891.

———. *The Junior Dean.* By Alan St. Aubyn (pseud.). 3 vols. London, 1891.

———. *The Master of St. Benedict's.* By Alan St. Aubyn (pseud.). 2 vols. London, 1893.

[Venn, Suzannah]. *Some Married Fellows.* By the Author of "The Dailys of Sodden Fen," "Four Crotchets to a Bar," etc. 2 vols. London, 1893.

[Bleackley, Horace William]. *Une Culotte, or, a New Woman: An Impossible Story of Modern Oxford.* By Tivoli (pseud.). London, 1894.

[de Winton, W. H.]. *A Green Bay Tree.* By W. H. Wilkins (pseud.). London, 1894.

Smith, Logan Pearsall. *The Youth of Parnassus and Other Stories of Oxford Life.* London, 1895. This is a collection of short stories marked by a tone that deprecates all pretension in university people, don and undergraduate alike.

Adams, Henry Cadwallader. *School and University: or, Dolph Woolward.* London, 1896.

Baker, James. *The Gleaming Dawn.* London, 1896.

Benson, Edward F. *The Babe, B.A.: Being the Uneventful History of a Young Gentleman at Cambridge University.* London and New York, 1896. The *English Catalogue* and *British Museum Catalogue* agree on the date 1897; my copy, however, is dated 1896.

Hardy, Thomas. *Jude the Obscure.* London, 1896.

Hemyng, Samuel Bracebridge. *Jack Harkaway at Oxford.* Part 4 of the Harkaway Series, published by E. J. Brett, "Boys of England" Office, Hogarth House, London. [1897?].

[Marshall, Mrs. Frances]. *The Proctor's Wooing.* By Alan St. Aubyn (pseud.). London, 1897.

Within Sound of Great Tom: Stories of Modern Oxford. Oxford, 1897.

Everett-Green, Evelyn. *A Clerk of Oxford and His Adventures in The Barons' War.* London and New York, 1898.

Gull, Cyril Arthur Edward Ranger. *The Hypocrite.* London, 1898.

Hemyng, Samuel Bracebridge. *Jack Harkaway's Strange Adventures at Oxford.* Part 5 of the Harkaway Series, published by E. J. Brett, "Boys of England" Office, Hogarth House, London. [1898?]

Collins, William Edward Wood. *The Don and the Undergraduate: A Tale of St. Hilary's College, Oxford.* London and Edinburgh, 1899.

Marshall, Archibald. *Peter Binney, Undergraduate.* London, 1899.

Sergeant, Emily Frances Adeline. *Blake of Oriel.* London, 1899.

[Belloc, Hilaire]. *Lambkin's Remains.* By H. B., author of "The Bad Child's Book of Beasts." Oxford, 1900.

Bibliography

Collins, William Edward Wood. *A Scholar of His College.* London and Edinburgh, 1900.
Allen, Inglis. *A 'Varsity Man: Passages in the Career of an Impressionable Undergraduate.* London, 1901.
Calderon, George Leslie. *The Adventures of Downy V. Green, Rhodes Scholar at Oxford.* London, 1902.
Cornwall, Mrs. Nellie. *The Little Don of Oxford.* London, [1902].
Butler, Samuel. *The Way of All Flesh.* London, 1903.
[Coke, Desmond F. T.]. *Sandford of Merton: A Story of Oxford Life.* By Belinda Blinders (pseud.). Edited by Desmond F. T. Coke. Oxford, 1903.
Gull, Cyril Arthur Edward Ranger. *His Grace's Grace.* London, 1903.
[Marshall, Mrs. Frances]. *The Senior Tutor.* By Alan St. Aubyn (pseud.). London, 1904.
Red Paint at Oxford. By "Pish" and "Tush" (pseud.). London, 1904.
Turley, Charles. *Godfrey Marten, Undergraduate.* London, 1904.
Baker, James. *The Inseparables: An Oxford Novel of Today.* London, 1905.
Taubman-Goldie, Valentine F. *Nigel Thomson.* London, 1905.
Coke, Desmond F. T. *The Comedy of Age.* London, 1906.
[Ball, Mrs. Oona]. *Barbara Goes to Oxford.* By Barbara Burke (pseud.). London, [1907].
Dickinson, Humphrey Neville. *Keddy: A Story of Oxford.* London, 1907.
The Massacre of the Innocents: An Oxford Conspiracy and Romance. By an Oxford Scholar. [London], 1907.
Portman, Lionel. *The Progress of Hugh Rendal.* London, 1907.
Woods, Margaret. *The Invader.* New York and London, 1907.
Ball, Mrs. Oona. *Their Oxford Year.* London, [1909].
Venning, Normandy. *The Spider of St. Austin's: or, Proxime Accesit.* London, 1910.
Beerbohm, Max. *Zuleika Dobson.* London, 1911.
de Wend-Fenton, West F. *The Primrose Path: Being the Adventures of Raymond Forsyth at Oxford, in London, and on the Turf.* London, 1911.
Gibbs, A. Hamilton. *The Compleat Oxford Man.* London, 1911.
Braithwaite-Batty, Mrs. Beatrice. *Mrs. Fauntleroy's Nephew: An Episode of Oxford History in the Eights Week.* London, [1912].
Broster, Dorothy Kathleen, and G. W. Taylor. *The Vision Splendid.* London, 1913.
Mackenzie, Compton. *Sinister Street.* London, 1913–1914.
Brown, Ivor. *Years of Plenty.* London, [1915].
[Sadleir, Michael]. *Hyssop.* By M. T. H. Sadler. London, [1915].
[Ward, Mary Augusta]. *Lady Connie.* By Mrs. Humphrey Ward. London, 1916.
Ritchie, Mrs. David. *The New Warden.* London, 1918.
Hopkins, Gerard. *A City in the Foreground.* London, [1921].
Nichols, Beverly. *Patchwork.* London, 1921.
Burford, Francis Rupert. *Forty Years Off: An Appalling Story of Love, Mystery, History and Crime at Oxford with Some Startling Sidelights on Cambridge.* Oxford, 1922. Not a novel, but certainly fiction, this is a fantasy relating a faked duel, a strike by the dons, imprisonment in the schools, and the like.
[Miles, Hamish, and Raymond Mortimer]. *The Oxford Circus: A Novel of Oxford and Youth.* By the late Alfred Budd (pseud.). Edited with Memoir but no Portrait by Hamish Miles and Raymond Mortimer. London, 1922.
Benson, Edward F. *David of Kings.* London, 1924. American title: *David Blaize of Kings.*
Golding, Louis. *Seacoast of Bohemia.* London, 1924.

Leslie, Shane. *The Cantab*. London, 1926.
Childers, James Saxon. *Laurel and Straw*. London, 1927.
Gibbs, Philip. *The Age of Reason*. London and New York, 1928.
Cannan, Joanna. *High Table*. London, 1931.
Masterman, John Cecil. *An Oxford Tragedy*. London, 1933.
Sayers, Dorothy. *Gaudy Night*. London, 1935.
[Stewart, John Innes Mackintosh]. *Death at the President's Lodging*. By Michael Innes (pseud.). London, 1937. American title: *Seven Suspects*.
Goudge, Elizabeth. *Towers in the Mist*. New York, 1938.
Knox, Ronald A. *Let Dons Delight: Being Variations on a Theme in an Oxford Common Room*. London, 1939. Another piece of fiction which is not a novel; the book is a collection of imaginary Common Room conversations which might have taken place at critical times in Oxford's history since 1588.
Costain, Thomas B. *The Black Rose*. Garden City, New York, 1945.
[Daniel, Dr. Glyn E.]. *The Cambridge Murders*. By Dilwyn Rees (pseud.). London, 1945.
[Montgomery, Robert Bruce]. *The Case of the Gilded Fly*. By Edmund Crispin (pseud.). London, 1944. American title (1945): *Obsequies at Oxford*.
Waugh, Evelyn. *Brideshead Revisited*. London, 1945.
Harrison, Paul. *Oxford Marmalade*. London, 1946.
Snow, Charles Percy. *The Light and the Dark*. London, 1947.
———. *The Masters*. London, 1951.
[Stewart, John Innes Mackintosh]. *Operation Pax*. By Michael Innes (pseud.). London, 1951. American title: *The Paper Thunderbolt*.
Balsdon, Dacre. *Freshman's Folly: An Oxford Comedy*. London, 1952.
Vulliamy, Colwyn Edward. *Don Among the Dead Men: A Satirical Thriller*. London, 1952.
Masterman, John Cecil. *To Teach the Senators Wisdom: or, An Oxford Guide Book*. London, 1952.
Cooper, William. *The Struggles of Albert Woods*. Garden City, New York, 1953.
Amis, Kingsley. *Lucky Jim*. London, 1954.
Farrer, Katharine. *The Missing Link*. London, 1955.
Stewart, John Innes Mackintosh. *The Guardians*. London, 1955.
McIntosh, Louis. *Oxford Folly*. London, 1956.
Robinson, Robert. *Landscape With Dead Dons*. London and New York, 1956.
[Stewart, John Innes Mackintosh]. *Old Hall, New Hall*. By Michael Innes (pseud.). London, 1956.
Wilson, Angus. *Anglo-Saxon Attitudes*. London, 1956.

INDEX

INDEX

Adventures of Oxymel Classic, Esq., The, 46–49; mentioned, 51, 60, 66, 71, 187
Allen, Inglis: *A 'Varsity Man,* 129, 131, 134
Amis, Kingsley: *Lucky Jim,* 175–176
Amory, Sir Thomas: *The Life of John Buncle,* 45
Arnold, Frederick: *Christ Church Days,* 114–115
Arnold, Matthew, 192, 193–194
Austen, Jane, 7; *Mansfield Park, Northanger Abbey, Pride and Prejudice, Sense and Sensibility,* 45
Adams, Henry Cadwallader: *Charlie Lucken at School and College, School and University, Wilton of Cuthbert's,* 120

Babler, The, 38
Baker, James: *The Gleaming Dawn,* 6; *The Inseparables,* 119
Balfour, Frederic Henry: *The Undergraduate,* 119
Ball, Mrs. Oona: *Barbara Goes to Oxford, Their Oxford Year,* 137–138
Balsdon, Dacre: *An Oxford Comedy,* 178
Beazley, Samuel: *The Oxonians,* 68
Bede, Cuthbert. *See* Bradley, Edward
Bee Bee. *See* Braithwaite-Batty, Mrs. Beatrice
Beerbohm, Max, 6, 136, 169, 180; *Zuleika Dobson,* 3, 131–133, 152–153, 197
Belloc, Hilaire, 159; *Lambkin's Remains,* 85–86
Benson, Edward F., 6, 150; *The Babe, B. A.,* 83–84, 127, 129, 186, 187; *David Blaize, David Blaize and the Blue Door, David of Kings,* 127–128
Bentham, Jeremy, 192
Bickerdyke, John. *See* Cook, Charles Henry
Bleackley, Horace William: *Une Culotte,* 73–74
Boating Life at Oxford, 116
Borrow, George, 7
Bradley, Edward, 5; *The Adventures of Mr. Verdant Green,* 78–81, 82–87 passim, 196–197 (mentioned, 97, 107, 178); *Little Mr. Bouncer,* 81; *Tales of College Life,* 81
Braithwaite-Batty, Mrs. Beatrice, 7, 145, 149; *Mrs. Fauntleroy's Nephew,* 138–140; *Passages in the Life of an Undergraduate,* 138; *Some Oxford Customs,* 210, 220
Brontë sisters, the, 7
Broster, Dorothy Kathleen: *The Vision Splendid,* 94
Brown, Ivor: *Years of Plenty,* 158–159
Bulwer-Lytton, Edward G. E. L., 190; *England and the English,* 203; *Kenelm Chillingly,* 9; *Pelham,* 8–9
Burford, Francis Rupert: *Forty Years Off,* 221
Burke, Barbara. *See* Ball, Mrs. Oona
Butler, Samuel, *The Way of All Flesh,* 9
Buxton, Harry John Wilmot: *The Mysteries of Isis,* 113–114, 186

Calderon, George Leslie: *The Adventures of Downy V. Green, Rhodes Scholar at Oxford,* 86–87
Cannan, Joanna: *High Table,* 175
Caxton, William: *Aesop's Fables,* epilogue to, 16
Chaucer, Geoffrey: *The Canterbury Tales,* 13–14, 17
Childers, James Saxon: *Laurel and Straw,* 175
Church, Alfred: *With the King at Oxford,* 5
Coke, Desmond F. T., 7; *The Comedy of Age,* 126; *Sandford of Merton,* 146–149; quoted, 7
College Debts, 115–116
Collins, Edward M.: *Colleges and Collegians,* 218
Collins, William Edward Wood: *The Don and the Undergraduate,* 124–125; *A Scholar of His College,* 125
Connoisseur, The, 39
Conybeare, William John: *Perversion,* 92
Cook, Charles Henry: *With the Best Intentions,* 82
Cooper, William: *The Struggles of Albert Woods,* 176

Cornwall, Mrs. Nellie: *The Little Don of Oxford*, 128, 145–146
Costain, Thomas B.: *The Black Rose*, 6
Coventry, Francis: *The History of Pompey the Little*, 43–44
Cowley, Abraham, 31
Crispin, Edmund. *See* Montgomery, Robert Bruce

Daniel, Glyn E.: *The Cambridge Murders*, 177
Dering, Ross George. *See* Balfour, Frederic Henry
Devil's Almanac, The, 41
de Wend-Fenton, West F.: *The Primrose Path*, 119–120
de Winton, W. H.: *A Green Bay Tree*, 150
Dickens, Charles, 7
Dickinson, Humphrey Neville: *Keddy*, 127, 170
Disraeli, Benjamin, 7; *Coningsby, Contarini Fleming, Endymion, Lothair, Sybil*, 8
Dodgson, Charles Lutwidge, 7

Earle, John: *Microcosmographie*, 24–25, 26–28, 37
Edgeworth, Maria, 7
Edinburgh Review, 53, 59, 63, 206
Edwardes, Mrs. Annie: *Girton Girl*, 137
Eliot, George, 7
Everett-Green, Evelyn: *A Clerk of Oxford and His Adventures in the Barons' War*, 6

Farrar, Frederick William, 4, 185, 186; *Julian Home*, 95–100; mentioned, 105, 107, 137
Farrer, Katharine: *The Missing Link*, 177
Fielding, Henry: *Tom Jones*, 41–42 (mentioned, 71 72)
Frederick: or, The Memoirs of My Youth, 61–62
Froude, James Anthony, 4; *Nemesis of Faith, Shadows of the Cloud*, 93

Gaskell, Elizabeth Cleghorn, 7
Gibbs, A. Hamilton: *The Compleat Oxford Man*, 134, 189

Gibbs, Philip: *The Age of Reason*, 175
Gissing, George, 7, 182
Godwin, William, 60; *Fleetwood*, 61
Golding, Louis: *Seacoast of Bohemia*, 174–175
Goudge, Elizabeth: *Towers in the Mist*, 6
Graves, Richard: *The Spiritual Quixote*, 45
Griffith, George: *The Life and Adventures of George Wilson, a Foundation Scholar*, 94
Guardian, The, 38–39
Gull, Cyril Arthur Edward Ranger, 7, 186; *His Grace's Grace, The Hypocrite*, 119

Hardy, Thomas, 7; *Jude the Obscure*, 9
Harrison, Paul: *Oxford Marmalade*, 178
Hemyng, Samuel Bracebridge: *Jack Harkaway at Oxford, Jack Harkaway's Strange Adventures at Oxford*, 118
Hewlett, Joseph, 4, 80, 100, 185, 186; *College Life*, 77–78, 99; *Great Tom of Oxford*, 78; *Peter Priggins*, 74–78, 80, 88, 100, 169
Heygate, William Edward: *Godfrey Davenant at College*, 90–91, 92; *The Scholar and the Trooper*, 5
Hobbes, Thomas, 31
Hobhouse, Christopher, 135-136
Hoccleve, Thomas: *De Regimine Principum*, 15
Holcroft, Thomas: *Hugh Trevor*, 60–61
Hopkins, Gerard, 165; *A City in the Foreground*, 5, 161–163, 169, 170–172, 197
Hughes, Thomas, 4, 6, 111–112, 126, 152, 197; *Tom Brown at Oxford*, 3, 105–113, 120, 152, 178, 184, 187; *Tom Brown's School Days*, 105, 110–111
Huxley, Thomas Henry, 192

Idler, The, 40
Innes, Michael. *See* Stewart, John Innes Mackintosh

Jests of Scogin, The, 18–19, 21
Jonson, Ben: *Every Man Out of His Humour*, 24

Index

Keddie, Henrietta: *A Young Oxford Maid in the Days of the King and the Parliament*, 5
Kingsley, Charles: *Alton Locke*, 9, 187–188
Kingsley, Henry: *Ravenshoe*, 218; *Silcote of Silcotes*, 219
Kipling, Rudyard, 7, 182
Knox, Ronald A.: *Let Dons Delight*, 222
Knox, Vicesimus, 57–58

Lang, Andrew, 186
Legrand, Martin. See Rice, James
Leslie, Shane: *The Cantab*, 151
Lever, Charles: *Charles O'Malley*, 68–69, 71, 74, 76
Lister, Charles: *The College Chums*, 118
Little, Thomas: *Confessions of an Oxonian*, 66–68
Lockhart, John Gibson, 4, 6; *Reginald Dalton*, vii, 62–65, 69, 152, 187, 207
Lyly, John: *Euphues*, 23–24

MacIntosh, Louis: *Oxford Folly*, 178
Mackenzie, Compton, 6, 180, 193, 194, 212, 213; *Sinister Street*, 154–158, 159–175 *passim*, 181, 197–198, 212
Marryat, Frederick, 7
Marshall, Archibald: *Peter Binney*, 84–85
Marshall, Mrs. Frances, 137, 186, 211; *The Dean's Little Daughter*, 144; *A Fellow of Trinity*, 140–142; *The Junior Dean*, 142–144; *The Master of St. Benedict's*, 144, 145; *The Proctor's Wooing, The Senior Tutor*, 144
Massacre of the Innocents, The, 116–117
Masterman, John Cecil: *An Oxford Tragedy*, 177, 180; *To Teach The Senators Wisdom*, 180–181
Memoirs of an Oxford Scholar, 49–50
Meredith, George, 7
Merie Tales of Skelton, The, 17–18, 21
Merivale, Herman, 4; *Faucit of Balliol*, 123–124, 189–190
Miles, Hamish: *The Oxford Circus*, 172–174, 197
Milton, John, 31
Montgomery, Robert Bruce: *The Case of the Gilded Fly (Obsequies at Oxford)*, 177
Moore, George, 7, 182

Morgan, Vaughan: *The Cambridge Grisette*, 73, 150.
Mortimer, Raymond: *The Oxford Circus*, 172–174, 197

Newman, John Henry, 4, 91–94 *passim*, 192–198 *passim*, 208; *Loss and Gain*, 92–93
Nichols, Beverly: *Patchwork*, 163–169, 171–174 *passim*, 197

Ouida (Marie Louise de la Ramée), 211
"Overburian characters," 24, 25–26, 37
Oxford and Cambridge Eights, The, 118–119
Oxford in 1888: A Fragmentary Dream by a Sub-Utopian, 208
Oxonian, The, 50

Parnassus Plays, The, 21, 24
Pattison, Mark, 52, 183–184, 186
Peacock, Thomas Love, 7
Portman, Lionel: *The Progress of Hugh Rendal*, 125–126, 152; quoted, 98

Rambler, The, 39
Reade, Charles, 7, 100, 192; *Foul Play, Hard Cash, A Simpleton*, 9
Reade, William Winwood: *Liberty Hall, Oxon.*, 3, 100–105, 186, 209
Red Paint at Oxford, 82
Rees, Dilwyn. See Daniel, Glyn E.
Rice, James, 4; *The Cambridge Freshman*, 81–82, 83
Ritchie, Mrs. David: *The New Warden*, 146
Robinson, Robert: *Landscape With Dead Dons*, 177

Sadleir, Michael: *Hyssop*, 158–161
Scott, Sir Walter, 7
St. Aubyn, Alan. See Marshall, Mrs. Frances
Saltonstall, Wye: *Picturae Loquentes*, 28
Sayers, Dorothy: *Gaudy Night*, 177
Sergeant, Adeline: *Blake of Oriel*, 145
Shakespeare, William: *Love's Labours Lost*, 24
Shorthouse, Joseph Henry: *John Inglesant*, 5
Smedley, Francis: *Frank Fairlegh*, 113

Smith, Logan Pearsall: *The Youth of Parnassus and Other Stories*, 220
Smollett, Tobias: *Peregrine Pickle*, 45–46
Snow, Charles Percy, 150; *The Light and the Dark*, 178–179; *The Masters*, 179–180
Spencer, Herbert, 192
Stevenson, Robert Louis, 7, 182
Stewart, John Innes Mackintosh: *The Guardians*, 176; *Death at the President's Lodging, Old Hall, New Hall, Operation Pax (The Paper Thunderbolt)*, 178
Stubbes, Philip: *Anatomie of Abuses*, 20
Sturgis, Julian: *John-a-Dreams*, 118, 170

Tatler, The, 38
Taubman-Goldie, Valentine F., 7; *Nigel Thomson*, 119
Taylor, G. W.: *The Vision Splendid*, 94
Thackeray, William Makepeace, 4, 6, 7, 9; *The Adventures of Philip*, 218–219; *The Book of Snobs*, 72; *Pendennis*, 3, 69–73, 74–81 *passim*, 107; *A Shabby Genteel Story*, 217
Tivoli. *See* Bleackley, Horace William
Tom Tel-Troth's Message, 20–21
Traill, William Frederick: *Tales of Modern Oxford*, 82
Trollope, Anthony, 7; *Barchester Towers, Doctor Thorne*, 9
Truth Without Fiction, and Religion Without Disguise, 88–89, 92, 94, 99

Turley, Charles: *Godfrey Marten, Undergraduate*, 129–131, 134
Tutor and the Student, The, 95
Tyrwhitt, Richard St. John, 4, 126, 165; *Hugh Heron, Ch. Ch.*, 120–123, 170
Tytler, Sarah. *See* Keddie, Henrietta

Usher, Frank: *The Three Oxonians*, 118

Vaughan, Herbert. *See* Morgan, Vaughan
Venn, Suzannah: *Some Married Fellows*, 145
Venning, Normandy: *The Spider of St. Austin's*, 128
Vivian, Herbert: *A Green Bay Tree*, 150
Vulliamy, Colwyn Edward: *Don Among the Dead Men*, 177

Ward, Mrs. Humphrey: *Lady Connie, Robert Elsmere*, 137
Ward, Robert Plumer, 4; *De Clifford*, 64; *Tremaine*, 207
Waugh, Evelyn: *Brideshead Revisited*, 175
Weatherly, Frederick Edward: *Oxford Days*, 116
Wilde, Oscar, 170
Wilkins, W. H. *See* de Winton, W. F.
Wilson, Angus: *Anglo-Saxon Attitudes*, 176–177
Within Sound of Great Tom, 145
Wood, Anthony, 16–17
Wood, Margaret: *The Invader*, 137
W. S.: *The Puritan*, 24

The Academic Profession
An Arno Press Collection

Annan, Noel Gilroy. **Leslie Stephen:** His Thought and Character in Relation to His Time. 1952

Armytage, W. H. G. **Civic Universities:** Aspects of a British Tradition. 1955

Berdahl, Robert O. **British Universities and the State.** 1959

Bleuel, Hans Peter. **Deutschlands Bekenner** (German Men of Knowledge). 1968

Bowman, Claude Charleton. **The College Professor in America.** 1938

Busch, Alexander. **Die Geschichte des Privatdozenten** (History of Privat-Docentens). 1959

Caplow, Theodore and Reece J. McGee. **The Academic Marketplace.** 1958

Carnegie Foundation for the Advancement of Teaching. **The Financial Status of the Professor in America and in Germany.** 1908

Cattell, J. McKeen. **University Control.** 1913

Cheyney, Edward Potts. **History of the University of Pennsylvania: 1740-1940.** 1940

Elliott, Orrin Leslie. **Stanford University:** The First Twenty-Five Years. 1937

Ely, Richard T. **Ground Under Our Feet:** An Autobiography. 1938

Flach, Johannes. **Der Deutsche Professor der Gegenwart** (The German Professor Today). 1886

Hall, G. Stanley. **Life and Confessions of a Psychologist.** 1924

Hardy, G[odfrey] H[arold]. **Bertrand Russell & Trinity:** A College Controversy of the Last War. 1942

Kluge, Alexander. **Die Universitäts-Selbstverwaltung** (University Self-Government). 1958

Kotschnig, Walter M. **Unemployment in the Learned Professions.** 1937

Lazarsfeld, Paul F. and Wagner Thielens, Jr. **The Academic Mind:** Social Scientists in a Time of Crisis. 1958

McLaughlin, Mary Martin. **Intellectual Freedom and Its Limitations in the University of Paris in the Thirteenth and Fourteenth Centuries.** 1977

Metzger, Walter P., editor. **The American Concept of Academic Freedom in Formation:** A Collection of Essays and Reports. 1977

Metzger, Walter P., editor. **The Constitutional Status of Academic Freedom.** 1977

Metzger, Walter P., editor. **The Constitutional Status of Academic Tenure.** 1977

Metzger, Walter P., editor. **Professors on Guard:** The First AAUP Investigations. 1977

Metzger, Walter P., editor. **Reader on the Sociology of the Academic Profession.** 1977

Mims, Edwin. **History of Vanderbilt University.** 1946

Neumann, Franz L., et al. **The Cultural Migration:** The European Scholar in America. 1953

Nitsch, Wolfgang, et al. **Hochschule in der Demokratie** (The University in a Democracy). 1965

Pattison, Mark. **Suggestions on Academical Organization with Especial Reference to Oxford.** 1868

Pollard, Lucille Addison. **Women on College and University Faculties:** A Historical Survey and a Study of Their Present Academic Status. 1977

Proctor, Mortimer R. **The English University Novel.** 1957

Quincy, Josiah. **The History of Harvard University.** Two vols. 1840

Ross, Edward Alsworth. **Seventy Years of It:** An Autobiography. 1936

Rudy, S. Willis. **The College of the City of New York:** A History, 1847-1947. 1949

Slosson, Edwin E. **Great American Universities.** 1910

Smith, Goldwin. **A Plea for the Abolition of Tests in the University of Oxford.** 1864

Willey, Malcolm W. **Depression, Recovery and Higher Education:** A Report by Committee Y of the American Association of University Professors. 1937

Winstanley, D. A. **Early Victorian Cambridge.** 1940

Winstanley, D. A. **Later Victorian Cambridge.** 1947

Winstanley, D. A. **Unreformed Cambridge.** 1935

Yeomans, Henry Aaron. **Abbott Lawrence Lowell:** 1856-1943. 1948